CONTENTS

CW01500833

T

PART TWO
FINDING HELP

Memoir
Both 2026

THE
PITS

THE
PITS

Life Literally Bit Me in the Ass

A MEMOIR

CHERYL EDWARDS

Copyright © 2024 by Huber House Press LLC

All rights reserved. In accordance with the U.S. Copyright Act of 1976, no portion of this book may be reproduced, stored in a retrieval system, or transmitted in any form or by any means, mechanical, electronic, photocopying, recording, or otherwise, without written permission except in the case of brief quotations embodied in critical articles and reviews. The scanning, uploading, and distribution of this book without the publisher's written permission constitutes unlawful piracy and theft of the author's intellectual property. If you would like permission to use material from the book (other than for review purposes), please contact Huber House Press LLC at permissions@HuberHousePress.com.

ISBN 979-8-9905081-1-8 (paperback)
ISBN 979-8-9905081-0-1 (ebook)
ISBN 979-8-9905081-2-5 (audiobook)

Library of Congress Control Number 2024918945

The events described in this book are real; however, some names and identifying characteristics of some individuals have been changed to protect people's privacy.

Editing by Danielle Lange
Formatting by Alfredo Sarraga Jr.
Cover design by Creative Covers
Front cover image by Stephanie Dubsky

First Edition
2024

Library of Congress Cataloging-in-Publication Data is available upon request.

For information about bulk purchases for educational, business, or promotional use, please contact Huber House Press LLC at info@HuberHousePress.com

Visit the author's website at www.thecheryledwards.com

Printed in the United States of America

PART SIX

DOGS AND ME BEFORE

PART SEVEN

THE WHY

DOGS AND ME AFTER

DISCLAIMER

We each view the world through a unique lens—our mindset. It's created by our past experiences, which guide our thoughts and attitudes. These mental impressions allow us to interpret the world around us and lead us to believe what we perceive to be accurate.

This book is a memoir and reflects the author's present recollections of experiences over time. Since memories fade, in some instances, the story may lack exactness. Some events have been compressed, some dialogue has been recreated, and some details may have been reported inadvertently in error. Regardless, the story has been told in a way that evokes the intended meaning and feelings, and the core narrative remains true to the author's experience. Also, in an attempt to protect privacy and maintain anonymity, the names and identifying characteristics of certain individuals involved have been changed.

Please note this book contains explicit content detailing a survivor's experience during and after a severe dog attack. The narrative includes graphic descriptions of violence, injuries, and emotional distress, which may be potentially unsettling for sensitive readers. These detailed accounts may be distressing and are not recommended for individuals sensitive to such subject matter discussions. Additionally, the book occasionally and authentically incorporates profanity, reflecting the author's intense circumstances. This material is not intended to offend but aims for healing and awareness and to honestly depict the author's traumatic ordeal. Readers are advised to proceed with caution, acknowledging the emotional impact of such content.

The author acknowledges the trademark status and trademark owners of various products referenced in this work. The publication and/ or use of these trademarks is not associated with nor sponsored by the trademark owners.

"Perception is reality."

—Lee Atwater

This is my experience, my story.

If you don't like it or disagree with it,
write your own damn book.

—Cheryl Edwards

This book is dedicated to those who have senselessly died due to dog attacks. If my story can bring attention to the problem so that even one life may be spared, all I have gone through will have been worth it.

This book is also dedicated to my husband, Dale, and our sons, "William" and "Harry." You are my whole world—whether you like it or not.

PART ONE

THE ATTACK

1. NO GOOD DEED

She remembered! I thought, fishing the silver key out from under the antique water pump decorating the front porch. As a real estate broker and former latchkey kid, I'd found trusting others to leave the key was usually half the battle.

Little did I know.

I paused at the front door, somewhat hesitant to tromp into another person's house, even with permission—another thing I learned from being in the real estate business for over twenty years. Even though owners usually aren't home for showings, it's still customary to ring the doorbell to announce yourself, just in case. However, even that's not foolproof, as I've surprised a few sound sleepers in my day.

I did a quick mental inventory. My Friend and her daughter were out of town, supposedly having left the night before. And her youngest son, who mainly lived with his father, was away at a lacrosse tournament.

Yup. Nobody's home.

After all, that's why I was there. Someone had to feed the dogs.

No need to ring the doorbell. Why would I when nobody was home to answer it? Besides, everyone knows that's a surefire way to get any dog riled up, let alone three pit bulls.

Once inside, I made my way through the foyer and living room, heading for the kitchen island. A quick tap at my sides reminded me I didn't have pockets in my gym shorts, so I tossed my purse, sunglasses, and her house key onto the marble-looking quartz counter. Four stools were evenly spaced along one side, and I recall noting how it was so big she probably could have fit two more. I loved this house.

Since she said the dogs would be in the garage, I paused when I thought I heard something, trying to figure out who or what it might be.

Even though I never ring the doorbell when visiting my parents or best friends, I still announce myself as I walk in with a cheery *I'm here!* Similarly, if one of the kids *had* stayed behind, I wanted to give them a heads-up to avoid catching them off guard. When I'd surprised those sound sleepers I mentioned before, it wound up scaring the crap out of all of us.

As for the dogs, while they knew me, I'm sure they weren't expecting me, so I suppose I wanted to give them some notice, too. Though, I doubt they cared who fed them, so long as someone did.

"Hey, puppers! Who's hungry? Who's gotta go potty?" I called out in a sweet voice.

No shocker, as soon as the first word escaped my mouth, they all started barking. My Friend's dogs ordinarily barked at people. Hell, most dogs ordinarily bark at people. So, as far as I was concerned, everything seemed fine.

Thinking back, I now realize it might have sounded a little more intense than regular barking, but then again, there were three of them. When their barking subsided as quickly as it had started, I took the outburst as their way of saying, *Of course, we're here. Now hurry up, lady! We're starving and about to pee our pants!*

I knew the home and its layout well because I'd sold it to My Friend's sister three months before. Heading for the garage, I worked my way down the main hall, passing the pantry, her daughter's bedroom, and the kids' bathroom. At the far end of the hallway was her son's bedroom, but just before that, off to the left, there was a small three-foot by four-foot hallway with two doors. One led to the three-car garage, one led to the laundry room, and both were closed.

This shorter hallway had a recessed wall. In the model home, the builder had installed a bank of built-in cubbies to hold coats, shoes, bags, and backpacks. Buyers with young families loved these drop stations, which were all the rage among builders. However, My Friend had other plans.

Being super crafty and not afraid to use power tools of any sort, she'd designed and constructed a built-in desk to fit the empty space. She'd told me about the desk, but this was my first time seeing it, so it drew my attention. I was impressed. Not only by her workmanship but also by how confidently she tackled more sophisticated home improvement projects. I can hang pictures, chalk paint furniture, and address anything that gives me an excuse to bust out my hot glue gun, but that's about the extent of my DIY skills. I'm no power-saw girl, that's for sure.

The plan, or at least how I saw it playing out, was to let the dogs in from the garage and then shoo them out the back door to tend to their business. Meanwhile, I'd throw fresh water and food in their bowls. Then, while they were busy eating their breakfast, I'd see myself out the front door and lock up.

When showing properties, dogs usually aren't left at home, but it's not uncommon for listing agents to warn that a cat might try to sneak out. Since I didn't know if My Friend's dogs might try to do the same, to play it safe, I thought it best to keep them preoccupied. Having just come from the gym, I'd already had my workout for the day, so I didn't need to be chasing any escapees down the block.

It was around 9:30 a.m. and sunny, but since there weren't any windows in the little hallway and since I hadn't flipped on the lights, it was darker than the rest of the house. That's why, aside from noticing the new desk, my eyes were also drawn to the line of bright light streaming in from the gap below the laundry room door. The gap was definitely taller than it should've been. The house had been brand new when she bought it, but sadly, it was way too common for subcontractors to cut corners, and I was disappointed that we hadn't caught that detail at her final walk-through.

Dancing in the light I could make out small shadows. I stared, confused, wondering if one of the kids *had* stayed behind. However, upon hearing snorting and the *tap-tap-tap* of nails on the tile floor, it clicked.

The dogs are in there! But wait. She said they'd be in the garage. She probably just changed her mind. Or maybe I remembered the directions wrong. Oh well. It doesn't matter.

Eager to get to the task at hand, I swung the door open.

2. SURROUNDED

The dogs immediately surrounded me. Kaya, the only female, barked nonstop. Her coloring was technically brindle but more black than brown. Even though the barking was annoying, I didn't sweat it. Since some dogs are barkier than others, I suspected that was just her nature. However, when her lips started to curl up on the sides, I could tell she wasn't happy. Still, I just took it as she missed her mommy and wasn't thrilled with the substitution.

Get over it, doggo. Mom's not home. It's me or nothing.

I reassured them with a sticky-sweet mix of "I know, I know," "It's okay," and "It's just me" in my higher-than-normal tone. It's the voice I usually reserve for talking to little kids and meeting new people, but unfortunately, it did little to calm the dogs down or win them over. I wasn't surprised. If I'm being honest, I'd had mixed results with the little kids and new people, too.

I reached out to give one of them a reassuring pat on the head, but their barking intensified before I could get remotely close. Now, even faster and louder than before, it was crystal clear—comfort from me was *not* what they were looking for.

Enough. Quit trying to make them love you, and just do what you came here to do.

That's when Red, the older, reddish-colored male, began jumping up at me. This was definitely no gimme-paw trick. He was coming at me with his face, and if I wasn't mistaken, he appeared to be aiming for *my* face. I could tell it wasn't to cover me in slobbery kisses, but I blew it off, chalking it up to his way of conveying that he wasn't happy, either. I silently blamed the other dog, Kaya, for overreacting first, as I knew dogs could pick up on each other's vibes.

Gee. Thanks a lot, girl.

I still didn't sense I was in danger, although there was no way in hell I could've imagined what was about to happen. However, I had to admit these guys were proving harder to handle than I expected. It bordered on overwhelming, and more than anything, I didn't appreciate the hassle. This was supposed to be a favor, a quick stopover on my way home.

Yet I could barely move. I wasn't just surrounded by three big dogs. Each of them was in constant contact with me, pressing and shoving their meaty bodies against mine.

When My Friend and I had made plans the night before, she'd mentioned that Red might prefer to hang out in the garage rather than in the house or the yard. He was getting up in age, and she thought he might be more comfortable where it was cooler or where he could be alone.

Our current situation was far too chaotic for the cramped hallway. And since it was easy to reach the door to the garage behind me without moving, I eased it open. I hoped Red would jump at the chance to retreat to the solitude of the garage, giving me one less dog to wrangle. And he did—kind of.

He started out the door but only made it three-quarters of the way through before looking back over his shoulder. Then, for whatever reason—fear of missing out perhaps— he made a U-turn, and we were right back where we'd started.

I still couldn't move without stepping on the dogs, so I told them, more forcefully this time, to knock it off and settle down. Again, it didn't help.

Since they say the best way to tackle a problem is head-on, I opted to stick with the original plan, making it my sole mission to get them out the back door. And the quicker the better, since I assumed that's where they wanted to be, hence all the fuss.

Seeing how the dogs were still pressed against me on all sides, they had to move before I could. As I leaned into them with my thighs, the pressure and weight of the dogs felt like I was trying to walk in deep water. Moving ever so slowly, I carefully nudged them with each step in the direction I wanted to go. I didn't want to shove them and piss them off any more than they already were, but I had to push them firmly enough that they got the idea. I'd liken it to moving a bee out of the way. You don't want to make any wild movements, make it angry, and risk getting stung, so you push it out of the way calmly and steadily. Same here. I was intent on remaining calm, wishfully thinking the dogs would then pick up on *my* vibe, follow suit, and settle the hell down.

This is how we made our way back down the long hallway and through the kitchen—all three dogs surrounding me, barking and ramming themselves into me. We moved like this literally the entire length of the house, which was over forty feet. I know because I still had a copy of the floor plan. Although technically, I imagine we walked even farther since we didn't follow a straight line. Instead, the four of us zigzagged our way through the house like a tumbleweed, a tangled mess traveling the path of least resistance, our direction dependent on whichever dog yielded the most.

As they rotated around me, I suspected they were working as a team, instinctually herding me—as their ancestors would've done with some runaway sheep—but it felt like being caught in a dog tornado. However, this was more of the F1 variety. It wasn't severe enough to warrant the National Guard, but I realized I should probably take precautions. And like a real national disaster, feeding the dogs had become super inconvenient and frustrating, so I hoped it would be over soon.

With the dogs constantly moving, it was tough to keep tabs on where their feet were at all times, and since I couldn't see my feet either, I walked with slow, careful steps. The last thing I wanted to do was step on one of them inadvertently, considering their teeth were never more than a few inches from my legs. I still didn't think the dogs would bite me just for the sake of biting me, but I wouldn't put it past them to lash out if I hurt one of them. Each step was like walking through a minefield. I knew one wrong move, and this operation was going to go south real quick.

Each dog took turns walking behind me, alongside me, and backward in front of me. This constant changing of positions seemed funny to me, but only in the preposterous sense. Probably because I did the same thing when I moved something heavy.

For instance, say I was helping to carry a couch, and I was the one walking forward. If it was too heavy, I'd get it in my head that the person on the other end walking backward had the "easier" end, so I'd want to switch positions. Then, after they changed with me, I'd start to think maybe I *did* have the better end to begin with, so I'd want to switch back again. I wondered if the dogs were doing the same thing.

When the four of us eventually made it to the sliding glass door at the back of the house, I metaphorically breathed a sigh of relief.

Finally! Time to get on with the plan.

3. FIDDLING WITH LOCKS

The muddy cowboy boots lying haphazardly on top of the multicolored rug in front of the door made it look like people and pups were expected to wipe their feet. This was already a bigger ordeal than I had imagined, and I needed less to contend with, not more.

Thank God these guys are headed out and not in.

Bumping and tripping over each other—no thanks to those damn cowboy boots—I worried I'd step on a paw or topple over them. Lord knows that was the last thing I needed. If these dogs were so ticked off when I was merely trying to feed them, I couldn't imagine how pissed they'd be if I tackled them, even if by accident.

At first, I thought the thick rug was the heavy braided kind. The ones everyone seemed to have in the 1970s. But the more we slid around on it, the more I suspected it was the newer variety made of scraps of fabric tied together. The dogs were still in herding mode, still circling and nudging me, and as they continued to dance around me, the more the rug bunched up around our feet. The twisted rug, combined with the weight of the boots, had cemented mine in place—and way closer together than I would have liked.

My situation left me no choice but to unlock the door from where I stood. While I could reach the lock with no problem, as with most sliding glass door locks, I had to fiddle with it a bit. First, there was a tiny plastic stick-like lever that I had to tick to the right or left, but I had no idea which direction meant locked or unlocked—I still don't. Then, just above that lock, was another that I had to slide up or down. Again, I hadn't a clue which did which. Hence my difficulty.

As a realtor, I open and close doors all day long. The problem is that not only is each sliding glass door different, but not every homeowner uses both locking mechanisms. So, sometimes, when I think I'm unlocking a door, I'm actually locking it. That's why I need to play with them a bit. Even though I consider myself a reasonably intelligent and experienced door unlocker, getting My Friend's slider unlocked, with the added stress of trying not to trip or fall, took longer than you might think.

Still convinced the dogs were just doing the pee-pee dance, whenever I did manage to open the door, I expected them to zoom right past me into the yard. I wanted to give them plenty of room to get around me, but at the rate we were going, it looked like I'd be trapped in place by the dogs, with no choice but to remain standing where I was, smack in their way.

Making matters worse, the curtain panels that hung next to the door covered the lock. So, while I could reach the lock just fine, I couldn't see it. My Friend had brought these curtains from their last house, but now, in the heat of the moment, they seemed more decorative than functional, and I cursed them under my breath for being pointless and in my way.

I attempted to unlock it by feeling my way, but after a few failed attempts, it was obvious I needed to hold the curtains back to see what I was doing. They were made of thick velvet, which pooled in a pile on the floor, making them extra heavy. I could have used two hands to hold them back, but I still needed to monkey with the lock, which I fiddled with single-handedly for another minute or so.

When the lock finally disengaged, it made a loud, abrupt sound—like a single clap, but more forceful and metal-sounding.

That's when the dog shit hit the fan.

4. BITTEN

As soon as the lock clicked, I felt a sudden stab of pain in my leg.

It felt like someone had shoved scissors straight into my calf muscle and not the super sharp kind hair stylists use; I'm talking an old, crappy, dull pair, like the kind you'd find in your grandma's junk drawer. If you've ever stabbed yourself in the leg with one of those big three-pronged forks used to hoist Thanksgiving turkeys or gotten your leg stuck in a medieval blacksmith's vice, I imagine it felt similar to that.

To say I was stunned would be a colossal understatement. At first, it didn't even register as a bite. I thought I'd been stung by a bee. Even though we were inside, considering there were no scissors or giant turkey forks nearby, that was the best guess I could come up with. Clearly, my mind was having difficulty making sense of the information it had been given.

Stupefied, I whipped around to look behind me to see what still had a lock on my calf. But just as I turned, whoever it was let go. Free from its grasp, I jumped, not just reflexively from the excruciating pain but also to get out of the way.

I figured it was Red. When I'd looked behind me, I caught him retreating, backing away, his head low to the ground, his hind end up in the air. He looked at me from the top of his eyes, like dogs tend to do when they know they're in trouble. It gave me the impression he didn't know what he was doing, was ashamed of himself, or regretted what he'd just done.

I rationalized that he must have been displeased that I had blocked his way outside or had taken too long to open the door. Either way, he wasn't wrong, so initially, I was more shocked than angry.

Only, this was no teething-puppy bite. It felt more like a shark bite or a right hook from Mike Tyson. It came out of nowhere and was packed with intention. I could tell this dog meant business.

Standing at the back door, the four of us had been practically tripping over each other. Maybe one of the other dogs bumped into Red, and he meant to snap back at them, but somehow, my leg had gotten in the way. Or, sliding around on the rug the way we were, maybe my leg had slipped into his mouth accidentally. As excuses go, clearly, I was reaching. Still, it never occurred to me that it was anything more than a case of mistaken identity.

After all, don't sharks eat surfers instead of seals by mistake all the time? Okay, maybe not *all* the time, but I've watched enough *Shark Week* to know how it works. Sharks are curious and hungry by nature, so when a surfer cruises by, sometimes sharks take a bite. The shark doesn't necessarily want to kill the surfer. It's just looking for more information. It's hoping the surfer tastes like seal.

Maybe Red was seeing if I tasted like chicken—or Alpo.

As gullible as it sounds, I still thought it was all a matter of wrong place, wrong time. Never in my wildest dreams would I have thought this was the start of something horrific. But like a shark that takes one test bite then comes back for more, and within seconds, the other sharks get in on the action, the frenzy had just begun.

5. THREE-ON-ONE

All three dogs started biting me. The bites came so fast and so often that I couldn't properly process what was happening. I didn't have enough time to think a complete thought, let alone make a deliberate move before they'd bite me again. My body was being jerked in one direction, my thoughts in another.

Time seemed to pass erratically.

Sometimes, it felt like it was all happening in slow motion, like I was watching someone else's dream—though not like some out-of-body experience where I was looking down on myself. It was more like I was watching the events unfold from the perspective of an astute observer rather than being the reluctant participant I was. It's in these moments I can recall precisely where I was standing, what I was looking at, and what I was thinking.

Meanwhile, other parts of the attack are a little fuzzier. In these instances, I can still recount what was happening, but more so in a general sense. During these times, it seemed like everything around me was happening in a flash—and in reality, it probably was—so I imagine specific thoughts and feelings didn't have time to register. I was operating on a primal level. Think crocodile brain, devoid of emotion.

Since the searing pain and racing thoughts monopolized my senses, my hearing seemed to take a backseat. Noises sounded muffled and distant. Specific sounds were hard to make out. Sure, there was lots of growling, snarling, and barking. But there was something else I couldn't quite place. It didn't sound human. It was guttural and more animal-like, yet it didn't seem to be coming from the dogs. I was confused.

Is that screaming? Has someone walked in on us? I glanced at the door, but nobody was there.

Is it me? Am I screaming? That can't be me.

I'm not a screamer. Not on roller coasters. Not when I was in labor. Not even when I tore my hamstring—on three separate occasions.

I've always been more of a teeth-clencher and grunter. Yet it appeared these sounds were coming from me.

How is this possible?

Here I was, trying with every fiber of my being to remain as calm as I'd been when we walked from the laundry room to the back door—as if, by doing so, I could somehow undo this whole shitty mess. Surely, if I was calm, the dogs would see that I wasn't a threat, and they, too, would relax. But no. Every time they locked onto me, I couldn't help but make those horrible sounds.

Until then, I'd never heard that sound before. Nor do I hope to hear it ever again. It was the sound of sheer terror, but something they've yet to replicate in any horror movie I've ever seen. It's no wonder it took me by surprise.

I guess it makes sense. These weren't your average dog bites. Usually, a dog breaks the skin and then immediately releases, having made its point. With these dogs, their jaws locked onto me, sinking their teeth deep into the muscle. So deep, it felt like they had grabbed a hold of my bones. For some reason, my wrists, hands, and arms were always their first choice. Multiply that by three dogs, and it seemed their bites were landing in all the same places, over and over.

And they weren't *just* biting me. These dogs wanted more. When they'd clamp on, they'd shake their heavy heads back and forth, throwing their entire body weight behind it. With all three shaking me simultaneously and in opposite directions, I felt like a human chew toy.

It reminded me of trying to wrestle a toy from a big dog's mouth when it didn't want to let go. It was hard enough to get one dog to release using two hands. With three pit bulls in full attack mode and both my hands trapped inside their mouths, there was no way I could break free. And when it was two dogs on one arm—one locked onto my hand, another hanging off my elbow—I felt my arms would be ripped from my shoulder joints completely or, worse, be torn in half.

Even standing was a struggle since they always had me by both arms, yanking me in all directions. And when they weren't shaking me to throw me off balance, they tried pulling me to the ground. Going down on their forearms, their butts up in the air, they'd force their heads to the ground, dragging with them whatever body part of mine happened to be in their mouth.

Most of the time, it was one dog on each arm, each dog tossing me around as they whipped their heads up and down and side to side. If the third couldn't get a good grip on my hands or arms because the other two were flinging them too violently for it to latch on, that third dog was happy to bite me anywhere it could squeeze in.

As two hung off my arms, forcing me down, bending me forward, the third would try climbing onto my back. My booty shorts were no match for their long nails, which made long scratches down the backs of my bare legs. On any other day, this would have hurt in itself, but today, I was only vaguely aware of the pain.

Instinctively, I knew if they got me to the ground, I'd never get up again. Therefore, I fought like hell to remain standing despite that third dog chewing on my legs, rear, and stomach.

It was a continuous battle, always trying to center my weight, constantly adjusting my stance depending on which dog yanked me harder. The problem was whichever dog pulled harder was ever-changing, so I had to walk a fine line. While I had to actively pull away from them enough to avoid falling in their direction, I also had to be careful not to pull too hard, out of fear sections of my flesh would be torn right off.

With each bite, I'd automatically and involuntarily thrust myself in the opposite direction out of sheer agony, but this only further complicated my literal balancing act.

When the attack originally started, my only thought had been to get the hell out of there. However, the more it dragged on, the more I realized escape wasn't a viable option—not when I couldn't even move. Three ferocious dogs weren't just hanging off me; they were attacking me in full force. The sad fact was, I wasn't going to get away unless these dogs *allowed* me to get away.

6. FIGHT

As the saying goes, fight or flight. Since I couldn't get away, I contemplated fighting back, although I'd be lying if I said I wasn't hesitant. Part of me feared I'd make them angrier and, in turn, more vicious. But this had been going on far too long, and I needed a new plan.

I envisioned myself punching them, causing them to back off so I could make my getaway; only, by now, my hands and arms were pretty mangled. Of course, I didn't see them mangled, or if I did, my brain didn't allow me to acknowledge the extent of my injuries. I was only aware they weren't working so great, as they were harder to control and weren't bending where they should.

I scanned the room, searching for something to grab, something I could use to deter them or keep them at bay.

Who did I think I was? A lion tamer looking for a whip and a small chair? Clearly, *somebody* had watched too many cartoons as a kid.

As the attack dragged on, the biting and shaking grew more intense. It was as if the dogs were trying to outdo each other, like a sick competition to determine who could bite harder, hold on longer, or shake me more violently.

The bites were happening so fast, so often, and so savagely I couldn't even formulate a complete thought. I barely had time for my eyes to focus on a specific object, let alone determine how it might be useful in defending myself before the dogs would jump on me and bite me again.

Then, just like that, I'd be jolted back to reality, and all thoughts of the object I was attempting to zero in on would disappear. Again, my mind would be flooded with overwhelming thoughts of the pain, the shaking, and my struggle to stand upright.

Up until this point, most of my ordeal occurred in the living room, specifically, the area between the sofa, coffee table, and an oversized chair—my very own Bermuda Triangle. Trapped in that one spot, I doubted whether I could make my way over to an object, even if I did manage to pinpoint something I could use. Not to mention, it's not like I had use of my hands to grab something anyway—seeing how they were constantly lodged in some dog's mouth. Nevertheless, I promised myself if the opportunity to fight my way out presented itself, I'd go for it.

When we'd somehow worked our way a few feet to the right, I caught a bit of a reprieve. Standing next to the sofa, the dogs couldn't get close enough to grab my arm on that side. Beyond grateful for a free hand, I scanned the area for something I could use to fend them off. They were still biting and pulling me every which way, so whatever it was had to be within easy reach—though it's not like I had incredibly helpful options to choose from.

Throw blanket or pillow? Quick! Throw blanket or pillow? Umm. Blanket!

It's funny how, even in the thick of it, I managed to note the blanket's bumpy texture, which was far too scratchy for my liking—so wool, if I had to guess.

By this point, my hands and wrists were a bloody, aching mess, so my goal was to wrap the blanket around my free arm and hand in an attempt to protect them from further damage. I even allowed myself to believe I could make a boxing glove out of it and literally fight my way out of the situation.

Looking back, it sounds like another dumb idea I probably got from cartoons.

However, no surprise, there'd be no boxing match. Since I only had the one lame hand to work with, trying to wrap the blanket around, it looked more like I was spinning cotton candy at a pop-up carnival in a Kmart parking lot. Needless to say, I only managed to flip it up and over once before another bite yanked me in the opposite direction, causing me to drop the blanket altogether.

Blanketless, but still with a free hand, I considered throwing one of the throw pillows at the dogs—no pun intended. But even if I could get close enough to reach the pillows again, I reasoned it was pointless. I'd played soccer in high school, not softball, so even when my arms worked fine, my aim was still crap. Besides, what if I *did* beam one in the face? One pillow wouldn't stop three attack dogs. Chances are, it would just bounce off them and onto the floor. Then I'd most likely trip over it since, truth be told, I hadn't been that great at soccer either.

On second thought, scratch that idea.

On the sofa table behind the couch, I noted the various decorative items on display. Though they were too far away, I considered my options just in case. While some were more delicate—mercury glass, I think—others were more industrial. I'd say farmhouse, but My Friend's style was more Restoration Hardware, less Hobby Lobby.

At first, the notion of a deterrent was invigorating. However, despite everything I was going through, I still couldn't condone breaking something of hers or hurting one of the dogs, even if given the chance.

In my mind, I'd already caused enough problems. How fucked up is that?

Standing in front of the couch, I caught a bit of a break. With the coffee table now behind me, it prevented those dreaded attacks from behind. Not seeing the dog coming and getting caught off guard made those bites from behind seem far worse.

I like to cut to the chase. No sugarcoated bullshit for me. Just tell me like it is. Trust me, after my upbringing, I can take whatever someone's dishing out. I know it sounds crazy, but I *wanted* to see the bites coming so I could brace myself—physically and mentally.

Being positioned in front of the coffee table got the dogs, literally, off my back, but I soon realized it was the worst place to be when one of them jumped on the sofa, and we were suddenly eye to eye. Petrified he'd go for my throat, I turned my head, squinched my eyes, and stumbled away with no real plan in mind—other than far away from that couch.

When I opened my eyes again, I was backed up against an ottoman. Or was it a chair? What matters is that I ended up twenty feet away from the sliding door—my original intended escape route. The closest door was now the front door but it was still ten feet away, and I was still trapped in place. That's when the thought hit me like a freight train.

I'm going to die today.

7. ONE-ON-ONE

Hank had my left arm in his mouth and was jerking it. Hard. Way harder than I'd been shaken up until now. He was a blue nose pit bull and the youngest of the three dogs. Going one-on-one with him, it was apparent he was way more powerful than the other two, and I couldn't help but suppose he was causing a lot more damage in the process.

By this time, I was exhausted from simply trying to remain standing. Each of Hank's bites seemed to deplete all the energy I'd been able to muster since his last. When he yanked on me, he seemed to be using every one of his sixty-eight pounds to drag me down. Every shake of his big, heavy head left me bumbling, scrambling for balance.

As insane as it sounds, I recall wishing I was back to being attacked by two dogs at once. At least with one dog on each arm, the weight was more evenly distributed. This way, when they tugged on me, it was fairly equal, and my torso stayed somewhat in the middle. When there were two, most of my effort was spent leaning back on my heels, trying to keep my head high. I couldn't prevent myself from pitching forward, but if I held myself at a steep enough angle, it was harder for them to climb onto my back.

With two dogs, I didn't have to worry so much about falling to the side. My feet were usually far enough apart that I only had to make minor adjustments. Simply shifting my weight from hip to hip, depending on who tugged more, seemed to do the trick.

When it was only one dog, I had to adjust my stance considerably and shift my weight wildly in the opposite direction with each shake. Anything to avoid toppling over.

Trying to constantly predict Hank's every move was exhausting. It was impossible to anticipate which way he'd pull, how hard he'd pull, how long he'd pull, and more importantly, when he'd slow it all down. Yet it was critical. Any change in his speed, direction, or intensity could lead to an overcompensation on my part and, with that, a greater risk of crashing to the floor or, worse, right on top of him.

Maybe it was because I'd known him since he was a pup, or perhaps it was the intimacy of this one-on-one, but with him latched onto my arm and the two of us face to face, staring into each other's eyes, I felt something shift inside me. The feelings of shock and horror fell away, not entirely, but enough that I now felt mostly sadness and disappointment in him.

I may have even pleaded with him out loud, saying something along the lines of "No-no, Hank. Not you, too."

I might have understood if he'd only been going along with the pack, but to come at me single-handedly was gut-wrenching. I'd thought we were buddies, so this felt like a betrayal. I never thought this dog had it in him to bite a person, let alone attack someone, and do it so viciously. But the fact that he did it *so well* is what rattled me to my core.

I could only endure his grip for so long. Each of his bites left me teetering on the edge of giving in. Not because I wanted to but because I had nothing left in me to draw from to fight him off.

Watching Hank in action up close like that, he didn't look like the dog I knew. He looked like a stereotypical pit bull, the kind that seemed to get other people so worked up. His big teeth, strong jaw, hard head, and thick neck were impressive, but when factoring in his compact musculature and sheer size, I could see he was perfectly created for this. He was, in fact, built for destruction. And as a specimen, I was oddly in awe of him.

That's when it occurred to me. If these dogs that I liked, which I thought had liked me, could not only do this to me but make it look so damn easy, it was going to be impossible to beat them at this game. Especially considering the game was three-on-one. It was then that tremendous doubt came barreling in. Not only could I see no way out, I was so damn tired of fighting. I was officially hopeless. Unintentionally, my brain flipped that switch. In that instant, I transitioned from survival mode to acceptance, and I started to prepare for the end.

8. ACCEPTANCE

The feeling that overcame me when I thought I was on the verge of inevitable death was surreal. It was like walking in a dream. My eyes turned away from the dogs and stared blankly into the distance. I went from being hyper-aware of each dog's every move to only having a vague sense of my surroundings. The bites were still coming, but I was no longer keeping track of who was doing what.

My eyes seemed to be stuck in tunnel vision mode. All I could see was this two-foot-wide path leading from where we stood, past the coffee table, and in the general direction of the television console beyond it. My peripheral vision was gone. I could no longer make out anything else in the room but this path. Everything else faded into blurriness, and no matter how much I blinked, I couldn't get it back.

This pathway had a weird, mesmerizing hold on me despite nothing of interest being there that would warrant that kind of attention. In fact, as had been the case since I opened that fucking laundry room door, all the action was still centered around me. All three dogs were either chewing on me or jockeying for a better position to grab ahold of me. As soon as one dog released me, another would pick up right where it had left off, leaving that first one in search of a different body part to bite.

Even though I was surrounded by chaos, everything seemed to stand still, and a tremendous peaceful feeling washed over me.

All noises faded to a low hum. I'm sure the barking and growling, as well as my heavy breathing and groans of pain, hadn't stopped, but they were now barely audible, like static on a radio.

My life didn't flash before my eyes, as they say, but I had a million thoughts racing through my mind in what seemed like one instant. They rushed in like rapid fire, one right after the other. I barely had time to acknowledge one before another would come crashing in behind it. Then that first thought, bumped out of the way entirely, would be forgotten just as quickly as it had barged in.

I suddenly had a lifetime to evaluate and little time to do it.

By now, I'd resolved myself to the fact that the dogs would kill me. I assumed if they kept tearing at me as they had been, they would eventually rip one of my limbs from my body, and I'd slowly bleed to death. Either that or eventually, I'd succumb to their weight, fall to the ground, and they'd rip my throat out. Since both sounded beyond horrific, I didn't allow myself to envision anything more specific than that.

I believe the human brain has this innate sense of what a person can and cannot handle, in the same way they say you can't die in your dreams. You might come close, but you'll always wake up before you die. That's because, supposedly, if you die in your dreams, you'll die in real life. Likewise, I don't think it was possible at that moment to think of what being mauled to death would've actually entailed without dying right then and there.

At the center of my desperation was the fact that I was all alone. There wasn't a single human being who was aware of what was happening to me. Therefore, no good Samaritans would be coming to my rescue.

My husband, Dale, was still asleep when I'd left the house to go to the gym that morning, so I didn't remind him I'd be stopping here on my way home. Truth be told, I couldn't recall if I'd even mentioned feeding the dogs at all. I figured he'd just assume that I'd swung by the grocery store or stayed at the gym to run extra laps around the block as I often did.

It wasn't like me to check in with him, so it would likely be hours later before he'd think something was wrong. Besides, he didn't have My Friend's new address, so it's not like he could come looking for me even if he had known my plans and grew suspicious.

To keep tabs on their spouses and kids, some of our friends had cell phone apps that allowed them to track each other's every move. We didn't. By the time Dale realized I was taking too long to get home, it would be too late. I was exhausted and wasn't going to hold up much longer.

I assumed my body wouldn't be discovered until My Friend returned from her trip a few days later, and just like that, I was sad all over again. Not for me, but for My Friend and her young daughter, who'd come home to find me dead in a massive pool of blood on their living room floor. I wondered how horrific that would be as I imagined my lifeless body sprawled out, cold and pasty white. Or would I be gray? The only dead bodies I'd ever seen had been covered in a thick layer of orangey makeup, making it impossible to tell what color they'd really been.

I then pondered whether the dogs would actually eat me since I never did get around to feeding them. I suspected three big dogs ate a lot, so if they made a meal of me, I wondered how much would be left after the long weekend.

Like some psycho, I also considered whether a human would taste better or worse than dog food. Dog food tasted like crap. I knew because I ate some on a dare in the second grade. Dog food, that is, not crap.

Disgusting tasting or not, they say when an animal eats a human, it can acquire a taste for it. That got me thinking about how long it would take before that kicked in. Would it be instantaneous? Would they take one bite of me, find me delicious, and then keep going because they couldn't stop themselves—like Dale and potato chips? Or perhaps the point of all this was simply to kill me, and after the dogs realized they'd done their job, they'd curl up in their beds and take a nap. Oh, how I hoped it was the latter.

I couldn't believe I'd ended up in this situation, and it made me think of that 1996 Alanis Morissette song, "Ironic." I was supposed to feed the dogs, not *be* the food for the dogs.

Had all those workouts and time spent pondering nutritional labels in supermarket aisles been a colossal waste of time? If this had been my destiny all along, I could have been eating pizza and brownies every day of my life, and it wouldn't have mattered. All this time, I thought I had been making myself harder to kill. Only I thought I was setting myself up for age ninety-four, not forty-nine.

Why now, and why in such an awful way? I couldn't wrap my head around the idea that my entire life had been leading up to this one moment. *This* was the big, grand plan God had in store for me? *Really?* If so, why were child molesters, rapists, and serial killers allowed to die of natural causes in warm beds? What could I have possibly done to deserve this?

I was also bummed not to be leaving behind a legacy of some sort. I'm not talking about a foundation or a cure for cancer, just something I could be remembered for. However, even if I had done something monumental or impressive with my life, I imagined it would still be impossible for anyone to remember me for anything other than being mauled by dogs. It made me furious to think that *this* would be my defining moment. Regardless of whether my accomplishments were big or small, ultimately, I wouldn't be remembered for anything *I* had done but rather for something that was done *to* me. I felt cheated in the worst way possible.

9. THOSE LEFT BEHIND

My mind continued to race. Knowing I wasn't ready to die gave way to thoughts of how my family would react. That made my heart ache so profoundly, I swear I could feel it deep in my soul. My kids. Oh God, what would happen to my kids? If they were still devastated over the loss of our thirteen-year-old cat, who passed away a year ago, this would surely destroy them.

I thought about my son, Harry, at a job training facility out West. Who would break the news to him? Would my husband do it, or would someone there be the one to tell him? Then I wondered which was worse—learning from a loved one by phone or from a stranger in person?

He worked hard to get there, so I hoped he'd continue. However, I worried he'd be forced to quit. If he couldn't concentrate, he'd likely fall behind. If so, I was afraid they'd ask him to leave. Typically, they didn't allow trainees to take time off from the program, but I wondered if they would make an exception in a case like this. What I wouldn't do to see him one last time.

Nobody's kids should be made to imagine a parent being mauled to death. Surely, this would haunt them for the rest of their lives. Perhaps they'd cherish our last words and focus on that instead. Then I wondered what those last words had been. Shit, I couldn't recall. I hoped it had been something profound and memorable and not something stupid like *Don't forget to take out the trash*. It was probably *I love you* since I always say that. I was so thankful I'd made a habit of always telling them I loved them. I just hoped they knew how much.

I wasn't worried about my husband surviving without me, as we were both independent, but I was sad that I'd be missing out on our future. We'd hit this stride after the kids graduated from high school. They say that's when most couples grow apart, yet Dale and I had grown closer. I suspect it's because that's when we started traveling more. We enjoyed exploring new places together and taking bad selfies on mountaintops. But we still had a long list of places we wanted to get to, and standing there in My Friend's living room, I couldn't help but wish we'd started sooner.

While he'd been a good dad to the boys, I didn't think he had the bandwidth to be both their dad and their mom, at least not the kind of mom *I* thought I was. I'd been trying to teach them to be proper humans, and though they were twenty-three and twenty-five, I was far from done.

There was so much more my kids would accomplish in their lives, and while I wanted to be a part of that, too, more than anything, I just wanted to be around to smother them with love. It was one thing to hope to dance with them at their weddings and snuggle their babies someday, but what about all those other everyday moments, the ones I was starting to realize I'd taken for granted?

Our family's love language had always been sarcasm. Nothing could brighten my workday like a snarky family group text. That and those stupid memes they sent me. Half the time, I needed someone to explain them to me, but that only made it all the funnier. Nobody could make me laugh like my kids. Damn, we'd had some good times.

No more family ski trips? No more family dinners? I still hadn't gotten around to teaching them how to cook. I mean, *really* cook. Their favorite recipes weren't written in any cookbook; they were straight from my memory. I thought they'd hand down my chicken piccata recipe for generations to come. I guess not.

Who'd tell them everything would be okay the next time some dumb girl broke their heart? Though I hoped one day they'd eventually find someone to love them as much as I did. Yeah, right. Impossible. These kiddos were my whole world.

I couldn't believe how fucking unfair it all was. We're all given this beautiful gift of life, but now, I felt as if I'd squandered mine. If I'd known I'd have such little time, I would have used it more wisely. Why hadn't I done more, seen more, learned more, and taken more chances? What had I been so afraid of? More importantly, what had I been waiting for?

I felt despair and regret. Immense regret. Harsh regret. I felt shame for not having done more with my life, but most of all, I regretted I wouldn't get to live a *long* life. I never expected to be dead before fifty.

Why hadn't I lived every day with the sense of purpose and urgency I felt right now? I had this live-life-to-the-max feeling practically pulsating inside me, but I had nowhere to channel it. And why was the Universe pointing this out to me now? Frankly, I would've preferred not to have realized this at all, rather than now when it was far too late. It all just seemed so cruel.

10. FLIGHT

I don't know how long I was zoned out, but the next thing I knew, Hank and Kaya started fighting each other, jolting me back to reality. I was still stuck in tunnel vision mode and getting mauled by Red. Lost in my racing, morbid thoughts, I heard it before I saw it. There's no mistaking the sound of two dogs fighting—their barks and growls project a ferocious intensity that drew my attention like a magnet. As they went after each other, they scuffled past the coffee table and wound up against the wall next to the TV console. For the first time since this shit show began, I finally had some distance between two of the dogs and me, even if it was only ten feet or so.

Red and I were still at the opposite end of the living room, my arm locked in his jaws, but I decided to make a run for the sliding door anyway. That is, as much of a run as one can manage with a sixty-five-pound dog hanging off their arm.

I wanted to stay as far away from the other two dogs as possible, so instead of walking through the living room, I backtracked a bit to walk behind the sofa and the table that ran along behind it. This buffer gave me the sense, albeit distorted, that I'd be hidden. Okay, maybe not exactly hidden, but at least trickier for them to get at.

There was only one problem with going in this direction. When Red and I emerged from behind the sofa, we'd be directly in their line of sight and a straight shot from where the other two were fighting. For this to work, I had to be quick about it. So, without another thought, I made a break for the door twenty feet away. But with Red in tow, of course, as he was unwilling to let go of my arm.

It sounds crazy, but I remember thinking how easy it was dragging the one dog around the house. Up until this point, I'd had over 200 pounds of ferocious dogs hanging on me and tearing into my flesh for who knows how long. Contending with one dog was way better than three, and that thought alone was enough to boost my spirits, restore some hope, and give me the gumption I needed to make it all the way.

I managed to slide open the back door with the one arm that wasn't locked in Red's jaws, and I felt a tinge of pride as this was no small feat, considering my motor skills were shot. By this point, nothing from my shoulders down was working the way it was supposed to, but I was determined to make the most of the opportunity.

Failing wasn't an option.

After I backed myself out the patio door, I used my free hand to pound on Red, aiming for anywhere I could land a punch. I say punch, but I was really just flopping my gimpy hand in his general direction. It was like batting at a mosquito and equally as effective. When I did make contact with his thick, hard skull, I'm sure it hurt me way more than it hurt him, so I was taken aback when he loosened his grip. It was probably just so he could get a better hold or catch his breath, but regardless, it was just enough.

I shoved him off me, which enabled me to slide the door shut between us. With Red locked inside with the rest of his pack, I felt somewhat triumphant, and for a brief moment, I was half-tempted to collapse with relief, believing I was finally safe. That is until I realized I'd just fucked up. And in a big way.

11. ONE FOR THE ROAD

The second I shoved Red off me, he snarled and lunged at me again. Hurrying, I fumbled to find the door handle without looking, and in doing so, I'd made a huge mistake. I'd grabbed the screen door handle, not the handle to the glass door, as I intended, having been too intent on watching the dog and not the door. But who could blame me?

Despite the epic fail, I was still somewhat relieved. This was the first time since I clicked that lock open that I didn't have a dog tearing into me. Too bad my joy was short-lived as I stood there, forced to carefully, yet quickly, consider my options.

I was afraid if the dogs saw me take off running in the backyard, it would trigger their chase instinct, like a rabbit decoy at a dog track. Or was that just in Bugs Bunny cartoons?

Seriously, Cheryl?

Even *I* was over the cartoon references. You would have thought the dogs had ripped chunks from my brain, and the only bits remaining were cartoon memories from the 1970s.

It didn't matter. There was no way I was trusting that flimsy screen door to hold the three of them back. I wasn't stupid. If they wanted out, they'd bust right through—taking that whole damn door with them.

But closing the sliding glass door meant pushing the screen door all the way open in order to reach the glass door handle behind it. It definitely wasn't ideal, though I couldn't see any way around it.

The problem was, opening the screen door again meant another bite from Red. He was still standing in the same place I'd left him with his nose up against the screen, snarling. The only thing separating us was the flimsy mesh.

Having been so focused on Red and the doors, I'd lost track of the other two dogs. Standing in the bright sunlight on the patio, it appeared much darker inside than out, so I couldn't make out anything beyond Red. I also couldn't hear the other dogs over Red's snarling and barking, mere inches from my face. For all I knew, the other two were right behind him. Regardless, I still had to switch the doors, and fast, before the others realized what was happening and rushed over to get me, too. For good measure, I said a silent prayer that they were still preoccupied or at least far enough away.

Again, I felt hopeful. I was closer to safety than I ever thought possible and committed to baby-stepping my way out of this. I told myself if I'd made it this far, I could undoubtedly manage one more bite if it meant my freedom. However, I also knew I no longer had the mental fortitude to handle another three against one or anything close to that level of intensity.

It's not like I envisioned myself being torn to shreds. I simply felt if all three of them came at me again, I'd die on the spot. Not from a heart attack, more like my mind would just shut down, and in doing so, I'd suddenly cease to exist, as if magically whisked away to Nothing Land, like a puff of smoke, ashes-to-ashes, dust-to-dust style. My mind couldn't—or wouldn't—allow me to imagine the alternative.

As expected, as soon as I slid the screen door back, Red was on me again, but this time, he was clamped onto my other arm. Knowing he'd grab me, I purposefully used the opposite hand to open the door. I couldn't bring myself to offer up that same fucked-up arm he'd been chewing on a few short moments before since it was still throbbing and burning with pain from the last big bite when I'd dragged him through the house by his teeth.

I pulled the glass door as closed as possible with the arm that wasn't in Red's mouth. He continued to shake the arm he had ahold of, but with the door mostly closed, my arm just slammed back and forth between the heavy steel door frame and the steel track running down the wall. I tried to jiggle it free from his jaws, but his shaking totally overpowered my feeble attempts to wriggle it, and I was too afraid to yank it from him. I thought if I pulled too hard, I'd help him to tear a chunk of flesh right off the bone.

I knew time was running out. The other dogs were bound to join in at any minute, so I snuck my foot through the crack at the bottom of the door. I wanted to kick him, but I found I didn't have the room to properly swing my foot in the small opening. Plus, coordination is *not* one of my many natural talents. However, even though I missed hitting him, I managed to cause enough of a distraction that he let go.

Still, I couldn't get the door closed all the way. It was somehow just as open as when my arm was stuck inside. Eyes darting around, I spotted the problem—that damn slippery rag rug. The same one I'd tripped over when I tried to open the slider the first time.

It was wedged in the opening at the bottom, preventing me from shutting the door. I had probably kicked it in the way when I pulled my foot out.

Talk about the gift that keeps on giving. Stupid rug.

I was already pushing my luck. I didn't think I could handle another bite from Red, and I definitely couldn't afford for the other two dogs to get in on the action. Though I was petrified one of them might push their snout in the opening and wedge themselves out the door, it would have to remain open those few inches. Not knowing how long I had before they'd figure all that out, I took off running.

PART TWO

FINDING HELP

12. OVER THE FENCE

I ran across the backyard toward the east side of the house, then up the side yard toward the street in front, only there was no gate. I had a fifty-fifty shot, but apparently, I chose to run up the wrong side of the yard.

Of course, I did.

Regardless, there was no way I was going anywhere near that sliding glass door or the backyard. Knowing my luck, just as I'd round the corner to head to the other side of the house, I'd bump smack into them, surely having figured out how to free themselves by now. And if they hadn't, seeing me run past was bound to inspire them to bum-rush the door.

Done with trying to outwit dogs, I decided, *Screw the gate*, and jumped the fence.

It's funny, for the longest time, that's how I told that part of the story. In simplifying it, by saying I jumped the fence, I inadvertently made myself sound like some expert pole vaulter—like it was all easy-peasy. Yet, considering my very less-than-Olympic track-and-field abilities, I'm surprised nobody ever questioned me. That is, until weeks later, when my gym coach and I were engrossed in my story. He probed me about the fence, asking if it'd been the chain link kind. Pfft, I wish. I went on to explain if it had been, I could've put my feet in the various holes, gradually working my way up and over the top.

Instead, it was the black aluminum kind where the bars primarily run up and down, with one horizontal bar a few inches from the top and another a few inches from the bottom. I stared at him stupidly when he asked where I'd put my feet to climb over. I didn't have a clue. There had been nowhere *to* put my feet.

Then he smiled at me and helped me see the only way I could have hoisted myself over that fence was by sheer strength. The muscle-up was a gym move, which I thought was way beyond my abilities. Yet, that day, not only did I manage to do it, but I did it with hands, wrists, and arms that were bloodied, swollen, bruised, and nearly broken.

What made this more impressive was that we had this conversation weeks after the attack. Even by then, I still couldn't wash my own hair because my wrists and fingers were too weak to withstand that kind of pressure. So, the fact that I had muscled my way up and over a fence immediately following the attack felt somewhat miraculous. Our coach had always told us we were stronger than we thought, and here was living proof. Adrenaline is a beautiful thing.

13. CHARADES

I may have been over the fence, but I wasn't out of the woods. My phone and car keys were in my purse, but that was all still inside the house—along with the three dogs who had just tried to kill me. So, to get home, I needed help to make that happen.

My Friend's neighborhood was brand new. Since the builders worked in phases, completing small sections at a time, so beyond her house, there was mostly vacant land. Even in the section where she lived, it was still hit or miss. A house that looked finished on the outside might only be half-finished on the inside, and with no way to tell which homes were done, I had no idea which were occupied.

Scanning the area for any signs of life, I spotted someone on a ladder in the driveway of a house still under construction. The house sat kitty-corner across the street, so I assumed he was in earshot. "Hello! Can you help me?" I yelled as I headed in his direction, giving little thought to what I looked like, only thankful to have found someone so nearby.

He had looked over at me when I called out to him, so I knew he'd heard, but when I got to his ladder, he ignored me. He just continued painting as if I wasn't there at all. I didn't have the time nor the patience for games, not usually, and definitely not today. I needed help.

So, since the front door was wide open, I wandered inside and found a Latina-looking woman in the kitchen. I can't recall what I said to her, but when she didn't reply, I suspected she didn't speak English.

My Español is normally rudimentary at best, but at that moment, it was failing me altogether. Still, I was undeterred. As anyone who knows me can attest, my charades game is fierce. So much so that when we vacation in foreign-speaking countries, I make it a point to chat up the locals. If we need directions or have questions, I'm the girl. Especially if it involves bartering since I like to think my negotiation skills transcend all language barriers—plus it's fun.

My friends and family make it seem like they're merely indulging me, but I think they're always secretly happy they don't have to do it themselves. They shake their heads and roll their eyes as in *Yup, there she goes again,* and then wave me off with a dismissive *Go do what you gotta do,* and off I go, smiling, jabbering loudly, my hands flailing in all directions.

I certainly wasn't up for a proper charades battle today. I could barely move my hands and arms, and when I did try, I'd mainly just fling blood everywhere. However, while I lacked my usual enthusiasm and animation, I still managed to gesture enough to convey I was looking to make a phone call.

Too bad the only phone number I could remember was Harry's in New Mexico. Although I didn't realize it at the time, I was in shock. I just assumed that years of having everyone's phone numbers programmed into my phone had finally caught up with me, and I'd forgotten how to remember altogether—the eventual and dreaded endgame to "use it or lose it." Being 1600 miles and two time zones away, Harry wouldn't have been my first choice, but it's not like I expected him to come to my rescue. I just needed him to call his father and tell him to pick me up.

Our little town was recently voted one of the country's fastest-growing communities, and developers were building more and more houses farther out east. However, unfortunately, the cell phone towers had yet to catch up, so reception could be sketchy, depending on the person's phone carrier.

Not surprisingly, the woman's signal was intermittent.

To make matters worse, I struggled to translate Harry's phone number. I knew all my Spanish numbers, but they weren't coming to mind fast enough. I could only manage to spit out a few before her screen would time out, or she'd lose the connection, and we'd have to start all over.

I could tell she was looking around for something to write with, and for a moment, I got excited.

Yes! Great idea!

As she wandered around, I readied myself for the pen or pencil which would finally get us over this hump.

First, I racked my brain trying to come up with a better phone number, and when none came to mind, I figured I'd stick with my initial plan and call my son out West. With that settled, I started thinking about where I'd write it down.

Kitchen counter? Nothing on it. Nice and flat. Perfect.

There was also the question of *how*, as in, how big I'd have to write it to ensure she could read it correctly since Lord Knows I'd be hard-pressed to win any penmanship awards these days. Trying to decipher my to-do lists, sometimes I even stumped myself.

But as she continued searching, the other aspect of that *how* stopped me in my tracks. That's when I realized there was no way in hell I could hold a pen or a pencil in my mangled hands.

Wallowing in my despair, I forgot she was still looking. So when she walked back toward me and eyed me apologetically to let me know she hadn't found anything to write with, I shrugged, letting her know it was okay. Disappointed and frustrated, we gave up on the phone altogether.

14. SHOCK

Bleeding steadily, I stood over the sink in the kitchen so as not to drip blood everywhere. Before now, I hadn't been able to look at my wounds. Not in the I-can't-look-because-yuck-gross, or in the I-can't-stand-the-sight-of-blood sense, but I literally had not been able to see my arms since the attack began. Either some dog had been blocking my view, or my arms were being whipped around so fast I couldn't focus in on them. Besides, I'd had more important things to worry about than evaluating my injuries. Important things like getting the hell out of there.

Now, with all the lines of blood trickling down my arms, it was hard to see what was what, so I was looking forward to rinsing myself off. I was not only hoping to get a good look, but I assumed the cold water would soothe the pain that seemed to grow more intense by the minute.

My arms were so limp and sore that I started to think the dogs had shaken them right out of their sockets.

I reached out toward the faucet handle but stopped abruptly, unsure how to turn it on. Part of me blames the plumbing industry. Nowadays, it seems every manufacturer has their own unique way of designing faucets. Even on regular days, I struggle when I encounter a new faucet. Fumbling around, I'll push and pull the levers every which way and wave my hands in front of it, jazz hands style, before figuring it out. But that day, I just stood there staring at it.

My brain seemed to only be capable of processing the primal urgency coursing through my body. It was stuck in fight-or-flight mode, and I couldn't penetrate that caveman layer to get to the practical, problem-solving layer that housed the information I was looking for. I hadn't a clue how to construct a strategy to even *attempt* to turn on the water.

I looked exasperatedly at the young woman standing on the other side of the kitchen island and gestured as wildly as I could muster toward the handle with my elbow before dropping to my knees in front of the sink. Suddenly dizzy, I instinctually crouched down to get closer to the floor.

The floor was covered in plain brown paper held together with royal blue painter's tape, presumably to protect whatever new and pretty flooring lay beneath. And with all the allure of a giant present, the former new-home sales consultant in me couldn't help but wonder what kind it might be. It was cool to the touch, so tile, most likely. I guessed it was the wood plank style, which was still super popular. But because the trend had been so overdone in recent years, I hoped it was finally on its way out.

By now, the pain was no longer coming in waves—it was constant, but the intensity varied. Since trying to move took all my concentration, I presumed my brain was filtering it to some extent. However, huddled down low like this, in a little ball, made the pain much worse.

After the gray-and-white-speckled fuzziness subsided and my vision returned, I stood to find that the nice woman had come around to my side of the island and turned on the faucet for me. So appreciative, I tried to muster a smile, but I'm sure my face was too twisted from the pain to look as grateful as I felt.

To my surprise, the water made the pain even more excruciating—though it probably had more to do with the adrenaline wearing off than the water itself. As soon as the blood washed away, it would reappear, but I felt tremendous relief in seeing that chunks of flesh weren't missing from my forearms. My fingers, however, bled too much and too quickly to make heads or tails of whatever skin or tissue may or may not lie beneath.

Clearly, I'm no doctor. The cold water didn't stop the bleeding as I had envisioned, and I felt a little dumb for even thinking that it would. However, in my defense, tenth-grade health class had been a *really* long time ago.

On top of that, I felt guilty for bleeding all over some stranger's new sink. I knew my blood wouldn't damage the stainless steel, but it would still be tarnished nonetheless and no longer the brand-new, fresh, unused sink the future owners expected. While they would never know, I would.

As I rinsed my arms, the young woman eyed me cautiously. Though we couldn't communicate, I could tell she wanted to help but didn't know how. I didn't blame her. I was also out of ideas.

I got the feeling I made her nervous, and it occurred to me that she was most likely wondering what had happened and why I looked the way I did. I wanted to reassure her that she wasn't in danger, but seeing how frustrating and poorly our attempts at a phone call had gone, I didn't have the energy to even try.

As strange as this sounds, I didn't want My Friend or the dogs to get in trouble over what had happened. If I gave out too much information. I was afraid I might inadvertently implicate them. So, to protect My Friend and her dogs, I consciously decided to avoid *any* talk of the incident or what may have led to my injuries.

As depressing as it was, it was apparent this situation wasn't getting me anywhere, so I resolved to hunt down help elsewhere. Not wanting this encounter to have been a *complete* waste of time, I scanned my surroundings again, looking for anything else that could be deemed useful. Since my arms were still wet with a mixture of water and blood, a clean rag or paper towels would have been nice. But considering it was a vacant, unfinished house, there was literally nothing to choose from.

As I walked out the open front door, the woman followed me outside and began speaking Spanish to the guy in the driveway, who now stood a little lower on his ladder, painting the garage trim. He didn't look at either of us when he replied, but I wasn't surprised. I already knew from my last interaction with him that he was unwilling to help.

I suspected he didn't want to get involved because of something having to do with his immigration status. Right or wrong, rather than think of him as a jerk, I preferred to believe he had a legitimate reason for ignoring me. At least that way, from a Karma perspective, I didn't have to hold it against him.

Considering our language barrier and my diminished brain function, it was clear I required a more user-friendly helper, anyway. So back down the driveway I went. *Plan B, here I come.*

15. PARANOIA

I wasn't just nervous. I was downright paranoid. As I trudged down the street past My Friend's house, I was convinced the dogs had found their way outside by now, and when they saw me walk by, they'd feel compelled to finish me off—fence or no fence.

The entire experience, thus far, felt like I was a participant in one of those nature films you'd find on Discovery Channel or National Geographic—the kind where the baby gazelle wanders away from its herd and finds–itself surrounded by a pack of hyenas. The poor thing cowers in the center while the hyenas take turns sneaking up behind it to steal a bite. Each hyena strives to outdo the last. All want to be the badass that will deliver the lethal blow, delighting the onlookers, like a dance battle or a piñata at a Cinco de Mayo party.

Somehow, the gazelle manages to break free. Then, right when I think it might actually survive and it's safe to pull my hands down from in front of my face, some overachieving hyena bounds out of nowhere and takes the gazelle down. By the throat, of course. It's always by the throat.

I felt like that baby gazelle. Even though I'd escaped, I was afraid the threat still loomed, so my guard was up—way up.

As I approached My Friend's house, her yard was quiet. I couldn't hear barking, and I didn't see any dog faces pressed against the fence, yet I was still careful not to cross to her side of the street until I was way past her property line.

For some reason, walking was throwing me for a loop. I imagine I hadn't thought about how to walk since I was eleven months old—it was just something I did. But suddenly, it was as if my brain had gone on strike. Nothing came to my mind automatically anymore. Every thought was a struggle. To walk, I had to break the process down into step-by-step instructions for my body to fully grasp the plan.

Okay, right leg, you start. Reach out. Get that foot out there. Yup, you got this. Okay, left leg, your turn. Same thing. Reach out. Push off. You're up again, right leg. Right leg? Hey, right leg, where'd you go? Stick with us. C'mon guys, keep it moving.

On the bright side, with my brain so preoccupied with figuring out how to move, it didn't have time to think about how my arms felt like they'd been run over by a goddamn dump truck. That alone would have compelled me to keep moving, but I spotted a man loading something into, or out of, the back of a pickup truck a few houses down, and he clinched the deal.

He didn't know it yet, but he was my plan B.

16. GOOD SAMARITANS

Constantly looking back, I kept a close eye and ear out for the dogs since I didn't put it past them to come charging down the street after me as I made my way down the road. And as I plodded along, straining to hear, I wondered if anyone had heard what had happened to me inside that house.

Most houses in Florida are made of concrete block, but that doesn't make them entirely soundproof. I usually ran a few miles in my neighborhood a couple nights a week and often heard dogs barking inside the houses as

I passed by. So surely, three big dogs ferociously barking should have been heard by someone, no?

Perhaps these dogs hadn't barked so much as they'd growled. But like a person who can't talk properly with food in their mouth, I didn't see how they could bite me and bark simultaneously. And with so much biting going on, I then wondered how they'd had time to vocalize at all.

As for me, again, I wasn't a screamer. I knew I had cried out, but I couldn't say how often. Recalling how the sounds I'd made had freaked me out, I questioned whether I'd blocked them out altogether because now, after the fact, I couldn't discern how loud I had been, either. Even so, I imagined there had to have been *some* sounds escaping from inside.

How could it be that in a neighborhood with hundreds of homes, nobody had passed by My Friend's house that morning? Nobody was out walking their dog, pushing a stroller, or riding a bike? Then again, maybe someone *did* hear something, but they'd chosen to ignore it.

What did I expect someone to do, anyway? In this day and age, who's going to ring a stranger's doorbell and ask the people inside if there's a problem? People are crazy. Do-gooders like that are liable to get a gun pointed in their face. In the end, I suppose I couldn't blame someone if they didn't want to get involved.

I guess it's a damn good thing I'd gotten myself out of there.

17. DODGING ME

I called out several times as I approached the man with the pickup truck. But when I got no reaction from him, I began to doubt whether he'd heard me. I supposed my voice could have gotten carried away with the wind. Either that, or he only *pretended* he hadn't.

When I was a kid, I had a paper route, and once a week, I'd have to go collecting. That's when you went to each of the subscribers' homes to collect the money to either pay for the newspapers you delivered that past week, or to pay for the papers you'd be delivering the coming week. This was the early eighties, and *The Courier Express* in Buffalo, NY was flexible like that. You could either pay in advance or pay in arrears. So long as you didn't get too far behind, you still got your paper.

As I'd make my way from door to door, usually sometime over the weekend, I'd look up the block and see people darting into their homes when they noticed me coming. Most ducked inside to grab their wallets so they'd be ready for me by the time I got to their house. But not all.

Others hid inside to avoid me. Unsurprisingly, the avoiders were usually the people in arrears.

I could stand at their door for what seemed like an eternity, ringing and knocking, but they'd continue to ignore me, pretending they weren't home.

Dude, really? I just saw you five minutes ago watering your lawn.

As with the avoiders from my past, each time the man with the pickup walked back into the garage, I was petrified I'd never see him again. I knew if he was dodging me, not only did I not have the physical strength to knock on his door, but I didn't know if I could bring myself to beg—even in my condition. Not when there was the chance he was avoiding me on purpose and might never come to the door. After what I had already been through that day, I didn't think I could handle any more rejection or disappointment.

I looked farther down the street, but nobody else was outside. If it wasn't going to be this guy, then who?

18. TWENTY QUESTIONS

By the time I reached him, he was standing next to the open passenger's side door, either on the phone or rummaging inside for something—it was hard to see exactly. Standing six-ish feet away, I waited a minute or so for him to emerge and take notice of me. Again, I'm not sure in what part of the brain manners are housed, but looking back weeks later, I found it ridiculous that I would yield to social etiquette in a situation like that. Ordinarily, I don't do anything silently—or patiently, for that matter—but there I stood, waiting silently and patiently for him to acknowledge me.

When he finally did, I asked, nicely and calmly—which was also not my usual modus operandi—if he could make a call for me. Only he didn't answer. Instead, he walked around the back of the truck to stand beside me and proceeded to slowly size me up and down before asking what had happened.

I'll admit I was annoyed. I wasn't in the mood for an interrogation. I'd merely asked a simple question—one that only required a yes or no answer. Not to mention, I couldn't see how what had happened to me was any of his business. Wasn't it impolite to ask me that? It's not like I had asked him what he was doing in his truck when I walked up.

This was transactional, not a social call. Therefore, within those boundaries, I was to mind my own business, and he was to damn well do the same, Hello? Couldn't he tell from the blood dripping down my arms that the phone call was more of a priority than any sidebar about what had happened? Besides, I'd given little thought as to how to explain all this, and I needed time to get my story straight.

I didn't want to get anyone in trouble, but I also wasn't in the mood to be judged as I still wasn't sure what stupid part I may have played in all this. I wasn't prepared for this line of questioning, and my brain *definitely* wasn't up to thinking on the fly. My only recourse was to dodge his questions the best I could. Meanwhile, he was throwing out all kinds of wild guesses. They came so fast and furious you would have sworn he was on a goddamn game show, and this was the speed round.

First, he asked if I'd fallen while running, and for a second, I looked at him like he was crazy. But when I realized I was still wearing my workout clothes, I supposed it wasn't that horrible of a guess after all. Though, I couldn't imagine how fast I'd need to run or how ridiculously clumsy I'd have to be to have inflicted this kind of damage on myself.

Then he asked if my boyfriend had beaten me up. My first reaction was to tell him I didn't have a boyfriend because I was married, a mere correction, but then I thought better of it. It sounded like something some snotty bitch would say to deflect some loser hitting on her in a bar, and I didn't want him to take it as such. At least I hoped he wasn't some creep trying to hit on me—says the not-that-horribly hideously-looking female, not wearing her wedding rings and dressed in skimpy workout clothes.

Shit. Oh well, creep or no creep, I need his help.

Before I could reply, the gravity of what he said sunk in, and I remember thinking, *Oh my God, that's right! There are actually assholes out there that beat women up and make them look like this.* Then I wondered how this man might react if that were the case. Would he be even more hesitant to get involved, worried he too might end up looking like me? Or was he the type of guy that would march over there and beat the living daylights out of the other guy?

I shrugged off each of his guesses—and there were plenty more—by saying things like "nothing," "no big deal," "long story," "it doesn't matter," and "I don't want to talk about it." When he eventually got around to asking if I'd been attacked, it took me by surprise. While I brushed it aside with yet another nonchalant comment, I had to look away so my facial expression wouldn't let on that he had, in fact, unearthed my secret.

His guesses came so fast I could barely squeak out a reply before he'd hit me with the next one. But as the adrenaline wore off, the pain seemed to take up all the space in my brain, and I found it super difficult to retrieve the words I was looking for. I knew they were in there, but I couldn't find them buried beneath that dense caveman layer.

I consciously tried to act as normal as possible, speaking at an average speed and volume and annunciating each word as I should. I felt like a teenager again, trying not to look and sound as if I'd had too much to drink when, in reality, I was plastered.

19. FAKING IT

Growing up in New York meant I talked fast and walked fast. Moving out of my childhood home when I was eighteen and holding down multiple jobs while putting myself through college meant I usually had too much to do and too little time to do it, so I learned to multitask early on. By the time I was married with a couple of kids, it seemed I was never *not* going a hundred miles an hour.

Up North, that pace is acceptable—even expected. Everyone rushes everywhere. Clerks and servers talk fast and move fast. Same with people on the street. Everybody has someplace better to be and something better to do, so nobody wants to be waiting around. It's a whole different mindset up there.

I don't know if it's because everyone is retired or because everyone is on vacation, but here in the South, I've seen people spend a solid five minutes waving each other on:

> *Go ahead.*
> *No, you go.*
> *No, really, you go.*
> *It's okay, I'll go after you. I insist.*
> *Are you sure?*
> *Yes, I'm sure, go ahead.*
> *Okay, but only if you insist.*
> *Yes, I insist, please go.*
> *Okay, thank you.*
> *No, thank you.*

That kind of crap drives me crazy.

Where I'm from, people appreciate it when others get to the point, but cross that Bible Belt, and suddenly you're abrupt or abrasive. Not that I care. I gave up giving a shit about what other people think of me a long time ago. People who know me know I'm not being rude; it's just a product of being busy and my way of trying to be as efficient as possible.

I still wasn't convinced this man with the pickup truck would help me yet. And since I was still trying to win him over, I figured I needed to be on my best behavior. So, knowing that being direct could be a turnoff for some, I tried hard to appear more polite and agreeable and less intense, pushy, and crazy.

Working in sales most of my life, I'd had years of practice luring bunny rabbits to eat out of my hand. That day, however, pretending to be a patient, pleasant person felt like treading water, and it was just as exhausting.

Despite the crisis mode I found myself in, I worked incredibly hard at appearing more fine than frantic. I thought if I could keep up the act, keep my head above water, so to speak, I could then breathe, talk, and act normally. However, underneath, I was doggy paddling my ass off so I wouldn't drown.

By working so hard to behave normally, my brain didn't have time to think about how much my body hurt. So I was sure if I quit pretending, I'd sink straight to the bottom where nothing but pain awaited me. In my mind, I had no choice but to keep up the overly nice-girl act.

20. NO ANSWER

Fortunately, I remembered my older son's cell phone number by now, and since William lived with us, he was a far better choice than Harry out West. However, my husband's number was still nowhere to be found. Though I'm sure the pain and this man's barrage of questions weren't helping matters.

Eventually, the man with the truck thrust his cell phone in my direction. *Finally!*

Even though I'd been waiting for this all along, I stared at it, frozen. I was too bloodied to want to touch it and too befuddled by the phone model, which was nothing like mine, to even begin to guess how to make the screen light up. Not to mention, I was far too damaged and uncoordinated to make any of my fingers hone in on a specific place on the screen. Even if by some miracle I did manage to land on the right spot, there was no way I'd be able to press and release the numbers as fast as the phone would require, with my fingers all stuck together with drying blood.

Thankfully, I only had to look up at him, dumbfounded, for him to offer to make the call on my behalf, even going so far as to hold the phone up to my ear. But when William didn't pick up, I was devastated. This was supposed to be the next big step in my grand rescue plan. That call had been my ticket home, and I'd wanted nothing more since I escaped My Friend's house, which I imagined had to have been at least a half hour ago. Just like that, I was right back to square one, no further along than when I'd hopped that fence.

I told William it was an emergency and to call me back at the number I was calling from as soon as he got the message; however, I was strategic about my tone. I needed it to sound urgent enough to get him to call me back immediately, but I also had to be careful not to make it sound too critical. If my helper got wind of my inner panic, I was afraid he might think twice about getting involved or, worse, abandon me altogether.

Luckily, this man then offered to call someone else, but when he suggested we call the police or 911, I shot him an alarmed look. Sheepishly, he gestured toward my tank top.

I always wore sarcastic workout shirts. At my gym, the workouts of the day, or WODs, were always strenuous. Yet, somehow, funny tank tops put me in a better frame of mind to tackle them.

The tank I'd worn that day was white, and despite being blood-spattered, you could still make out the red letters that said, "Call the cops because I'm killing this workout."

Yup. I'm definitely living that Alanis Morissette song. It doesn't get more ironic than this.

I smirked back at my helper. Even under the circumstances, I couldn't deny it was funny, but I pleaded with him not to call the police, telling him, "I prefer to keep it a private matter." Whatever the hell that meant.

It took all my energy just to keep my shit together.

I was trying so hard to act calm, cool, and collected, but my mind and body urged me to moan, drop to my knees, and pound the ground with my fists out of sheer frustration. On top of fighting back those thoughts, I now had to somehow convince this man *not* to call the police while simultaneously trying to come up with a new number for him *to* call. It's too bad this brain of mine wasn't up to multitasking for me like I was used to.

So, in order to focus better, I took a few steps back from him and the truck. Eyes closed, I paced around on the front lawn, trying to tune him out as he yammered away.

Please, God, I pleaded. *Please help me remember Dale's phone number. Please!*

Lo and behold, it worked! Only he didn't pick up, either.

My bad. Perhaps I should've been more specific. Something like, *And one more thing, God, if it's not too much trouble, can you make him pick up for a change?* However, my imaginary sarcastic retort quickly morphed into concerns about blasphemy, followed by Catholic guilt.

Dale and William were both on the shy side. They hated if their phones rang in public and how people would inevitably turn to look at them. Again, I didn't give a crap, so it always annoyed me how the two of them set their ringers to silent or vibrate. Mainly because they never seemed to pick up when I called. Case in point.

Granted, I usually just needed them to check the refrigerator for milk, pick up something while they were out, or listen to one of my a-funny-thing-just-happened stories. The purpose of my call was just to save someone time or aggravation, or to make them laugh. If they didn't pick up, it was never life or death, just inconvenient and annoying.

This time, however, I was *pissed*. Weren't cell phones explicitly invented so we could make calls in an emergency? Whelp, it doesn't get any more emergency-er than this! *What. The. Fuck.*

21. PLAN C

I knew I had to get to the hospital, but I continued to refuse this man's offers to call 911 because I still didn't want My Friend or her dogs to get in trouble. Out of options, I told him if either of them called back, to please ask them to drive in this direction and to be on the lookout for me as I'd be walking home. With that, I started down the driveway.

I didn't live that far away. Later, Google told me it was only 1.8 miles. I knew walking on the winding sidewalks would take longer, so I considered taking a shortcut and going—as my grandmother would say—as the crow flies.

Obviously, I wasn't thinking straight. To do so would involve traipsing through swampy scrub and wooded areas. On top of that, since the roads in My Friend's neighborhood curved in every direction, I only had a general idea of where my house was at. Thankfully, as I made my way down the driveway, debating where to enter the woods, I began to see it for the stupid idea it was.

Fortunately, I had enough sense to realize there was a major possibility I'd get lost or wind up way off track, thus defeating the whole purpose of cutting through. Also, I was still lightheaded, so I considered what might happen if I fainted.

Would I come to after dark and be unable to find my way out?
Would I be covered in red ant bites, mosquito bites, or worse?

We were always finding water moccasins, aka cottonmouths, in our neighborhood. If those nasty snakes liked hanging out in the landscape beds around my house, I figured there had to be plenty more living in the tall marshy weeds I was now staring at.

On top of snakes, we also had boars, bobcats, and coyotes living in the woods behind our house. While I was pretty sure they didn't eat people, I also didn't think My Friend's dogs would eat people, either, and look where that had gotten me. Especially now that I was dripping with blood, I didn't want to take a chance. Lord knows the last thing I needed was to go toe to toe with another pack of wild dogs.

If only this man could see my dumb idea, like a real-life thought bubble floating above my head. Surely then he'd feel obligated to offer to take me home. Or so I hoped. I was still too afraid to ask him outright out of fear of rejection.

When the second man strolled out of the garage, I presume he'd asked the first guy what was happening. At least that seemed most likely, but by this time, I was already at the bottom of the driveway and out of earshot. Apparently, the rejection I got from the man at the first house must have made quite an impression on me because I was convinced this new guy, a little older and thinner than the other I'd been speaking with, had come outside to tell the man of many questions to stop talking to me, mind his own business, and get back to work.

22. HOMEWARD BOUND

Thinking I'd gotten as far as I'd get with these two men, I conceded it was time to move on. Again. That's when this new guy took me by surprise. He walked right up to me and asked what he could do to help, even going so far as to ask if he could drive me to the hospital. Still trying to downplay my situation, I told him that wasn't necessary but that I'd be super grateful for a ride home. Still afraid he'd ultimately say no, even though he'd volunteered, I assured him it wasn't that far. I even offered to ride in the back of the truck so as not to mess up his interior, but my heart fell once again when he walked away without saying a word. I assumed I'd scared him away or had asked for too much. Yet, there he was, less than a minute later. This time, he was holding a couple of towels.

He ushered me into the front passenger seat of a black BMW sedan. It had been parked in the driveway, too, closer to the house, yet somehow, I'd failed to notice it altogether. He placed one towel on the car seat for me to sit on and the other on my lap to rest my hands and arms.

I liked—scratch that—I loved that he didn't interrogate me about what had happened. Since I didn't have to focus so much on deflecting a bazillion questions or concocting answers, I could finally relax a little. At long last, I was heading home. It felt good to let my guard down.

Thankfully, he did the majority of the talking. Mostly general reassurances that everything would be okay with a smattering of small talk about the house he was remodeling. Though it had been brand new, apparently, the finishes hadn't been to his liking. He probably asked me some questions, too, but I can only recall apologizing repeatedly. I felt terrible about staining his nice towels and the constant dinging of the seatbelt reminder as neither of us attempted to buckle it around me when he'd loaded me into the car.

Surprisingly, I didn't mind the conversation as it made for a nice distraction from the pain that continued to build. So much so, I couldn't even recall the name of my street, nor my left from my right. The only directions I could offer him were to gesture with my head which way to turn.

My Friend and I didn't live that far from each other, but driving between our houses took longer than one would have thought. We lived off the same main drag, but because it was a divided road, you had to drive in the opposite direction or past where you wanted to be. The object was to get to a place where U-turns were allowed. Then, once on the proper side, you could turn down the street you wanted to be on.

The closer we got to home, the less I felt this man would abandon me, so I no longer felt immense pressure to pretend this was all no big deal. The more time passed, the more it hurt, so I allowed myself to moan and rock a little.

Living in a gated community isn't as fancy as it sounds; it's just one of those things they do in Florida. As residents, we're given a sticker for our car window, and when we drive slowly past a sensor, the sticker triggers the gate to open automatically—no people required. Guests, on the other hand, have to pull up to a kiosk in another lane, where an operator greets them. Then, after verifying the resident is expecting said guest, the operator remotely opens the gate.

As soon as the operator came over the speaker, I verbally vomited all over her, quickly explaining who I was, how I lived there, and that I wasn't in my regular vehicle before yelling out my four-digit code. But wouldn't you know it, just as she opened the gate for us, another vehicle drove up in the resident's lane and through the open gate intended for *our* car. Since the gate closes automatically after each vehicle, that meant we were locked out again.

Seeing how we had already driven past the kiosk and another car had pulled up behind us, we now had to make a U-turn, circle back around the landscape median, and get back in line to talk to the operator again. The area is narrow and not built for U-turns, so it turned into more of a six-point turn thanks to another car that had pulled up behind us.

I swear. Can just one thing go right today?

Again the operator came over the speaker and started to rattle off her usual lengthy greeting, including the same questions we'd just answered. *Oh, hell no!* If she thought we had all the time in the world to go through that whole process for a second time, she had another thing coming.

Instead, the driver and I simultaneously screamed into the speaker how we had already done this and that someone had hijacked the open gate intended for us. To convince her to move a little faster, we were also sure to let her know it was an emergency and we didn't have time to dick around.

Thankfully, she let us right in.

"Which house is yours?" he asked.

Ordinarily, I would have told him, *the one with the dark red truck out front* or *the one on the left with the paver drive,* but still frazzled from the gate debacle, I had no words. As he crept along, I could only thrust my chin towards the windshield in rapid succession to indicate we had a ways to go.

As we neared my house, I wanted to tell him it was the tan one with the three-car garage, but those words weren't possible, stuck somewhere in the far reaches of my brain. Frustrated and disappointed in myself, I must have shaken my head, which he mistakenly took as another gesture to keep going because he hit the gas despite us only being a few houses away.

I envisioned zooming past my house and wondered how the hell I'd ever get out of this guy's car if I couldn't verbalize which house was mine. With the panic building and my house quickly approaching, I eventually managed to yell, "Stop!" The word only finding its way to my lips when we had nearly passed my house, causing his car to chirp as he slammed to a halt a few yards past my driveway.

He walked around and opened the car door for me, catching the towel that fell to the ground as I stood. Incredibly relieved that I had finally made it home, I found my words at last. I apologized again for ruining his towels and thanked him profusely for the ride. He wished me well, and I headed toward our open garage door.

I had zero thoughts regarding what was to come next. I was just excited to see my family.

23. HOME SWEET HOME

When I got out of the helpful stranger's car, Sharon, my next-door neighbor, was walking their dogs and called out to me from the sidewalk between our two houses. We were both usually busy with work and didn't run into each other that often, so she was probably looking forward to catching up. If we hadn't seen each other in a while, it wouldn't be unheard of for us to stand there for thirty minutes, somehow managing to talk about everything and nothing at all.

Today, I rushed right by her, yelling over my shoulder something about it not being a good time or maybe later. Since it was Saturday morning, if I had stopped to chat, we probably would've made plans for the four of us to go to dinner that night. We were all suckers for good Mexican joints and pitchers of margaritas. Then again, who isn't?

Fortunately, the door leading from our garage to our house was open, though I recall being a little ticked at the time. Memories of my father's voice bellowed in my head, *Shut the door! You're letting the cold air out. Do you think I'm made of money?* While I couldn't help but wonder how long they had left it open and how much air conditioning *had* been sucked out into the garage, I was just as defiant now as I'd been back then.

This is my house, so I'll do what I please. If I want to leave the garage door open, I will!

Even though I'd promised myself ages ago that when I grew up, I'd be nothing like him, I had to admit, I didn't like the idea of air conditioning the entire neighborhood, either.

My thoughts then turned to our cats and whether one of them had made a break for the promised land when nobody was looking. *Great.* As if I needed to contend with that on top of everything else.

Walking into our hallway, I kicked the door shut behind me.

My eyes are super sensitive to the sun, so I usually don't set foot outside without my sunglasses—big, oversized ones that make me look like a fly, or so my kids said. But, today was far from usual, so my sunglasses were still lying on My Friend's kitchen island. After being outside in the bright light for so long without sunglasses, standing in our hallway with no windows, no lights, and dark wood floors, it took a minute for my eyes to adjust. When they did, I saw the outline of Dale standing in the kitchen in front of our pantry. His back was to me, and his cell phone was pressed to his ear; however, when the door slammed, he turned to notice me and immediately hung up.

I found out later that he'd been on a bike ride when I called earlier, so he was just now getting around to calling the guy with the truck back when I walked in. Dale was the president of the association for our beach condo, so the property manager often pawned her more troublesome calls off on him. So, when he hadn't recognized the number I'd called from, he assumed that's what it was and thought it best to deal with it when he was back at his desk rather than mid-bike ride.

I walked toward him, past the laundry room, the kids' bedrooms, and their bathroom. I only managed to blurt out, "They attacked me," before he started swearing. While it's well-known that I have the mouth of a sailor, Dale only cusses when he drinks. That's another reason I like going out for margaritas since that's when Fun Dale comes out to play. Today, however, even *I* had to admit his language was a bit over the top. It went a little something like, "Are you fucking kidding me? Holy shit, look at your arms. Your arms are broken. Unfuckingbelievable. We need to get you to the hospital."

24. MAN WITH A PLAN

I'd say I felt relief, but that word doesn't do it justice. It was a much bigger feeling than that. In fact, no word in the English language even comes close to describing the extent of my relief.

Not only did Dale have a plan, he took no time putting it into motion, grabbing a stack of towels and ushering me back out the door as if we were in a hurry to get to the beach. Again, so I wouldn't bleed all over the car, he wrapped one around my arms and laid another on the seat. The SUV was Harry's car, but it used to be mine, so it was comfy and loaded with options. He then placed another towel over my shoulders to help keep me warm because, unbeknownst to me, I was trembling.

On the way to the hospital, Dale peppered me with questions, too, but this time, I didn't mind because I could finally be myself. I no longer had to dance around the incident, afraid I might get My Friend or her dogs in trouble, nor did I feel like I had to act in any particular manner in exchange for help.

While I could speak freely, I still spoke abruptly and used as few words as possible as there was still that strange barrier in my head, so selecting words and creating sentences was difficult. Besides, I preferred chanting, moaning, and rocking to speaking, as they seemed to help me cope with the pain and shaking. Coincidentally, this was also my go-to method when I was in labor all those years ago. Lamaze breathing never did shit for me.

We weren't that far from our house when he started making calls. I remember it clearly because Dale, typically a man of few words who speaks slowly, was rambling on and on and talking way faster than usual. It all struck me as bizarre.

Meanwhile, I'm the complete opposite. I'm loud, and I talk fast. Since I can also listen fast, I appreciate when people around me talk fast. So much so that I'll often jump in and finish their sentences if they're taking too long. Yup, I'm one of those assholes. But in my defense, it's something I'm working on. This is why I was so surprised. Usually, it's Dale telling *me* to slow down, not the other way around.

I assumed I'd fallen behind in the conversation because I hadn't been paying attention, so I began to listen more carefully. I hoped the context of what followed would allow me to piece together what I'd missed, only I couldn't process all the words as fast as they were coming. As I turned toward him and was about to tell him to stop, back up, and slow down, I realized he wasn't talking to me. He was speaking into his phone.

Any confusion or anxiety I felt subsided, and I was thankful I could go back to not paying attention.

I also recall being strangely fascinated that he could simultaneously talk on the phone and drive, as if it were some incredible feat, even though in my line of work, I did it all the time. In fact, I often did so while chugging water, eating, rummaging through my bag, writing notes, and driving over the speed limit—as any passenger of mine can attest to.

Eventually, I surmised he was talking to My Friend.

Harry and My Friend's oldest son had played travel hockey together, and part of being a parent of a kid on a sports team means having every other parent's contact information programmed into your phone. The hockey dads usually called each other to talk smack after the games. Meanwhile, us hockey moms managed logistics. Things like locating lost equipment, carpools, sleepovers, and where to meet up for meals between games.

It finally sunk in that Dale had called My Friend to tell her what had happened. *Duh, of course. That totally makes sense.* Yet, at the time, it never would have occurred to me to call her. My brain just wasn't working like that. Logic and taking charge were usually my strong suits, but not today.

The way Dale talked nonstop as if the conversation was one-sided, made me suspect he was leaving her a message because she hadn't picked up. There seemed to be a lot of that going around today—people not answering their phones when you wished they would.

I snarkily thought to myself, *See? How does it feel?*

Dale's voice sounded intense, more forceful than usual, so I wondered if it annoyed him that he couldn't speak with her directly, especially about something as important as this. At least, I *hoped* it did, seeing how I was still annoyed that neither he nor William had picked up for me earlier.

Dale also left a message for her soon-to-be ex-husband, asking if he or their son could access My Friend's house to retrieve my purse and car keys. Dale was in full problem-solving mode, and apparently, next on his agenda was figuring out how to get my car home.

25. SETTLING DOWN

While Dale made his calls on our way to the hospital, panic started to creep in as I felt a warmth spreading down my backside.

Shit! Is that blood? Am I bleeding from somewhere I don't know about?

I didn't think I was injured that badly, but up until now, I'd been too preoccupied with negotiating a ride home to know for sure.

As I debated interrupting Dale's call to break the news that I was likely gushing blood from some unknown source or that I'd possibly peed my pants, it slowly sunk in. Again, the old noggin wasn't clicking like it usually did, so it took me a few minutes to realize Dale had turned on the heated seats.

Granted, it was November, but here in Florida, it rarely gets cold enough to justify heated seats. However, it *was* too cold to be prancing around in short shorts and a tank top. While my outfit wasn't helping my shivering, by now, I knew it was just the adrenaline working its way out of my system since I'd had similar experiences after my emergency C-sections, a scary run-in with a squatter in a vacant house, and shark diving off the East Coast a few months before.

The heat felt terrific, and while it didn't stop me from shaking, it certainly took the edge off.

From the moment I walked into our house, my husband immediately swooped in and took care of everything. He anticipated needs I didn't even know I had, yet somehow, they were exactly what I'd needed. I'd say I was grateful, but again, in this instance, that word wasn't big enough to describe the extent of what I was feeling.

As I began to relax, engulfed in the warmth of the seat, there was a significant shift in my frame of mind. I no longer felt like I had to evaluate and calculate my every word and every move as I had for the last hour or so. And not having that constant pressure of basic survival looming over me felt fucking amazing.

Until now, I'd felt as if I was constantly bracing for what was about to come next, like when a person knows they're about to be punched in the stomach, so they tighten their core, hoping it might hurt a little less. The problem was, during this whole ordeal, since I honestly had no idea what was coming next, there had been no way to prepare for it.

All morning, I had been trapped in this state of freaky, heightened awareness and crushing anxiety. So realizing I no longer had to think or do any damned thing whatsoever, was comforting beyond belief.

PART THREE

THE HOSPITAL

26. EMERGENCY ROOMS

We drove to the emergency room closest to our house. We'd been there a few times before, mostly for our kids' sports injuries. But, thankfully, those visits never amounted to more than a sprain or a mild concussion.

Glancing around as we walked through the automatic double doors, I was surprised that the waiting room wasn't busier. Off to the left were rows and rows of standard-issue doctor's office chairs, light gray aluminum frames with curved edges, and padded teal vinyl seats. Normally, I wouldn't have noticed the chairs because there would have been butts sitting in them. But today, the large waiting area was—at least by emergency room standards—almost empty. Plus, I was still in that hyper-aware mode, taking note of everything around me. While I had never used cocaine, I imagined this was what it felt like.

We approached the window that housed the triage nurse, or what I like to call the emergency room gatekeeper, although less Sigourney Weaver in *Ghostbusters* and more troll under the bridge. Usually, you hand them your driver's license and insurance card, give them a brief description of the problem, and then they grunt for you to take a seat while you wait your turn.

The problem with emergency rooms is that it's difficult to keep track of who's next. A dedicated fan of the nineties television show *ER*, thanks to that hunky George Clooney; it conditioned me to believe the next person up was always the gunshot or car crash victim being rolled in by the ambulance drivers. However, in my real-life, middle-class suburbia version, anticipating who was next in line, in terms of seriousness, wasn't so easy. Unless they had a gaping wound, most people's ER issues, not unlike their other issues for that matter, were usually well hidden. I couldn't tell a heart attack from a stroke or appendicitis from a kidney stone. And while I hoped nobody would be left sitting around a hospital waiting room when they needed help, the sad truth was, they probably were. Because, let's face it, we were all there for some emergency or another.

Hanging out in the waiting room during previous visits, I was always on the edge of my seat. Each time the ER gatekeeper called another person, I'd ponder whether their injury trumped mine or whether the gatekeeper had skipped my turn by mistake. Unable to resist the temptation; eventually, I'd saunter up to the window again to ensure they hadn't forgotten about me, which didn't help. When am I going to learn, that never helps? So the next time the gatekeeper called someone else's name instead of mine, not only did I wonder about the severity of their injury and their rightful place in line, I now questioned whether the gatekeeper was skipping me on purpose; her way of punishing me because she thought I was a dick.

However, on the day of the attack, we didn't have to sit in the waiting room at all. We weren't just buzzed in through the massive double doors; they even sent out a couple triage nurses to escort us personally. So either they had nothing better to do, or I looked way worse than I thought I did.

27. I'M NO SNITCH

Checking in immediately like that meant we didn't have to crouch down to speak through a hole in a plexiglass window. Instead, a nurse plunked me down in a wheelchair directly behind her desk. They offered Dale an actual chair beside me, but he chose to stand. He handled the business side of things, providing them with my name, address, and insurance information, along with answering basic medical questions and signing the multitude of medical releases. Meanwhile, the other nurse got to work, taking my temperature, noting my blood pressure, and shining a mini flashlight in my eyes.

Her desk was about four feet away from where they'd parked me up against the wall, so to enter my info into her computer, she slid back and forth on her wheely stool. Way more fun than a dumb chair, for me, wheely stools rank right up there with chocolate cake, kittens, and rainbows, all of which are guaranteed to make me smile. Despite my age and ragged condition, I allowed myself to daydream about how many times I might make it around without puking, falling over, or chipping a tooth—provided I got a proper windup, of course. On those shiny terrazzo floors, I bet it would've been lots.

I knew at some point someone would ask about the dogs and want me to give up their details. In fact, I expected it to be part of the intake process. However, even in my state of confusion, I still, from a logistical standpoint, couldn't see how they would force me to tell them since I was pretty sure waterboarding wasn't allowed. Besides, what if I didn't know whose dogs they were? And how would they know if I knew them or not?

Never one to shy away from confrontation, I prepared for battle once again, ab muscles engaged. Or so I thought. After two C-sections, I hadn't felt my ab muscles in over twenty years despite all the planking. I was torn. I'm honest—some would say brutally honest—so, for me, lying wasn't an option. But I wasn't about to throw My Friend under the bus, either.

Again, I'm a huge believer in God, Karma, the Universe, or whatever else might lend me a spiritual boost. I call it "fire" insurance. I'd rather play it safe and find out someday that it was all one big lie rather than the other way around. With that, if someone up there was keeping score, I felt I was already at a disadvantage with all my swearing, so I didn't want to make matters worse by lying.

Of course, it didn't take them long to start lecturing me on the importance of my reporting the dogs. First, they told me it was my duty to tell on them for the sake of my community. Blah, blah, blah. I vote and show up for jury duty when my name is called. How's *that* for civic responsibility?

Then they came at me with, "What if they attacked someone else?" I'll admit, this one gave me pause. However, even after all that I'd been through, I still didn't think these dogs were a danger to anyone else. For starters, they'd never attacked a person before, and most importantly, they were safely locked inside the house by themselves. At least, I hoped they still were and hadn't nosed their way out that slit in the door.

I continued to think I'd done something unwittingly to cause the attack. Knowing how some people were so quick to crucify the entire pit bull breed, I didn't want the dogs to be punished for something that was my fault.

Besides, I wasn't sure how this whole reporting process would play out. I was smart enough to realize once I let the cat out of the bag, I could never take it back. And once that process was set in motion, I suspected nobody would have the power to stop it.

When their attempts to guilt me into railroading the dogs and My Friend didn't work, they pulled the rabies card. Little did they know I had an ace up my sleeve, too. It turns out my there's-no-way-in-hell-I-can-hold-a-pen-to-fill-out-your-stupid-form card trumped all of their cards. Then I doubled down when I practically hissed back, asking whether this could be taken care of *after* I saw a doctor. Then it was game over. Clearly, these nurses were smart enough to admit that whose dogs they were was *not* the priority here.

Dale was still in form filling-out mode, signing all the medical permission slips necessary for me to see the doctor, so they added the doggo tattle tale form (aka our county's Animal Bite Report Form) to his pile. I let the nurses believe he would fill it out while we were back there with the doctor, though I knew that was never going to happen. I think Dale may have started to fill it out, but when she was at her desk with her back turned to us, I shot him a look that said, *Don't you dare.*

28. MAKING ME COMFORTABLE

Finally situated on a gurney in the back, the doctors first wrapped me in warm white towels. However, they were careful not to cover any of my wounds.

Not to sound like a snob, but these towels weren't the plush bath sheets we had at home. Instead, they reminded me of motel towels—thin, small, and scratchy. I often regretted buying those giant fluffy towels, as I'd been disappointed in every other towel ever since.

They laid one towel across my shins, and they placed the other across my chest, but it only covered me from my neck to my belly button and shoulder to shoulder. I was still freezing and shaking, but I now suspected it was more from it being so damn cold in there than from the adrenaline or shock.

Before I knew it, I was whisked away for X-rays. My arms, wrists, and hands were already so black and blue, swollen, and distorted that they assumed something had to be broken. However, when the report came back negative, they couldn't believe it, so they sent the films to a specialist for a second opinion.

Word of my attack got around the ER quickly, and as my story spread, all the nurses, doctors, and X-ray techs, basically anyone who came in contact with me, made it a point to tell me how lucky I was to be alive. As if I needed to be reminded, having just endured what I had.

They'd forced me to give up my warm, albeit scratchy, towels in the imaging department, so when I returned to my room, I was again freezing cold and shaking, along with trying to cope with the unbearable pain.

Next up on the list of fun activities they had planned for me were tetanus and antibiotic shots. According to the nurse, one was known for being quite painful, so someone set out to hunt down some lidocaine or something similar to help numb the area.

Pfft. Please.

I practically laughed in their faces, assuring them that nothing could hurt any more than my arms were already hurting. "Let's skip the numbing stuff and just get to it," I told them. I realized certain things needed to happen, but the sooner I could be done with all of it, the better.

Before the attack, my inner pain scale ranged from, say, a paper cut to childbirth. But the attack now set that bar considerably higher. Lying in the hospital bed, I couldn't rock from side to side as I'd done standing in that man's driveway or back and forth as I'd done during our car ride to the hospital. This had been my unconscious way of purging the pain, so without being able to do so, my body inevitably resorted to moaning and shaking my head from side to side.

I begged and pleaded with the staff to give me something for the pain, which, by that time, was excruciating. Dale, who knew I hated taking any medication and would never beg anyone for anything, essentially ordered them to give it to me. Lidocaine, be damned.

Along with the pain shot came an anti-nausea pill, or maybe it was a pain pill, and the shot was the anti-nausea medication. Regardless, when the pain medication didn't work, the doctors suggested we wait a little longer, spewing some crap about how it needed more time to work its magic. When I didn't buy it, they then promised me if it didn't kick in within fifteen minutes, they'd try a higher dose or track down something different, something more potent.

Time was definitely not on my side; the more time passed, the more it hurt. The way I saw it, in fifteen minutes, they could give me more of whatever placebo bullshit they'd just given me, or I could be fifteen minutes closer to getting home.

Crazy hippie women pooped out babies without drugs all the time—in bathtubs, no less. I got this.

Impatient as always, I pressed them to continue with whatever was next on their agenda, further explaining how anything they were about to do to me would only hurt a fraction of what I'd already been through.

Uncomfortable beyond measure and sick of being cold, I longed to be bundled up in warm clothes and curled up on my couch. Like the kid's games Sorry, Trouble, and Parcheesi, where the object of the game is to make it home, that was my goal, too.

29. THE MOSH PIT

I was not at all prepared for the commentary that ensued as my story made its way around the ER. Perhaps their many questions were an attempt at bedside manners. Whatever their reasons, the chatter seemed misplaced at the time.

For starters, it seemed everyone had better things to do. Important things like positioning the large X-ray equipment at precise angles, shooting controlled substances into my veins, and sewing my ass back together. Things that I thought required their full attention.

I'm the kind of person who has to turn down the radio in my car to read house numbers. However, apparently, all these folks were the kind of psychos who could sing along while they did their calculus homework.

Since my brain obviously needed to chill, I allowed Dale to do most of the talking. However, when I was alone with the staff, like in the X-ray room, I felt compelled to try to answer their questions to avoid appearing rude. I understood they were naturally curious about what had happened, but why not just whisper to each other in the hall outside my room? Isn't that typically how stories spread in big box environments like this? At least, that's how it was done in high school and back when I worked in corporate America. I would've been cool with that. As long as the conversation didn't involve me, I could not have cared less.

The uncomfortable feeling I got from their questions was overwhelming, but I brushed it off since so many other feelings were coming and going, and all of them were way bigger than usual. I was still processing a crazy amount of pain, plus the shock and terror of it all. I was also experiencing immense feelings of relief that it was all over, and extremely grateful to finally be getting help. On top of all that, I longed for home.

I was terribly sad my life had taken this crazy turn, and I was desperate to go back in time and undo it all. I also felt guilty that this was somehow all my fault, and I feared how this would impact my future.

I can best describe my brain at the time as a mosh pit. Picture sweaty feelings dressed in jeans and black tees crowded into my head. They're slamming into and bouncing off each other, each trying to make it to the front of my mind. Yet, each feeling can only hold my attention for a few seconds, body surfing its way through my brain before another feeling comes flying in to take its place.

I was angry with the hospital staff for asking me all these questions. Had this been any other day, I would have told them to back off and give me some space. Yet, today, I couldn't find the words to do so. Nor did I dare to offend them because I was so desperate for their help.

In my superhero-like, hyper-aware state, I wasn't just hearing the words they spoke or the questions they asked. I heard beyond that. I heard the undercurrents of questions. I heard how they expected me to answer, and I heard their next question before it even formed on their lips. "Whose dogs?" and "What were you doing there?" when decoded were actually *Are you dumb? Why would you do that? How did you let this happen?* and *What did you do to cause this?*

I sensed I was being judged and that they thought I was too dumb to notice. I then imagined how a rape victim must feel when people scrutinized the length of her skirt or how much she'd had to drink. When, in fact, none of that fucking mattered because there's nothing she could have ever done to have caused *that.* I'm not saying my experience comes even remotely close to being raped. I'm simply saying victim shaming in any instance is abhorrent and appalling, and it needs to stop.

30. MY SPOKESPERSON

Dale became my biggest advocate that day and for that, I will always be eternally grateful. Those who know me know I'm a feminist. It's not that I feel compelled to slap on a vagina hat, rip off my bra, and yell at spectators as I parade down Main Street. It's because I believe *I can take care of myself,* and *I can do it myself.* I never expect or want other people to do something for me, especially if I'm perfectly capable of doing it for myself. I'm not fragile, and I'm certainly not helpless.

I didn't have a stellar childhood. Nobody advocated for me back then, so I learned the hard way not to count on the people closest to me, even when I needed it the most. So, after being shot down so often, I eventually stopped expecting anyone to help me. That's why I either avoid situations where I'll need help, or I go into situations prepared to do it all myself.

As the doctors milled about, they continued with their random questions. Sometimes their questions pertained to the attack, sometimes they had to do with my medical history, other times it was just small talk. I wanted to be polite and cooperative, but the more the pain escalated, the harder it was to find and spit out the right words.

Thank God for Dale. After twenty-five years of marriage, he knew most of the answers, so he jumped in and responded for me. And when he didn't know the answer or if he felt it wasn't necessary, he deflected their questions altogether.

Usually, I would've detested someone speaking for me. It still makes me smile to think of the stockbroker I dated in college and how I left him sitting at a fancy restaurant one night when he tried to order for me without consulting me—as if I couldn't read a menu and decide for myself. Jerk.

However, on the day of the attack, I greatly appreciated Dale taking control. Even more so because I didn't have to ask for his help.

31. SCRUB-A-DUB-DUB

I have to say, the doctors did an excellent job of explaining each aspect of the treatment process beforehand, and next on their agenda was cleaning my wounds with a sponge.

Oooo. That sounds nice. Lord knows I could use some pampering right about now.

Granted, I didn't expect candles with Barry White crooning in the background, but the way people made sexy jokes about hospital sponge baths, I *was* expecting a few bubbles and a sea sponge. You know, one of those funky-shaped tan fuzzy ones with the big holes. The kind they sell in bath boutiques along with organic, gluten-free, tropical fruit-scented vegan bath bombs.

So you can imagine my surprise when what they whipped out was a pack of sponges you'd find alongside the Scrubbing Bubbles at Walmart.

Huh? I thought, disappointed and confused. *Maybe they're medical grade.*

Nope. These were standard-issue—a rectangular yellow sponge on one side with a dark green Brillo pad on the other. Funny, I wouldn't have thought they could use regular sponges for this sort of thing. *Damned budget cuts. Oh well. A sponge is a sponge, I suppose.*

The doctors needed to get a good look at each wound in order to evaluate them individually before determining how to repair them. That meant washing off the blood so they could see what they had to work with. Only the blood was mostly dried by now, so they used, you guessed it, the scratchy side. The same side you'd use to scour a ring of soap scum off your bathtub or some caked-on, baked-on lasagna off a casserole dish. With the luck I'd been having that day, this seemed par for the course.

Greeeaaat!

As one would expect, the scrubbing just made my wounds bleed all over again. That led to even more scrubbing. And so it went as if they were sanding layers of varnish off an antique table.

So long, epidermis, it's been fun.

The room wasn't the kind surrounded by curtains; it was an actual room with walls, but it was just as small. Therefore, with a whole medical team tending to me, it was pretty crowded. One person scrubbed, one disinfected, and several others either bandaged me, ran off to grab more supplies, or barked out orders to someone else in the group. Some sat, some stood, and some squatted, but they all huddled around, peering down at me in my bed. It reminded me of the ceramic Nativity scene I set out on the sofa table each Christmas.

This must be how baby Jesus felt. . .Yikes! You're not allowed to think that. Are you trying to land in Hell?

As they worked on me, the sense of urgency dissipated, and this new mood helped me relax. The new vibe was casual, and everyone milled about slowly, which was fine by me, considering I'd had enough excitement for one day. No, make that for a lifetime.

I knew I was feeling more comfortable when I thought, *When did all the doctors get to be younger than me?* Usually, a thought like that would've made me feel old. Today, however, it gave me hope that the fun me was still in there . . . somewhere. I thought about testing the one-liner out on all the Doogie Howsers puttering nearby, but I was still too overcome with pain to formulate a sentence—at least one I was guaranteed to deliver in the way I needed to if I wanted to pass it off as a joke. The last thing I wanted to do was to offend them, considering they were still poking and prodding me. As they say in comedy, timing is everything.

32. BITE MAPPING

I wasn't surprised that I was so obsessed with getting a good look at the damage. I'm not at all squeamish when it comes to blood or needles. Some might say I have what's called morbid curiosity.

Most of my girlfriends like to watch sappy rom-coms, while I prefer shows like *Dr. G: Medical Examiner*. It's not that I'm into chopping up bodies. I'm not a psychopath. I've just always been super intrigued by people's insides.

I even took our boys when they were in middle school to see the *Bodies* exhibit when it came to town. You know, the one where they used actual cadavers and peeled back the layers of skin to showcase the body's various systems. I found it fascinating how one's lifestyle could affect a person's longevity and how all these underlying diseases could run rampant in people without them even knowing. Maybe that partly explains why I am, to some degree, a health fanatic. And apparently, my apples didn't fall far from the tree because our boys thought those skinless bodies were pretty cool, too.

The doctors and nurses scrutinized each of the sixty-plus holes—yes, we counted—noting out loud the depth of the puncture wounds and the direction in which my flesh was torn. Then they'd search in that same general area, looking for other holes with similar characteristics, allowing them to draw imaginary half circles connecting the dots, which they would officially call a bite.

The punctures left by the pointed canine teeth were easy to identify because they were deeper and more extensive.

In some places, we could even see where the dog's smaller middle teeth—in addition to all four canines—had broken the skin. Those bites made perfect ovals encompassing the top and bottom of my arm and were way easier to count. Since it took a lot of pressure for all those teeth to make contact, it also explained why those areas were a lot more painful.

My hands and wrists had been bitten repeatedly and, consequently, felt like they had gone through a meat grinder. At first, I felt relieved when the doctors noted how those bites were shallower than the ones on my arms. That is until they went on to explain that the wounds were only shallower because the dogs' teeth had hit bone, thus preventing them from biting down any deeper. *Ahh.* It was all starting to make sense.

Where the skin was torn, it was hard to decipher which holes matched up with which bites. In some instances, it appeared the shaking had led to the tear, while in others, it looked as if different teeth had landed in the same spot at different times, shredding the skin entirely.

Altogether, we only counted twelve distinct bites. The rest were random wounds, most likely from partial bites where the dogs couldn't get a good grip.

I don't know if it's because I like puzzles or because I'm a no-nonsense gal, but I thoroughly enjoyed the bite mapping. It was nice to set aside the emotion of it all and let my left brain stretch its legs. A little math, a little science, and a little logic worked wonders to balance me out. At the very least, our little game was a fantastic diversion from the stinging antiseptic they were slopping all over me.

33. LUCKY

From the moment I walked in the door, the hospital staff repeatedly told me how lucky I was:

> lucky to be alive
> lucky because it could have been worse
> lucky they didn't go for my throat
> lucky I didn't lose a limb
> lucky they didn't puncture an organ
> lucky nothing is broken
> lucky I didn't get bit in the face
> lucky I didn't need a skin graft
> lucky my blood and the dogs' slobber had probably
>   made it too slippery for them to get a good grip
> lucky some of their teeth had landed in the gaps between
>   my fingers, sparing me from further damage

Don't get me wrong, I was grateful my injuries weren't worse, but *lucky*? The word reminded me of cheap silverware because it left that same cold, metallic taste in my mouth. The idea that anyone could look at me and think *lucky* repulsed me.

Lucky is supposed to mean finding a good parking spot at the mall or winning a few bucks on a scratch-off ticket. It's a fun little word meant for happy things. I didn't think the word had what it took to do the heavy lifting needed to associate it with not getting too terribly maimed or dying when attempting to feed a friend's dogs.

I understood the hospital staff was trying to make me feel better, but I couldn't help but think they were playing me. Their statements felt way outside the boundaries of "lucky," yet the way they continued to pummel me with that kind of talk made it seem like they were trying a little too hard to make me believe it—like some cult indoctrination.

34. THE PATCH-UP

Some of my wounds started bleeding after they were scrubbed, while others had never stopped. For the stubborn bleeders, they applied direct pressure. Again, I found it ironic that even though everyone in the room was convinced my bones were broken, they assigned a big, burly male nurse to jam his thumb into my most painful places.

Umm. Excuse me? Shouldn't we wait for that second opinion to come back on those X-rays before y'all go doing that?

Direct pressure just seemed so uncivilized and outdated. Oh, I'm sure it came in handy during the Civil War, and we all know it worked well for that little Dutch boy who stuck his finger in the leaky dam, but now?

With all the medical advances, it was hard to believe that this was still the most effective way to stop the bleeding. At least Wild West gunslingers and outlaws were given whiskey and bullets to bite down on.

To everyone's surprise, the only place the dogs had torn my flesh to the point I needed stitches was my ass. That had always been my problem area, and I constantly complained to my gym coach that we weren't doing enough glute exercises to tighten my tush. It's not that I was expecting to build a badonkadonk like JLo's— although that would've been fine by me. All in all, I was just trying to fight off the blasted gravity that was causing my once perky rear to slide down the back of my thighs. Well, on the bright side, at least now there was a little less to slide.

There was one other particularly nasty tear on my right middle finger, but unlike my fanny, there wasn't anything to stitch back together. However, they did find some miscellaneous skin wadded up in the general area, which they flattened out the best they could and placed back in the gash. I was told the wad was too mangled to reattach itself, but they hoped it might help protect it from getting infected until new skin could grow back.

The doctors said they couldn't do much about the punctures. Apparently, wounds like that had to ooze to prevent infection, so stitches weren't an option. For those still bleeding heavily, glue and clear plastic tape were used to hold them together to somewhat control it.

I say somewhat because I was still bleeding enough that the doctors wrapped my wrists and hands in gauze, making it look like I was wearing big white mittens. Then, to help take some of the pressure off the I-can't-believe-it's-not-broken arm, they outfitted me with a sling. And that was that. I was as patched up as I was going to get.

35. FOR BETTER OR WORSE

I hadn't peed since I left the gym, which had been hours ago, so I asked if I could use the restroom while we were waiting on my discharge papers. I was essentially done. I'd been officially treated, so the old me—Independent Me—thought Dale was acting a little overprotective when he volunteered to go with me, but I cut him some slack. I'd been through a lot, so I supposed I could see where he was coming from and allowed him to tag along.

I quickly learned it was a good thing he *had* offered as he came in handy when I had to open the door, shut it, and lock it. Then, turning my back to the toilet, ready to pull my shorts down, it hit me. I had no use of either of my hands. *This* was as far as I could get when going to the bathroom on my own. My contribution to the process consisted of walking up to the toilet and turning around to face the other way. *That's it.*

Independent Me screamed to myself, *You've got to be fucking kidding me!*

Again, without saying a word, Dale slid my shorts and underwear down in one fell swoop. I was always teasing him about wanting to "do it" in public, knowing he was far too shy to ever take me up on it. So I tried to lighten the mood by cracking a joke—something about how it looked like he had finally changed his mind. Needless to say, he wasn't amused.

As if the mood wasn't squashed enough, sitting down to pee, I was surprised to see a maxi pad staring back at me since I'd totally forgotten I'd worn one that morning.

Our gym coach always posted the following days' workouts online the night before. He did it so we'd know what to expect. However, I used it as more of a what-to-wear guide. For instance, if there were box jumps, I'd wear tall socks. One day, I fell off my wooden box, took a chunk out of my shin, and swore I'd never do that again. As they say, live and learn.

Similarly, on days that involved a jump rope, I usually wore a pad just in case. Okay, apparently, I had *two* problem areas I needed to work on: my glutes *and* my pelvic floor. Don't judge. Ask any woman who's had a nine-pound baby use her bladder as a trampoline and a hammock every day for nine months, and she'll probably tell you the same thing.

The pad had started out as one of those super thin ones, but it had grown so thick it reminded me of a waterlogged diaper after my kids got out of the pool. Yes, I'm so old; when my kids were little, swim diapers hadn't even been invented yet.

I reckoned I had peed a little with each bite, involuntarily, like when a doctor bounces that little triangle hammer off your knee, and your foot kicks out. I pointed out my discovery to Dale, and after he wiped me, he threw the pad in the trash, no questions asked.

Obviously, *this* was the shit they were talking about when the pastor had said, *For better or for worse,* all those years ago. By this time, I imagine we were both beginning to realize this road to recovery would be way bumpier than we initially thought.

36. MARCHING ORDERS

They instructed Dale and me several times on the importance of keeping the wounds clean to prevent infection. The bandages were to remain for as long as I was bleeding, and I was not to mess with the surgical tape. They assured me the heavy-duty clear tape would curl up at the edges and fall off on its own when it was ready, and by that time, everything most likely would be all scabbed up.

Since the stitches in my butt weren't the kind that dissolved on their own, I'd have to have them removed in a week. However, they said I didn't have to return to the hospital; my regular doctor could take care of that if I preferred.

I learned the doctor had used non-dissolving stitches because they're stronger, don't pull apart as often, and can help reduce scarring. It's not like I was a porn star and required a scar-free ass, but I appreciated the consideration, nonetheless. If ever I was looking for a career change, it was nice to know I had options.

They also sent me home with a couple of prescriptions. One was for an antibiotic, a giant pill I had to take twice a day. The other was for Percocet, which I was supposed to take every four hours to stay ahead of the pain. They also recommended icing my hands, wrists, and arms as much as I could stand.

The last of my instructions threw me for a loop. Petting my cats or allowing them anywhere near my wounds was a no-no, as was handling their toys, bedding, food bowls, or litter box.

No scooping cat poo? No complaints here. Sorry, Dale. Doctor's orders.

I tried negotiating with them on the kitty cuddles, but they were adamant. Supposedly, with the number of open wounds I had, the risk of infection was too great to chance it.

Fine. Whatever. Let's get out of here.

PART FOUR

MY FRIEND

37. FRIENDS

Our family had known My Friend and her family for fifteen years. Our sons were the same age and played on the same hockey team, so they often hung out together on weekends.

Back when our family lived in suburban Western New York, we'd had a one-acre lot, so when it came time for house hunting in Florida, none of us had been thrilled with the smaller lot sizes in most communities. However, what our Florida home lacked in a backyard, we thought it made up for in neighborhood amenities, including pools, playgrounds, basketball courts, tennis courts, a sand volleyball court, and even an outdoor hockey rink. While we had plenty to amuse kids, we also had a homeowners association that was a stickler for rules. Think sixth-grade safety patrol—minus the neon-orange sash. *Walk, please!*

My Friend's house, the one prior to her divorce, sat on seven acres and had its own pond. My kids, who grew up riding their four-wheelers in our backyard up North, loved going to play at My Friend's house. There, they could run around, fish, hunt for critters, get muddy, and be as loud as they wanted. The best part was, there were no busybody neighbors to care what they did or how they did it. Her house was country living at its finest, so it's no wonder all the kids preferred to hang out over there.

Growing up the baby of something like ten kids, I imagine that had a lot to do with her laid-back parenting style. Don't get me wrong, she was an awesome mom— loving, attentive, and fun. She also kept a clean house, was a great cook, and all three of her kids had impeccable manners. If I was the jealous type, which I'm not, I'd probably hate her since she seemed to do everything better than the rest of us moms. I only say laid-back because nothing seemed to rattle her.

38. MOTHER NATURE

My Friend was raised in rural south Florida, so dealing with critters wasn't just something she had experience with; she would have put Steve Irwin to shame. Me, on the other hand, like most northerners who find their way to the Sunshine State, I was scared shitless of being assassinated by the Florida wildlife.

Even My Friend's then four-year-old daughter knew how things worked in the wilderness, as evidenced by the jelly jar she thrust in my face one night at hockey practice. She then proceeded to tell me about the rattlesnake that had been in their yard until "Momma went *chook-chook bang*," as she simultaneously demonstrated how to pump a shotgun like some pint-sized Annie Oakley. Meanwhile, I just stood there in awe, holding a—what was now apparent—rattle floating in clear goo.

I admired My Friend, how she handled the various and never-ending projects that coincided with maintaining their chunk of land, and how nonchalant she was about her frequent run-ins with what I considered scary nature.

I was most interested in the elusive black widow spider. Everyone warned me about them when I first came to town, but I'd yet to come across one. My Friend assured me they were, in fact, everywhere if you knew where to look. To prove it, she brought one to hockey practice the following week along with its spiky, round white egg sac—again in a sealed jelly jar. While it was thrilling to roll it around slowly with my nose pressed to the jar and get a good look at her red hourglass, I made a mental note to politely pass on any homemade jam if she ever offered.

Another time, she'd been tanning a rattlesnake skin when the hockey team made the playoffs. And since it needed to be treated every day, she brought it with her to the out-of-town tournament and rolled it out on the bathroom counter each night, thoroughly freaking out the other hockey mom bunking with her in the process.

Harry, having started school in New York, where they had different cutoff dates for entering kindergarten, had graduated from high school a year earlier than his hockey teammates despite them all being the same age. Since he had been away at college, I was bummed I hadn't been there to see that snake story unfold. Pun intended.

39. PARTNER IN CRIME

I have a variety of friends. For instance, my favorite shopping buddy is the one who dresses impeccably and always seems to know the answer to which shoes go best with any outfit. Then there's my CEO friend who told me to suck it up and stroke the check when I forgot to file my annual reports for my business entities and had to pay $1200 in late fees. I also have my party friends and church friends—yet never the two shall meet.

When My Friend found a dead boar lying on the side of the road, I immediately pegged her as my don't-ask-any-questions-but-meet-me-in-the-middle-of-the-night-and-oh-by-the-way-bring-your-shovel kind of friend.

On her way home from dropping the kids at school, My Friend would stop to poke the boar with a shovel she kept in the back of her truck specifically for occasions such as this. For weeks, she waited for the boar to decompose in the hot Florida sun until she could finally dislodge the skull from its body. When the time came, she heaved its head into a Hefty bag, lugged it home, and disposed of it at the edge of their property. Then she waited for the vultures, insects, and sun to work their magic, later turning it into home décor.

Hearing this, I thought, *Damn! She is definitely going to be my first call, and Dale had better be on his best behavior.*

PART FIVE

THE
AFTERMATH

40. ABBREVIATING

When we got home from the hospital, Sharon's husband, Robert, was walking their dogs between our houses. Dogs who clearly had tiny bladders since she'd just been walking them a few hours before when Mr. BMW had dropped me off.

When Robert saw me get out of the car all bandaged up, he rushed over to get the scoop. After our brief encounter earlier, Sharon had told him she thought something was up, and my mummy-ish getup now confirmed it.

I wasn't in the mood to chit-chat, but I didn't want to be rude, so we talked with him for a few minutes in the driveway. I gave him an abbreviated version of what had happened, nothing too specific. "I tried to feed My Friend's three pit bulls, and they attacked me." Not surprisingly, Robert had lots more questions, but I let Dale tackle those. He, too, kept his answers brief and then hustled me into the house.

Little did I know that one sentence would become my go-to line, like an elevator pitch or a marketing slogan. I wound up using this line repeatedly because it covered all the bases. It answered where I was, whose dogs they were, what I was doing there, and how it happened. It also explained why I looked the way I did.

While it might not have told them everything they wanted to know, 90 percent of the time, it was usually enough to satisfy their curiosity and shut them up. That was the best part—having a shocking explanation stunned people for a second or two. And with them speechless, even if for only a moment, it gave me time to make a getaway before they could hit me up with any more questions.

So far, this whole day had been about doing things I *had* to do, like a super shitty to-do list:

Do burpees at the gym. Check.
Run an errand on the way home. Check.
Save myself from three attack dogs. Check.
Hitch a ride home. Check.
Hang out at the hospital for two hours. Check.

That was enough for one morning, and I figured it was high time I did something I *wanted* to do. After all, I'd earned that right, hadn't I?

While I said I wanted to curl up on my couch and watch some mindless TV, what I really wanted was to forget this ever happened.

41. GOOD IDEAS

Back in the day, our boys used our old blankets to build forts or crash pads for their dumb stunts. From age five to thirteen, our boys acted like mini Evel Knievels, and in taking them to see all those *Jackass* movies, we probably only made matters worse. Now in their twenties, nobody was jumping ramps on skateboards anymore, but we still kept old blankets on hand. We found they came in handy to take to the beach or on the occasional camping trip, for moving furniture, and apparently in instances like this.

Dale knew how much I'd been looking forward to crashing on the couch, probably since I hadn't shut up about it the whole ride home from the hospital. So the first thing he did when we got inside was dig those old blankets out of the linen closet and spread them over the couch cushions so I wouldn't get blood all over them.

This struck me as another brilliant idea, the same as when he'd called My Friend from the car on the way to the hospital. Though neither idea was particularly ingenious, I found it impressive. I was only living moment to moment, my mind too pooped to think things through, consider consequences, or come up with plans, so I was fascinated that he could do all that. Not to mention, this way, all I had to do was plop down.

42. YADDA YADDA

Next, Dale had Sharon come over to babysit me while he ran to the pharmacy to fill my prescriptions. Of course, she also wanted to hear all about what had happened, and since Dale would be gone for way longer than my one-liner could carry us, I had to offer her more.

Usually, I could babble on and on about pretty much any topic—just ask anyone who knows me. But talking about the attack was different. I could only cover the basics, as if I were a newscaster covering the highlights of some latest catastrophe.

My Friend was out of town. I went to feed her dogs. Biting, shaking. Yadda, yadda. Scary, scary. Over the fence. Ride home. Hospital. The end.

I couldn't bring myself to go too deep or into detailed descriptions. I couldn't even think about it on that level. My brain wouldn't let me anywhere near the nasty stuff. Picture one of those mazes from *Alice in Wonderland*. If a memory proved to be too traumatic, my brain would throw a thorny hedge in my way, making it impossible for me to access the information. In relaying the story, if I came across one of those dead ends and couldn't get to what came next in the sequence of events, my thoughts would automatically pivot in another direction.

Like a pinball machine or a Roomba, my thoughts bounced around, looking for the path of least resistance. I knew what was beyond those thorny bushes, but I didn't try to push my way through. Pushing required more effort than I was willing to give. Instead, I'd heed the warning and reroute my thinking to something more mundane.

Oddly, I also noticed it seemed impossible to talk about the experience in any capacity without shaking my head. Was I trying to shake it from my memory? Or maybe I was in such serious denial on the *inside* that it was manifesting itself outward. If so, that would explain the thoughts of *No, no, no!* that were still screaming in my head and radiating within me anytime I got too close to the rough stuff.

43. NO CRYING ALLOWED

Despite the brutal attack and subsequent memories, I had yet to cry. I said earlier I wasn't a screamer. Well, I'm not a crier, either.

Obviously, I'm not entirely immune to tears. If I see someone else crying, chances are I'll well up, too. That's another reason I steer clear of those sappy Hallmark movies. I mean, *besides* the crappy acting and predictable plots.

I'll also cry when I get super frustrated, but I can count on one hand the number of times that's happened in the last ten years.

I blame my fucked-up childhood, being born in the you-better-not-cry-or-I'll-give-you-something-to-cry-about generation. At least, I think it was my entire generation. Then again, maybe it was just *my* parents who were assholey like that.

In my experience, crying, feeling sad, or feeling depressed never changed a goddamn thing. All the pouting in the world wouldn't have made my life any easier or my parents any less selfish. Crying *never* made a situation less sad. If anything, it made me feel worse. I guess you could call me practical and results-driven. Since there really wasn't any *point* in crying, I just didn't do it.

My neighbor Sharon, on the other hand, had a Norman Rockwell-ish childhood and, coincidentally, loves pathetic Hallmark movies, so it's no surprise that even my brief summary of the attack was enough to make her cry. I can still recall how incredibly weird it felt having to comfort someone else over something that had happened to *me*.

44. MOMENT OF TRUTH

On the day of the attack, My Friend had been visiting her friends and family on the other coast of Florida. Obviously, she dropped everything when she got Dale's message and drove straight home. Therefore, it wasn't long after we arrived home that she showed up. I figured she'd have to be the one to eventually retrieve my purse and car keys from inside the house, but I didn't expect to see her so soon.

All morning, my mind had been swirling with emotions, and it hadn't yet settled on any one feeling in particular. On the one hand, I was sad and angry it had happened, but on the other, I was incredibly relieved and thankful it was over. Even though I still couldn't pinpoint what I'd done wrong, I assumed the attack had been my fault, so I also felt guilty and wondered if My Friend would forgive me. On top of all that, knowing how much she'd been looking forward to her weekend plans, I felt terrible for wrecking them.

Her face crumpled the second she walked in the door, making it impossible to read her. While we usually got along effortlessly, there was now this walking-on-eggshells vibe between us, which was almost palpable. Seeing how my thoughts on the matter were all over the place, I was nervous about where *she'd* land on the spectrum.

This was a big deal for both of us. It's not every day a friend's three dogs maul another friend and try to kill her. What was the protocol in an instance like this? What were we supposed to say? It's not like anything we said could ever undo what had happened. So, how were we supposed to stuff this back into the proverbial genie bottle and move on?

As it turns out, we didn't have to say a word. The look on each of our faces said it all. We both felt horrible— so very sad and so very sorry. Then, just like that, when My Friend burst into tears, the eggshells were gone.

She moved toward me, her arms outstretched, in preparation for a big hug, and I rose from where I'd been seated on the couch to meet her. As much as I wanted to reciprocate, I couldn't do much beyond the initial thought. In a sling and heavily bandaged, there was no way I could lift my arms or put any pressure on them, so I just stood there awkwardly. When it dawned on her that I couldn't hug her back, she stopped abruptly, presumably out of fear she was hurting me. This made her cry even more.

She told me she thought I'd be mad at her. I wasn't. How could I be? It's not like she knew the dogs would attack me. Seeing how upset she was, I tried to downplay the whole thing. Not only did I not want her to feel bad, I really wanted her to stop crying.

I give her credit. Despite her emotional initial response, she didn't want my dumbed-down newscaster version; she wanted all the details. And though I didn't want to upset her further, she needed to know. She wasn't asking for curiosity or entertainment's sake. Like me, My Friend wanted answers. She was equally as shocked as I was that they'd turned on me, so we felt compelled to get to the bottom of what had gone wrong, even if only to prevent this from happening ever again. Also, I was beginning to realize I needed some closure if I was going to try to forget this ever happened.

Yeah, right.

Getting the entire story out and nailing down all the specifics was emotionally draining. Every horrific detail was excruciating, not only for me to relive but for My Friend to imagine since she was experiencing the shock and horror for the first time—and through *my eyes*, no less.

Strangely, I felt like I was in a better frame of mind compared to her. The worst was behind me. I was happy to finally be safe and warm. Plus, I'd had a few hours to settle into my situation.

She cried. I cried.
She blamed herself. She cried. I consoled her.
I blamed myself. She cried. I consoled her.
We then talked about how much worse it could've been,
    and we both cried.

The saddest part was that even after all our overanalyzing, we still didn't have the first clue as to why it had happened. Ultimately, we were left with no choice but to chalk it up to a freak accident, a perfect storm, if you will. We latched onto that idea and held it tight. There was comfort in knowing nobody was to blame and there was nothing either of us could have done to prevent it.

During our discussion, we took turns rerouting the conversation to focus on the positives. I think it was instinctual, not only to preserve our friendship but our sanity as well. We found solidarity in discussing what went right, thus preventing the situation from becoming far worse. We were thankful she had asked me to feed the dogs instead of one of her kids' friends, which she had also considered. We were also grateful I was in good physical shape to endure what I had and that the two dogs started fighting, allowing me the chance to get away.

It was basically our pathetic attempt at looking on the bright side.

45. GYM RAT

I've always been fit. While it's true I was gifted with a small frame, I also worked hard at being healthy. In college, I'd go for long bike rides, play racquetball, and jog. Occasionally, I did aerobics with my roommate, but considering we usually downed a large pizza after, I doubt that counted.

When my kids came along, exercise was more about chasing them around, with only an occasional fitness class or tennis game thrown in here and there. Slowly, our lives grew more hectic, and before I knew it, what used to be "me time" turned into sitting on my keester while driving kids to practices and cheering them on at games.

In my later years, I joined our local YMCA and resumed running, even competing in a half marathon when I was forty-seven—if only to check it off the bucket list. That is until a knee injury eventually got the best of me, and I had to give up running altogether.

On top of that, around the same time, a torn rotator cuff snuck up on me without my knowing—another testament to my high pain tolerance and my aversion to doctors. However, after some time, I surrendered and went to the orthopedist, who, aside from forbidding me from performing a lengthy list of activities, assigned me some rehab exercises for my knee *and* my shoulder.

Sidelined from almost everything, unable to do what I liked to call "burn my crazy," and no longer working out regularly, I started to see some unwelcome changes in my body. Changes that my halfhearted attempts at better eating couldn't thwart. So in the summer of 2018, when I saw an advertisement for a CrossFit gym that guaranteed they could get my butt in shape, I scheduled a meeting with the owner.

To be accepted into the program, I had to commit to attending classes a minimum of three times a week for six weeks and follow the assigned meal plan. I'm not talking about meal-replacement shakes. This was all real food, but super clean stuff. It was all sugar-free and low-fat but all-natural—nothing packaged, processed, or laden with preservatives. Everything also had to be measured, although I was shocked and delighted by the generous portions.

Our 7:00 a.m. class consisted of all newbies, so we were all struggling—I mean learning—together. The owner, our coach, like Ghandi, was a wealth of knowledge and patient as hell. The classes were tough, but over time, I got better at each of the moves. Each class consisted of lifting weights, followed by an intense cardio workout. The name of the game was to push yourself, either by adding more weight, completing more reps, or doing it faster—however, never at the expense of good form. Our coach was a stickler about performing each exercise correctly to ensure we didn't get hurt, and my broken body appreciated that.

It didn't take long for me to see results, and the more results I saw, the more hooked I became. I was soon going to class every day, and before I knew it, I'd turned into one of *those* people who rambled on and on about their daily workouts. I told everyone and anyone about how fantastic my gym was, how outstanding the program was, and what insanely challenging things I did at the gym that day—whether they cared or not.

46. ADRENALINE JUNKIE

People who poke around my Facebook page will see I've gone cliff jumping, sky diving, and walked on hot coals. I've even swam with sharks—not in a cage or aquarium— but in the open ocean, where they chummed the water with bloody fish parts to lure them to us. It was thrilling to be surrounded by twenty or more sharks, so close we could barely swim without kicking them. Well, at least this adrenaline junkie thought it was thrilling.

I had always enjoyed living life to the fullest, doing exciting things other people might have considered scary, difficult, or crazy. Being adventurous made me feel more alive and recharged my batteries. It also gave me a sense of accomplishment and reinforced my belief in the old adage, mind over matter.

CrossFit was no different.

Every day, I'd look at the workout before class, and every day, I'd have my doubts. I'd question not only whether I was physically capable of doing each of the moves but also whether I could push myself as hard as I'd have to in order to finish. So, on the days I could complete the workout, which, oddly enough, was *every day*, I always felt super proud of myself. I liked referring to myself as an old dog learning new tricks. I loved seeing how far I could push this old body of mine. It made me feel like I was exercising my mind, too, as it never ceased to amaze me what I could do when I put my mind to it. Stretching my self-imposed limits to their max, whether in the gym or on a high-risk adventure, was a major confidence booster for me.

47. FIT

On one hand, the attack couldn't have happened to a better person. By November 2019, I'd been at this gym for over a year, and despite slacking off on the strict meal plan, I was probably in the best shape of my life. Granted, my body fat percentage wasn't the eighteen I had whittled it down to during that initial six-week challenge, but I was still under 22 percent. Not bad, considering I didn't know many other women my age who could say that.

The morning of the attack, I attended the 8:30 a.m. workout, the only class they offered on Saturdays. Since the owner promoted positivity and camaraderie— another reason I loved my gym—when we were done, it was customary to stay and cheer on the others until the last of us had completed the workout. Therefore, I can't say *exactly* when I left the gym that fateful day; only that sometime after the last high five, I set off to feed the dogs.

I know it sounds insane, but My Friend and I spoke at length about how grateful we were that I was the one who got attacked. While what I endured had been horrific, we figured my gym training had kept me alive. Mentally, I had been conditioned not to give up. Physically, I had been strong enough to keep my balance so the dogs couldn't take me to the ground—and having that extra muscle probably prevented them from tearing pieces off.

I'd heard it about a thousand times, but it was true. It could have been so much worse.

Her dogs could have killed me. Had it been one of her kids' friends who went there to feed the dogs instead, I doubt they would have survived. For that reason alone, I felt my being attacked was the best-case scenario. Even knowing what I know now and having gone through what I've gone through, I'd take that over someone's dead kid any day.

48. CHECKING IN

On the day of the attack, while I was at the gym, Dale had made plans for us to meet up with friends but later canceled while we were at the hospital, briefly explaining what had happened. That's all it took for word to spread—like herpes.

For the first few days, I just wanted to rest and pretend the whole thing had never happened; however, everyone I knew seemed to be calling or texting to check up on me.

So and so from the gym texted after our usual morning class to say they missed me and wished me well. Another friend running errands wanted to know if she could pick me up anything while she was out. Someone else tried to cheer me up by sending pictures of fishbowl-sized margaritas from one of our favorite hangouts. Even a friend from high school, whom I hadn't seen in over a year, messaged me to let me know she was in town and was hoping to see me.

My phone constantly buzzed and beeped from early morning until late at night.

I know I should've been grateful that everyone cared, but I mostly saw it as a sad reminder that they were out there living their lives, and I wasn't. The only thing in *my* foreseeable future was lying on my couch with ice packs covering my arms.

I couldn't move my hands or fingers well enough to hold the phone to talk, so I had no choice but to let the calls go to voicemail. Then, to play the messages, I'd use my elbow to steer my limp hand above my phone, using only the outside of my right thumb to press the voicemail and speakerphone keys. Operating a phone was like playing one of those claw-and-crane, toy-grabber games you'd find in an arcade. Too bad I sucked at those.

If I was still numbed up from the ice packs that Dale tried to keep in constant circulation, I'd sometimes try to type abbreviated texts back or reply using the talk-to-text feature. I also liked the generic automatic reply options. The kind where you only have to hit one button, and it shoots back a *thanks*, *okay*, *yay*, or *no problem*. While they weren't always the most appropriate replies, they were far easier to knock out.

As the days wore on, I grew increasingly resentful of everybody's check-ins. They meant well, yes. I got that, so fortunately, I had enough restraint not to act like an asshole when they called, but it still irritated the crap out of me.

It felt like that stupid game we play at the grocery store. The one where the cashier asks how we're doing when, honestly, they couldn't give two shits. Then we say we're fine even if we're not fine. Nobody likes that game.

My friends and family weren't calling to hear me complain about the pain. Nor did they want to hear about how I couldn't bathe myself or feed myself. I felt like they were calling so they could feel good about *themselves*, and my role was merely to validate that *they* were the kind of good friends who checked in on another friend.

And, like the grocery store game, the pressure was on me to not burst everyone's bubble. I was supposed to tell them something that would make them feel good. They wanted me to reassure them that I was okay, feeling better, or that I'd be back to normal in no time. But I wasn't okay. I felt horrible. And with every day that passed, I was increasingly and painfully aware that I'd never be normal again.

There I was, struggling not to think about it twenty-four hours a day, yet the people who *supposedly* cared about me the most kept dragging me right back there. I imagine I could've told them all to go to Hell. After all, fewer friends would have meant less dreaded Christmas cards to write out. But instead, I tried to sound chipper and steered the conversation toward any progress I was making.

I was sick of discussing the horrendous event, my current problems, and whatever future disabilities I might have been looking at. They didn't want to hear all that, and talking about those things wasn't doing me any good, either. Therefore, each day, I forced myself to come up with one good thing I could brag about to everyone, no matter how small.

I can get off the couch by myself now—if I push off with my face. Yay, me.

49. FLASHBACKS

For the first few days, I planned to sleep on the couch Dale had covered with old towels—having ruined the old blankets on day one—at least until the bleeding stopped so as not to stain our good bedding. What I *didn't* plan on was not sleeping at all. I wanted to sleep. I needed to sleep. And since I was totally exhausted, I didn't have trouble falling asleep. The problem was that as soon as I'd drift off, I was right back in My Friend's living room getting mauled all over again.

I didn't want to think about the attack; if anything, it was the exact opposite. I wanted nothing more than to forget, but my subconscious was calling the shots these days, not me—at least not Old Me. It's like when you tell someone, *Don't look* or *Don't move,* but they instantly whip their head from side to side or start jumping all around; every time I closed my eyes, the attack was all I could think about.

The flashbacks caused me to cry out involuntarily, and I'd jerk awake, hyperventilating, my heart pounding. I didn't hyperventilate to the extent I needed to breathe into a paper bag. Instead, it was more like being a kid again, swimming laps underwater in a friend's pool and seeing how many times I could go back and forth in one breath before I'd be forced to pop up, gasping for air.

My brain was deceiving me yet again. Whatever part was in charge of playing back that horrible movie in my mind must have also been in charge of telling my body to breathe because, apparently, I couldn't do both at the same time—like that worn-out old line about walking and chewing gum.

When my friend Kellie, whom I'd known since I was twelve, came to see me the day after the attack, I was delirious from not sleeping and barely able to hold up my end of the conversation. Frustration practically bubbled inside me, which didn't help. I couldn't stop the intense pain, and I couldn't stop the flashbacks, but until I got a handle on both, sleeping would remain impossible.

The pain meds were supposed to help with pain *and* sleep, but I couldn't keep them down. Poor Kellie had the thankless job of holding my hair back when I'd barfed up my last dose. Lucky for me, she had lots of hair-holding practice thanks to our rebellious juvenile delinquent high school days and a few Caribbean booze cruises when we'd been older—but clearly not wiser.

50. MAD MEN

Unfortunately, a few years before, Kellie had lost her mother-in-law to colon cancer, a horrible and painful disease. The oncologist had advised her mother-in-law to leave the television on while she slept since it was supposed to distract her mind from the pain, so she suggested I give it a shot.

Desperate to try anything, as soon as she left, I began searching Netflix for the perfect show. I wanted it to work so badly that I gave it all the optimism I could muster. Like that book, *The Secret*, I thought for it to work, I needed to show the Universe I honestly believed it would work. So, to prove I'd bought into the idea and was 100 percent committed, I looked for a series with a lot of seasons. If— crap, I mean *when*—this worked, it would have to hold me over for several weeks. That's how long the doctors said it would take for the pain and pressure from the intense bruising and swelling to subside.

The series also needed to have an even tone—no arguing, screaming, or loud noises. I'd had my fill of mayhem the day before, plus I didn't want it waking Dale in the other room. Not to mention, the entire purpose was so I could fall asleep while watching. If I *did* manage to fall asleep, the last thing I needed was to be woken up again by the sound of gunshots or childbirth. For whatever reason, actresses seem compelled to break the sound barrier when birthing babies, and it drives me crazy.

My last requirement was that the series had to have very few plot twists and turns. Since I only planned on watching it during those hopefully very few and very brief moments between sleep, I didn't want to be entertained so much as I wanted it to calm me down and help me fall back asleep—like a binky. I also wasn't looking for a show where I'd feel forced to pay attention and lost if I didn't. That would just stress me out and piss me off. Then, I *definitely* wouldn't be able to fall asleep.

I took a chance on *Mad Men*, and boy, was I right. If anyone could keep his cool, it was Don Draper. On top of that, everyone seemed to talk in monotone. *Perfect.*

During the periods I slept, I never missed too much of the story that I couldn't follow along again when I woke up. Every episode was pretty much the same: a little drinking, a little advertising, and a lot of secretary screwing. Rinse and Repeat. It was precisely the mindless deliciousness I had been looking for. Even their outfits were a snoozefest: housedresses and plaid sport coats. Yawn.

While my plan didn't work entirely, it did allow me to sleep for small chunks of time. Sometimes, it was only ten minutes, and sometimes, I could make it an entire hour, but I'd still wake up in terror. There seemed to be no way around that. However, when it happened, I'd simply watch TV until I could fall asleep again. Rinse and Repeat.

51. MIND TRICKS

Even though I didn't feel like Old Me at all, I tried brainwashing myself into believing I was the same person I'd always been—the only difference being, now I was covered in bite marks. Each time I woke up, the first thing I did was look at the clock. If I had stayed sleeping for an extended bout, my inner coach would cheer for me and pat me on the back. However, if I had only slept for a few minutes, my inner coach, like my son's hockey coach, would whap me upside the head with a clipboard, leaving me feeling defeated and deflated. Think Homer Simpson. *D'oh!*

This was the game I played until 5:00 a.m. since I'd convinced myself that nobody under eighty officially wakes up before then. That is unless they're hosting a morning talk show, catching an early flight, or their house is on fire.

If I gave in and officially started my day at some insane hour, in my mind, I'd be conceding, admitting to the Universe that I was somehow allowing myself to be terrorized.

Nope. Not on my watch.

This whole victim mentality hadn't sat well with me from the get-go, and I didn't want to give my problems any more power over me than they already had. I hated losing, especially to myself.

A firm believer in all things woo-woo, I've always been a big proponent of mind over matter, and this entire ordeal had been my biggest test so far. *If you don't think it, don't say it, and don't believe it, it won't come true.* That's one of my mantras. Not that I ever meditate. It's just one of those beliefs that really strikes a chord with me. Just ask my kids.

Nobody in our house is allowed to verbalize bad luck. Not on themselves out of fear it'll come true, and not on anyone else out of fear Karma will boomerang it straight back to them tenfold. As soon as they utter the words, I insist they apologize, urging them to *Hurry, take it back, take it back!* They have to do it fast because, once it's spoken, it isn't long before the celestial winds carry it away and send it on its mission, making it impossible to take it back.

I have no idea what brand of spirituality this is derived from. Something African, maybe. My rugrats made me watch *The Lion King* like 4,000 times, and well, that's how Rafiki found out Simba was still alive. Oops. Spoiler alert. Sorry.

Failing at something as basic as sleeping took a horrendous toll on me. So once the clock hit 5:00 a.m., I'd quit trying to sleep and would just get up. I'd convince myself, fake-it-until-you-make-it-style, that I wasn't giving in to my nightmares. Instead, I was just one of those early risers, like those entrepreneurs they profiled in business magazines. People like that got up early on purpose because they had lofty goals and important shit to do. Even if my lofty goal was only to take a shower that day, if it was after five, I'd bully myself into believing I, too, got up that early because I wanted to and not because I was tormented by bad memories and pain. Besides, my couch wasn't as comfortable as I'd hyped it up to be, at least not long-term.

52. SLEEPING

There's something about sleeping on a sofa that makes you feel like an unwanted houseguest, even in your own home. So when I returned to my bed a few weeks later, it was nice to feel somewhat normal again. I say somewhat because I still couldn't put any pressure on my arms. Not because it was "doctor's orders;" physically, it just wasn't possible. Getting into bed was more of a lie-down and scooch, like an upside-down inchworm kind of ordeal, while getting out was more of a slither off the side and let gravity do the rest kind of thing.

When lying on my back, it was too painful for my arms to be down at my sides. The blood, rushing downward, even those few inches, was enough to make them throb unimaginably, so for the first few weeks, I had to sleep with them folded across my stomach.

Though I was back in our bed, I still watched *Mad Men* with the volume on low. Thankfully, Dale is patient and can sleep through anything. Side note: this also meant he could sleep through crying babies (ours in particular), cats barfing, and any alarm clock ever made. So, while it sounds endearing now, the thought of murdering him in his sleep had crossed my mind a time or two.

It had been a long time since we'd had to deal with screaming babies, so these days he was mostly on my good side. I say mostly because if Dale laid off the cat treats before their nighttime zoomies, we probably wouldn't have to deal with cat barf, either.

Nevertheless, I didn't want to wake him, so I kept the volume low. While he wasn't awake-awake, I worried I was preventing him from getting that proper REM kind of sleep. Though knowing him, he'd probably just suck it up rather than ask me to turn it down.

Lying there, my mind wandering as it does when one can't sleep, I thought of the difference between him and my mother. She's the type of person who would pretend I *was* keeping her awake even if I wasn't. She's the definition of a martyr, and growing up, it drove me insane. Then, as I grew older and saw it for the manipulation it was, it just made me angry. Dale was the opposite. He often pretended things didn't bother him even when they did. I wasn't sure how I was supposed to feel about that, but thanks to her, having the TV on, even with the volume on super low, made me feel guilty.

Months later, as I slept, I'd still cry out involuntarily from the zingers of pain that shot down the nerves running through my hands and arms, but I was thankful I could finally sleep on my side again. Though unfortunately, it seemed like the nightmares were here to stay.

53. TOUGH LOVE

While the nightmares and flashbacks came during the day, too, nighttime was the worst, especially when trying to fall asleep. It was there, in that sweet spot, when I was partly sleeping yet partly still awake, that the memories would slide into my subconscious undetected.

If I had to get up to go to the bathroom at night, after inchworming my way back into bed, memories of the attack would inevitably flood my brain. It didn't matter how exhausted or sleepy I was. I'd still struggle to fall back asleep. My brain, having to work in overdrive to fight off the flashbacks, often left me more awake than when I'd initially gotten up to go to the bathroom.

By the time the pain or flashbacks reached peak intensity, I'd find myself so wide awake I'd feel compelled to get out of bed and find something else to do, like go to the bathroom, get a drink of water, or get a fresh ice pack. This was another head game I played with myself. I'd use these little missions to try and reset my brain. Sometimes, it was enough of a distraction to break the cycle, and I *could* get back to sleep. Other times, it would pick up right where I'd left off, like pressing pause on a super shitty movie.

When I couldn't sleep, I'd be furious with myself. Logic told me it was *my* brain, so I should be able to control what it was thinking. Only I couldn't, so I'd ultimately resort to bossing it around like a lousy babysitter, telling it things like *Knock it off, Cut it out, Stop it, You're acting dumb, Enough already.*

Suppose I got to the point where I was talking some serious smack to myself, and it was only an hour or two before my alarm was to go off. In that case, I'd usually just get up—even if it was before my self-imposed rule of 5:00 a.m. In terms of setting my mood for the day, I was way better off getting up earlier than I had planned. If I laid there for several hours playing the flashback, negative self-talk game before I got up, it always left me feeling battered, defeated, sad, and angry—and that's no way to start your day.

I was so adamant about not allowing the flashbacks to control me that I'd seek out things to do, like tidying the house or reading emails, to convince myself I'd intentionally chosen to wake up for these other purposes instead.

They don't call me a control freak for nothing.

54. LUCKY THIRTEEN

The doctors said I wasn't allowed to take a bath out of fear of infection. It's funny. I was never much of a bath girl. However, just when I'm in the market for a passive, half-assed way to semi-bathe, they go and yank it off the table—just my luck.

Showering, I quickly learned, was now one of the many things I used to take for granted. Because I needed so much help, it now required the careful planning of a full-blown event—minus the canapes.

As Dale undressed me for my first shower after the attack, and my pajama top fell to the floor, he stepped back, staring at my naked midsection. And no, he wasn't gawking at my boobs. For one, Dale's a butt guy. And two, it wasn't an *Ooo, sexy mama* look. It was more of a *Ruh-roh, Raggy* look.

He tried to be smooth about it, quickly glancing back up at my face, but it was too late. I immediately knew something was wrong. I'd seen the flash of concern on his face. Then, I saw him purposefully set it aside as he gauged what to do next. I know because he got the same look when we assembled Ikea furniture and wound up with too many extra parts afterward.

The hospital had missed a bite on my upper left abdomen, and Dale didn't want me to shower since it hadn't been properly disinfected like the rest.

I'd been looking forward to showering for days, and I wasn't about to let him burst my bubble, so I made a deal with him. After the shower, he could slather that bite with whatever stingy antibiotic crap he could find in the medicine cabinet, so long as my hair got washed. When he didn't respond, I doubled down and added, "Even if it's expired."

Our medicine cabinet seemed to be some sort of time machine where as soon as we put something inside it, it automatically expired. Dale knew this, too, but he agreed, confirming what I already knew: I'd missed my calling as a hostage negotiator.

Whelp, if I died from a bacterial infection, at least now the mortician would have a fighting chance at a proper hairdo.

Looking back, I suppose the water wouldn't have hurt anything, but we didn't know that. We had no formal medical training. We just knew we didn't want to make a bad situation worse. Also, considering its proximity to some vital internal organs and how we were lectured ad nauseam on infection, we were nervous. However, it was all for nothing, as it eventually healed just fine, aside from leaving another nasty scar.

55. IN A BIND

When it came to bathing, I was useless. My wrists wouldn't bend to allow me to roll a bar of soap around in my hand, nor could I flip a shampoo bottle upside down. And since I couldn't withstand the slightest pressure, even pushing down on a pump dispenser was out of the question.

Eventually, as the weeks wore on, I figured out that I could use the heel of my palm to pump soap onto one of those plastic-netted loofah balls, which I gently slid around my body. Again, it was one of those things I had previously taken for granted. I was thrilled to be showering by myself again, despite the moderate difficulty—and moderate pain, as the netting often tugged at the loose surgical tape.

Washing my face, on the other hand, took way longer than I thought it would. I'd try every day, but I couldn't bear to put any pressure on that right hand. Attempting to slide a washcloth around my face felt like someone was stomping on my hands with steel-toed boots. While my left hand could handle a bit more pressure, it had zero flexion, so I couldn't maneuver it to reach anything on my right side.

As my strength and mobility slowly returned, I eventually made it all work. But I still had to contort my left arm across myself in such a way it reminded me of that game Twister.

Washing my hair was no better, but again, I kept trying, hoping one day it would click. At first, I couldn't bend my fingers on my right hand to move the shampoo around, but as they grew stronger, I found I had bigger problems. The surgical tape that covered my wounds had started to lift in places. While it was no longer sticky enough to stay stuck to my skin, it apparently had *no problem* sticking to my hair.

No matter how often Dale trimmed the excess tape flaps, time and again, I found myself naked and wet, shampoo burning my eyes, with my hands essentially glued to the top of my head. I'd learned the hard way not to shower when Dale was on a conference call or when I was home alone. Needless to say, my inner feminist was not a happy camper.

Even months later, washing my hair still hurt that right middle finger that had been mangled, but at least I could finally stop howling or crying out in pain.

56. NATURE CALLS

Potty breaks were also a big problem, so Dale was in charge of all things bathroom for the first week or so. The missing skin on that right middle finger, combined with my severely limited finger and wrist mobility, made pulling clothes up or down ridiculously hard. The best way to do so from a pain perspective was to use my thumbs and index fingers. However, such a delicate grasp didn't give me much leverage. Since I could only grab a small section of material at a time, tugging only moved that section so far while the rest of my pants remained firmly in place. Eventually, I could do it myself, but only by methodically working my way around the waistband, moving each section up or down, inch by inch.

Obviously, that took forever, so rushing to the bathroom with a full bladder was no longer an option. So I wouldn't pee my pants; bathroom visits, like showers, had to be planned out well in advance. I felt like I was potty training myself.

Do you have to go? Are you sure? Do you want to try? Let's just try while we're here.

It didn't help that the dogs had taken a chunk out of my butt cheek, right where my rear rested on the edge of the toilet seat. That meant every time I sat on a toilet, I yelped a little from the pain. Getting my pants and underwear caught on the stitches when sliding them past always led to more squealing—resulting in some awkward looks from the other ladies standing at the sinks in public restrooms. That is, after I began to venture out more.

Those stitches took so much abuse that, somewhere along the line, one of them got ripped out before they were ready to be cut out. The doctor told us he'd put four in, but there were only three when it came time to take them out. But that's a whole 'nother story.

57. SWELLING

Not only was I messed up on the outside, I was messed up on the inside as well. Even though they weren't broken, my bones felt as if they were shattered. It hurt from the inside out in a way I'd never experienced before. Therefore, the doctors wanted me to ice my arms, wrists, and hands as much as I could tolerate for the first few weeks.

In the beginning, my mobility and strength were no match for the suction of a refrigerator door, let alone for wrestling an ice pack out of our freezer, which was overstuffed with who knows what. Welcome to life in the lightning capital of the U.S.

To keep your freezer contents from thawing when the power goes out, they advise you not to open it, the object being to keep everything as cold as possible. That's all well and good, but when the power comes back on, everything freezes up again, so then I have no way of knowing if it had gotten a *little* unfrozen or if we're talking *botulism-level* unfrozen. So there it stays because I'm not wanting to throw out a perfectly good roast, but I'm also too chicken to eat the chicken.

Since I hadn't yet figured out how to get up off the couch by myself, icing only happened when Dale remembered to walk over and plop an ice pack on my arms. Sadly, the ice didn't actually help much with the pain. If anything, it may have even made it worse, in that brain freeze or frostbite kind of way. But it was supposed to reduce the swelling and the constant unbearable pressure, so I kept at it.

My lack of hand function weeks after the attack made me think there was more damage than we'd initially thought, so I called the orthopedic practice where I'd gone for my knee, shoulder, and hamstring issues.

I was super relieved when the orthopedist, who specializes in hands, said that it was still related to the extensive bruising and swelling and recommended physical therapy a few times a week to help speed things along. It felt good to be doing something proactive.

In case it's not obvious yet, I'm not a patient person.

58. PHYSICAL THERAPY

Physical therapy was an emotional roller coaster. The exercises they proposed were so incredibly basic that I couldn't see how they would help. So, as the therapists explained each of them, I rolled my eyes. I reminded them I was a CrossFitter, as if to imply that the exercises were somehow beneath me and to assure them I could do whatever stupid thing they wanted me to do. To prove it, I silently promised to complete double the reps they assigned. *I'll show them.*

Touching my thumb to each of my fingers on the same hand seemed geared more toward people with brain damage, and taking turns using each of my fingers and thumb to move some chip clip-like clamps from left to right seemed just as silly. And who couldn't hold a contraption that looked like a kite string roller out in front of them, twisting it back and forth to roll and unroll the string wrapped around it?

Me, that's who. All that shit was crazy hard.

It was all so depressing. These were simple exercises, and I knew this because I *didn't* have brain damage. I should've been breezing through them, so the fact I struggled, yet again, with basic movements was hard to accept. I began to doubt that I was as strong as I thought I was, physically—or mentally. My self-esteem took a big hit. I was angry. I expected more from myself.

59. HELPLESS

For the first ten days or so after the attack, Dale basically did everything without my having to ask. I'm talking all household chores, as well as taking care of me. Having moved out of my childhood home at eighteen, I'd always been highly independent, so as understanding as he was about it, it was starting to get on my nerves.

By week two, I attempted to do more for myself, but I was definitely sucking at it.

Flipping through the *SkyMall* catalog—back when it was an airplane seatback pocket staple—I always gravitated toward the section with the various framed motivational quotes. The kind you'd find sitting on some middle manager's desk in the 1990s, no doubt an obligatory gift from the office staff. Sure, they were cheesy, but you had to admit the words were simple yet powerful.

Stuff like Wayne Gretzky's "You miss 100% of the shots you don't take" or Albert Einstein's "You never fail until you stop trying." I bought into all that shit hook, line and sinker.

I never minded doing difficult things and failing at them. Hey, at least I tried, right? But when the *thing* is something easy, somehow, the act of failing felt far worse than if I'd never tried in the first place.

That's how I felt trying to do the physical things required of me, both in physical therapy and in my day-to-day life. Being unable to do something I had done a gazillion times before, and usually with little or no thought, left me feeling discouraged, frustrated, and angry.

I hated asking for help, even when it came to the tough stuff, so asking for help with easy things was infuriating. And God forbid if I had to ask *after* failing to do it myself. Woo-wee! If that happened, everyone had better look out because I'd be pissed.

For me, asking for help was synonymous with being helpless. Helpless meant weak, and both screamed vulnerable. Even worse were the problems and baggage that usually followed. Been there, done that. That's a nope for me.

60. MIDDLE FINGER

My biggest challenge by far was my right middle finger, the one where the dogs ripped the skin off one side, but with nothing to stitch, the doctors just filled it with random skin bits and hoped for the best.

Most people treated me like I was being dramatic if I complained about it, and I get it. They were probably thinking, *Yeah, so what? Who needs that part of that finger, anyway?* I know because, initially, I'd thought that, too. Only it turned out I used the side of that finger for a ton of things. I just didn't realize it until it wasn't there.

I had no idea that's where: a pen rests when you write, a mug handle rests when you drink, and a cell phone rests when you hold it.

You use it to: flip switches, open drawers, and open doors.

It's also where: a toothbrush rubs, a lipstick tube rubs, glasses rub when you take them on or off, a seatbelt buckle rubs when you fasten or unfasten it, and a plate or bowl presses when you pick it up.

Every single eating utensil rests there, too.

Every time I turned around, I couldn't do something because I was missing the side of that stupid finger. My middle finger. Again, the irony was not lost on me.

61. DIFFICULTIES

My husband traveled a lot for work, so I had to rely on our older son, William, for help when Dale was out of town. That is, if William was home, not working, not playing hockey, and not out with friends.

Feeding the cats and zipping zippers were still flat-out impossible for the first month or so. The only laundry I could get out of the washer and dryer were light things like tees and socks—no jeans, towels, or tangled messes. Lifting detergent and tilting it to pour was also out of the question, so a shout-out to laundry pods for the clean underwear.

Folding clothes is also insanely difficult when your wrists don't bend as they should. Same with sweeping, washing dishes, scooping cat poop out of the litter box, and you could forget vacuuming altogether.

So many everyday tasks required me to move in ways my wrists couldn't anymore: dressing, turning pages in a book, twisting doorknobs, opening car doors, placing my handbag on my shoulder, picking up a laptop, and using scissors. The list goes on and on.

I know because I was attempting to do everything myself since I was hell-bent on believing that doing all the normal things would, by definition, make me normal again. Still incredibly desperate to put this entire ordeal behind me; it's another horrible example of me trying to brainwash myself.

See? I can do this. I'm fine. There's nothing to see here. Move along.

As it turned out, even with physical therapy, it was several weeks before I could close my hands and several more before I could ball them into a fist.

62. AS GOOD AS IT GETS

The therapists set the bar pretty low early on, prepping me all along with talk of "realistic" expectations. My frustration over being unable to do more was met with statements like *This might be as good as it gets*, and *You're lucky to have made it this far.*

They constantly—and not so subtly—told me that thanks to scar tissue, I probably had all the range of motion I'd ever get back. When the physical therapists stopped pushing me and were no longer impressed by my accomplishments, I took it personally. It felt like they were giving up on me, like I was hopeless.

I was torn. I wanted to get better, but I also didn't want to throw money out the window if therapy was no longer helping. By this time, the medical bills from the ER visit were rolling in, and I was spending hundreds, if not thousands, every week on my various doctors' appointments.

It was true I was no longer making the long strides like when I'd started, but I believed I still had potential. At least *I* wasn't ready to give up on me. Despite what my parents used to say, I wasn't a quitter, but I also didn't want to risk catching the therapists' negative outlook or complacent mindset, either. So, when I left physical therapy after only a few months, I thought it was for the best.

63. FUN IN THE KITCHEN

As time progressed, I got strong enough to lift more things, but my un-bendy wrists were still problematic. Everyday tasks took twice as long because I had to invent modified ways to do them.

While I could lift a plate straight up and out of the dishwasher, I couldn't turn it to place it horizontally in the cupboard.

Opening containers was the worst. I had better luck opening Tupperware with my teeth than with my hands. Trying to open a bottle or jar was so bad that I'd turn it into a joke, asking my family to place bets on my chance of getting it open. They'd shout out my odds from across the room like they were at one of those divey off-track betting joints. I know because my mom enjoyed a brief stint as a bookie when I was in my early teens and would drag me along as she hurried to get her bets in before the deadlines. And if the jar was new and vacuum sealed— forget it. It was never going to happen.

Watching me try to pour something had to be comical, as finding unique ways to get the job done became my specialty. My strategy depended on how heavy it was, the size of the container I had to pour it into, and how important it was that I didn't spill it. Dumping water on the kitchen counter was one thing. Dumping an entire bottle of olive oil on the stovetop was a whole 'nother ball game, especially since I still couldn't wiggle my wrists to properly clean it up.

I could only lift and tilt containers so much with my hands before I'd have to resort to folding and twisting my entire body like a master yogi. Needless to say, I made a lot of messes, but the feeling of accomplishment I got from doing it all by myself was worth it.

Cooking, which used to be one of my favorite things to do, became something I loathed. Even stirring something in a bowl or tossing a salad hurt. The utensils either rubbed my middle finger or my wrists just wouldn't bend like that.

I began to see eating healthy as a disadvantage when I discovered fresh vegetables were my kryptonite. I'd always been a whiz with a knife, but even months after the attack, a bout of chopping veggies left me feeling like I'd run ten miles. The pressure I had to exert to press down on the knife, plus the up-and-down rocking motion, was exhausting. Afterward, my hands would ache so much I'd be forced to ice them for the rest of the night.

I've never been one of those people who follows a recipe. I'm more of a taste-as-you-go-and-just-keep-an-eye-on-it-while-it's-cooking kind of gal. However, repeatedly opening the oven door, sliding out a rack, or lifting the bakeware in and out of the oven multiple times to check on it was no longer an option. After the attack, if I went to the trouble of taking something out of the oven, it stayed out, even if it wasn't quite done. It's a wonder none of us died from salmonella.

I had hoped my Crock-Pot would be my new go-to, hands-off way to cook. But when trying to brown a hunk of meat beforehand, I nearly set my house on fire. Thanks to gravity, I had no problem dumping it into the hot pan, but I didn't have the strength or the coordination to flip it or lift it back out. I could see being outwrestled by Hulk Hogan, but being outwrestled and apparently outsmarted by a three-pound chuck roast was fucking depressing. After that, I stuck to soups.

I also attempted to cheat the system by using other kitchen gadgets, but sadly, the hand mixer and my electric knife were too "powerful" for me to control. Not to mention, the vibrations made everything hurt worse than if I had done it the old-fashioned way.

Even though I was doing a crappy job at most things, I still insisted on doing them myself. In my mind, the only way to get better was to keep practicing—and I prayed it would all eventually get less painful, too.

64. NERVES

My hands were a lingering problem for me. They didn't even feel like my hands anymore. It felt like someone had superglued someone else's hands onto the ends of my arms, even after I could open and close them again. It was like I was wearing bionic hands, but not the state-of-the-art kind. These were more like some cheap, crappy Chinese knock-off variety that weren't made well and didn't work well.

It's tough to explain, but it was as if my fingers no longer lined up correctly with the ones next to them. They felt like they were rubbing and bumping into each other in places where they hadn't before. Similar to when the dentist leaves your mouth hanging open too long, and when you finally close it again, your bite feels off, like your teeth forgot how they were supposed to line up.

It felt like wearing a pair of winter gloves. My fingers were there, but they felt fat, weird, and distant. For a long time, I thought it was a result of all the inflammation, but after the visible swelling subsided and they still didn't feel right, I figured there had to be more to it.

It wasn't like they saw these kinds of injuries all the time, so nobody could say for sure, but the therapists assumed it was due to nerve damage. Some thought it was due to bruised or severed nerves that had yet to repair themselves. Others thought the nerves had grown back but in a different configuration than before.

They said as nerves heal, they can feel somewhat overactive. So, while they felt dull and lifeless initially, with time, it felt like electric shocks were constantly shooting through my arms and hands.

Whether I was waiting for them to grow back or waiting for them to settle down, either way, I was looking at another case of *Only time will tell,* or another one of those *This might be as good as it gets* scenarios.

65. SCAR SCRAPING

I joke that my superpower is making scar tissue. With each surgery, each torn hamstring, even when I bonked myself in the forehead with my trunk lid (don't ask), I always wound up with too much scar tissue, which proved troublesome later on.

Therefore, it wasn't a surprise that as all my puncture wounds healed, I developed lumps of scar tissue around each. So much so that it attached itself to my muscles and tendons in several places.

The physical therapists worked on those areas but could never loosen them up enough to make much of a difference from a mobility standpoint. They said I needed to work on them at home, but I quickly learned it isn't possible to inflict that kind of pain on yourself.

It's the same reason we don't see women waxing their bikini lines at home. Sure, slathering hot wax *on* is no big deal, but when it comes time to rip that shit off, after staring at it for twenty minutes, you'll need to call your best friend to come over and do it for you. Trust me. I know.

I eventually reached the point where the folks at the PT group admitted they'd probably gotten me as far as they could. According to them, to see any further improvement in my mobility, I'd have to tackle the scar tissue—and apparently elsewhere.

Fortunately, a therapist who worked out of my gym a few days a week specialized in Active Release Technique (ART). He'd helped me with my back issues in the past, so I met up with him to discuss my new problem. He straight-up guaranteed he could get the scar tissue to release, but he warned me it would hurt.

Dude. Seriously? Need I remind you how I got this way in the first place? Bring it on.

He first tackled the nickel-sized lump of scar tissue that had formed on the top of my left wrist, the worst of my issues. This lump had affixed itself to the tendon below, which prevented it from sliding within some sheath—or so they said. I could only grasp bits and pieces of all the hand physiology everyone was throwing at me before my eyes would glaze over.

To get that scar lump to release, he lifted, stretched, twisted, and poked at my skin using his "medical device," which was eerily reminiscent of the plastic scraper tool our high school janitor had used to scrape gum off the cafeteria floor. My therapist was right. It definitely didn't feel pleasant.

He also worked on the weird quarter-sized lump of scar tissue in my forearm, which made me look like a junkie who had mistakenly shot a gobstopper up her arm. This was my second-worst problem area because, for whatever reason, it was ridiculously tender. I could barely slide a sleeve down over it without flinching from the pain, so you can imagine how much it hurt for him to repeatedly pinch, poke, and prod at it with his gum scraper.

66. NO PAIN, NO GAIN

The ART therapist, as well as my gym coach, couldn't believe I allowed him to do what he did without jerking my arm or crying out, even though I warned them I had a crazy-high pain tolerance. What can I say? I had been through the wringer:

I broke my two front teeth clear off in a
     fifth-grade playground accident, though
     I probably did myself a favor with that
     one since they were huge. On Julia
     Roberts, they make for a big, beautiful
     smile. On me, they were horse teeth.
Once, after being dropped off from a
     babysitting gig, I slammed my thumb in
     the dad's car door and had to jog along
     next to it until he realized. And that was
     back when cars were still made from
     molten steel.
I managed two C-sections with no pain
     meds. I'm talking after, not during. I'm
     no saint.
I broke my foot but didn't realize it until
     the following day when it looked like
     Fred Flintstone's.
I also ran for months after I tore my
     hamstring because I didn't know I had.
I lifted weights with a shredded rotator
     cuff because, again, I had no idea.
I even got the tip of my tongue cut off
     with a pair of sewing scissors when I
     was ten for being "sassy." Seriously, why
     would I ever make shit up when real life
     is this entertaining?

You get the idea.

Though this technique was insanely painful, I went
into each session with a positive attitude. After being
in labor with the first kid for over twenty-eight hours, I
felt I could endure anything for half an hour. Especially
since, as far as I knew, this was the only way to free that
tendon. Much like the only way to get a baby out is to

endure delivery, I figured the end result would be worth the pain, so I just sucked it up.

There were definitely days when I questioned whether childbirth had been worth it—thanks to those middle school years (ugh)—but I never regretted the scraping. My scar tissue loosened with every visit, and after four or five sessions, my range of motion was almost back to normal.

I also had hard lumps in a few other areas where the scar tissue had attached, like under the skin on my left palm, the inside of my left wrist, the palm of my right hand, and the back of my right hand. However, since none of those areas seemed to affect my mobility, I didn't see the sense in digging into it further. Digging. Get it?

67. THE CLAW

Since the attack, my right ring finger had been noticeably fatter than my left. At first, my medical team and I thought it was from swelling, but as the months wore on, it never subsided—neither did the pain. If anything, it ramped up. It felt as if I'd jammed it. Lord knows I'd done that enough times playing basketball with our boys in the driveway. Even bumping it the wrong way when grabbing a glass, picking up my purse, holding onto a steering wheel, or doing other day-to-day activities made me see stars.

I hoped the healing was just taking a little longer than expected. However, six months after the attack, not only did I still have tremendous pressure and pain in that one finger, but it was now involuntarily curling up and in, towards my palm, reminding me of a claw.

The tighter the claw got, meaning the closer my finger got to my palm, the more it hurt, so I tried to catch it in the early stages of curling. During the day, it was easier to manage. Since I was always using my hand, I could feel the tenderness mounting and could quickly intervene.

The only way to ease the pain was to forcibly bend the finger back, pushing it a little beyond the straight-up position, giving it the intense stretch it felt like it needed. Stretching it reminded me of how my back or legs would get stiff after sitting too long in a movie theater or on a long car ride and how good it felt to walk afterward.

When I bent my finger back to where it was supposed to be, my knuckle would crack a few times, and it felt like something was tearing deep within along the underside of my finger. I cringed each time, hoping I wasn't doing more damage, but bending it was the only way to solve the problem, at least temporarily, so I often did this ten times a day.

At night, however, I was at a disadvantage. When sleeping, I couldn't see it starting to curl, nor was I aware of the mild initial cramping. It wasn't until the pain got so severe that it woke me up that I'd realize what was happening, but by then, the finger was usually pinned to my palm in full-claw mode. Catching it late like that meant it would hurt a lot more to bend it back, so I had to take my time and play with it for a bit before attempting to get it completely straight.

The doctors had already ruled out swelling as the underlying cause. They now suspected the tendon running through my hand to that finger had been damaged or wasn't sliding as it should due to the excess sticky scar tissue in my palm. So back to the ART therapist I went, only to learn that he couldn't help because the skin in people's palms is too tight to lift and shove his scraper under. Well, damn.

Dead set on regaining proper use of my right ring finger, I explored other options. I saw a chiropractor once a month for my scoliosis, so I consulted with her. She gave me some stretching exercises and attempted to break up the scar tissue with ultrasound therapy, but neither did much good.

Someone else suggested I see a hand surgeon. I didn't even know those existed. Silly me, I thought being a surgeon qualified you to cut anything you wanted. Okay, I knew brain surgery was its own thing, and frankly, that made sense. Brains seemed like they'd be a little more specialized. But hands? In the end, I was glad it turned out to be a real thing.

What the hand surgeon lacked in bedside manner, he made up for in expertise when he immediately diagnosed me with a trigger finger. The middle schooler in me made a wisecrack about it being itchy, which he was too mature to get, too busy to acknowledge, or he'd heard it way too many times to even fake amusement.

I was outfitted with a special brace and told if it didn't work, I'd be looking at surgery to correct it. It took a month or so, but fortunately, it did the trick.

68. TAKE WITH FOOD

I liked the pain pills at first. While they didn't help with the pain much, they did make me drowsy, and I needed all the help I could get to fall asleep. However, I was forced to give them up entirely the day after the attack when they started to make me throw up, even if I took them with food.

In college, I took a nutrition class, thinking it would be a good "filler" class to round out my summer schedule. Instead, it led to a lifelong obsession. I became fascinated with foods and their impact on our overall health—positive and negative. While I've always been mindful of what I eat, that's not to say I don't eat unhealthy foods. I do. But to give my brownies a healthy boost, I often mix in shredded zucchini, sweet potatoes, or black beans—much to my kids' disappointment.

"You are what you eat" isn't just a catchy saying. It's science. Our bodies use the nutrients in food for energy, growth, and cell repair. Healthy, nutrient-dense foods help our bodies function as nature intended and promote healing. Why do you think they say that homemade chicken soup can cure colds and sugar fuels cancer?

I knew I needed to nourish my body so it could heal itself, yet I wasn't eating much after the attack. For starters, I couldn't hold a fork or spoon, and feeding myself with my hands turned out to be way more trouble than it was worth. Besides, I wasn't that hungry. And it's not like I was burning through my energy stores just lying around on my couch, so I wasn't too concerned about my lack of appetite. But when I started throwing up what little food I *did* eat, from a healing perspective, I knew something had to give.

69. WHO BABY?

Pain meds and I have a complicated history. After my first C-section, unbeknownst to me, they were pumping me with intravenous morphine to the point I couldn't keep my eyes open.

Here's what I remember from that first night in the hospital:

Nurse: [Flips the light on.] "Look who's here to see you."

Me: Zzzz

Nurse: [Baby crying in the background.] "Open your eyes. It's time to feed the baby."

Me: [Unable to open both eyes, though I did manage to pop one open for a quick second to peer at what she was shoving in my face. Then, sounding like I'd tossed back a fifth of bourbon.] "Cute baby. Who baby?"

Nurse: "It's your baby."

Me: [Big delay. The nurse thinks I'm taking my time waking up, but I've passed out again.]

Nurse: "Time to wake up and feed the baby."

Me: [Grunting] "No baby."

Nurse: [More stern, this time.] "Come on, Cheryl. Wake up. He's hungry. The baby's hungry. It's time to wake up and feed the baby."

Me: Zzzz

When my IV bag ran low, the machine next to me would beep until a nurse showed up to swap it out for a new bag. I was awake to the point where I knew what they were doing, but I couldn't open my eyes to see or open my mouth to speak. And so it went for the entire night.

The following day, after a shift change, I presume, it took the new crew a little too long to get around to my beeping IV stand. Luckily, the drugs had worn off just enough that I could finally talk, although it was still too hard to keep my eyes open. I complained to the nurses that they were giving me too much and that I didn't want it, but those bitches wouldn't listen. They swore it was "standard procedure," acted like I was overreacting, and replaced the bag anyway. It took an order from my OBGYN, who visited later in the day and wondered why I was half comatose, to finally put a stop to it.

The next time I had a C-section, I didn't have that problem. I had pre-negotiated a no-drugs-after deal with my doctor and reminded every nurse who came within ten feet of me just to be sure.

70. CUSTOMS

I'd had another awful experience with pain meds when I had LASIK in the mid-1990s. I like to say the procedure wasn't legal in the United States then, but technically, it just wasn't FDA-approved yet, so we had to drive to Canada to get it done. Again, that isn't as adventurous as it sounds. Since we lived in the suburbs outside of Buffalo back then, it was only a short drive across the bridge.

The procedure was supposed to reshape my corneas with lasers so I could see better far away. If everything went according to plan, I'd gradually regain my sight in a few days and never have to wear glasses again. However, during the procedure, if I blinked, moved, or didn't stare directly at the red light, I could be blinded for life. So if a patient wasn't a nervous wreck *before* the doctor explained the procedure, they sure as hell were *after*. And since not everyone is cool with that kind of pressure, the doctor made everyone take Valium beforehand. Presumably, to help minimize freakouts—and lawsuits from blind people, too, I suppose.

An hour or so after the procedure, as we approached the border, I was still totally out of it. While I may have been heading back to my native land, I probably looked like I was returning with one less kidney than when I'd left, the victim of some black-market, involuntary organ donation.

Dale was super on edge. I needed to look the part of an un-stoned, consensual female. If not, he knew, as the driver, he'd be in a heap of trouble until I sobered up enough to back up his story that I was just sick of being nearsighted.

In the customs line, while still on the bridge, he grumbled for me to wake up and get my shit together, but I could barely keep my eyes open and only mumbled back incoherently. All I wanted to do was sleep, but his voice was getting louder and louder. As we slowly crept toward the row of booths, he grew even testier, repeatedly reminding me of what I had to say.

Then, just as the customs agent ducked down to peer in our window, Dale gave me a good hard shove, and I opened my eyes as wide as possible. I probably looked more like a surprised Chihuahua rather than a young woman *not* being held captive against her will, but I did as I was told and rattled off my name and citizenship. I'm proud to say I even smiled and nodded, though they may or may not have been at the appropriate times. With access granted, no sooner had we pulled away than my head hit the headrest, and I was off to la-la land once again.

71. JUST SAY NO

Aside from those few instances, I hadn't had much experience with pain medication. Even when it comes to headaches, I'm more apt to drink a glass of water than pop a pill. Since I was a bit gun-shy after those bad experiences, any pain medications my family was prescribed usually wound up in our medicine cabinets, where they'd remain unused, forgotten, and—you guessed it—expired.

I assumed I'd had those adverse reactions because I wasn't used to meds or they'd given me too high of a dose for my small frame. At five-six and topping out at around 150 pounds when pregnant, I imagine it didn't take much to knock me out.

It wasn't until years later that I read something interesting in a pharmacology book and considered how it might pertain to me. No, I didn't read pharmacology for fun; this was required reading. At the time, I was a pharmaceutical sales representative, and my company had us learning the ins and outs of a new drug we were launching.

In one of the case studies, they talked about how some people had more or fewer liver enzymes, which affected how their body metabolized drugs and determined the extent of any side effects.

You don't say.

Since then, I vowed to remind all doctors that a little goes a long way when prescribing me pain medication. Only I hadn't been prescribed anything in so long, and with my brain on the fritz, I completely forgot to mention it at the hospital after the attack.

The vomiting, unbelievable drowsiness, and inability to keep my eyes open reminded me that pain medication was not my friend. So the day after the attack, I quit that shit cold turkey and never popped another pain pill again, not just for the pain from the dog attack, but from then on.

To this day, I even take over-the-counter cold medication sparingly.

72. THE PINK STUFF

Our family was an insurance company's dream. We paid our monthly premiums through my husband's employer but rarely used our health insurance. It's not like we were hippie-dippie people who didn't believe in Western medicine. Nor were we the type to "drink the Kool-Aid," thinking there was a magic pill for everything, either.

Fortunately, none of us had any serious or chronic conditions that demanded much attention. We went to the doctor, but only when warranted, not for every little thing. If the kids needed physicals for school, sure. If one of them had a cold, heck no.

Most of the stuff that ailed us was the kind of stuff a doctor didn't want to see us for, anyway. That is, if they're a good one. We're talking upper respiratory crap, sprains, and those miscellaneous aches. It seemed no matter what we went to the doctor for, we always got the same advice. We were either told to rest it, ice it, elevate it, drink lots of fluids, or take whatever over-the-counter medication made the most sense. Apparently, every ailment and boo-boo we came down with would ultimately work its way up and out over the next few weeks or heal on its own.

So, going forward, we smartened up and would treat ourselves at home for the first week or two. Most of the time, the doctor's usual advice of rest, ice, or whatever else Dr. Google suggested would do the trick and spare us the hassle of a trip to an actual doctor's office, which was even better since we loathed that whole ordeal.

So much so that when the kids' pediatrician moved out of state and I had to interview new doctors, one of the questions I asked was, "If I bring one kid in and he winds up having strep, then two days later, the other kid comes down with a sore throat, do I have to take off work and drag him back here for a culture, too, or will you just call in another prescription for the pink stuff?"

Maybe unemployed or retired people had hours to spend at the doctor's office, but I sure as hell didn't. When the kids were younger, Dale and I both worked full-time, and we only got so many vacation days. Taking time off from work to cart ourselves or the kids to a doctor's appointment seemed like a waste of a day off. Color us silly, but we preferred saving our vacation days for fabulous, fun family adventures rather than pissing them away in crowded germy waiting rooms.

On the other hand, it seemed some of our friends and family loved going to the doctor. I imagine some went because they didn't take care of themselves and wound up with legitimate health problems. I suspected others went because they were worrywarts and *imagined* they had legitimate health problems. And the rest went because it gave them something to do and something to talk about.

We were none of the above.

73. NO THANKS

Right from the start, My Friend was kind enough to offer to pay my medical bills. Her offer was very generous, but taking her up on that would've been weird.

I was brought up in a time when talking about money with friends and family was considered tacky or taboo. So that meant that lending to others, borrowing from others, or accepting money from others was definitely out of the question.

I didn't want to pooh-pooh the idea entirely because that would've been rude, so my official response was, "Thank you, but this is why we have health insurance." When My Friend pressed, I told her the easiest thing was for me to run everything through my insurance first, and then, if anything wasn't covered, she and I could talk about it later.

At least, that's what I *told* her.

I never actually planned on having that conversation with her down the road. Again, that would've been weird. "Do you want to get together on Saturday? Oh, and by the way, you owe me $5,000. Pay up." Yeah, no.

While my reply made sense, it also bought me a little time. While I didn't want to take My Friend's money, I also didn't want to make a financial obligation without running it by Dale. It's not like I had to ask permission to spend money. However, in the past, when I'd made large purchases or hefty donations without his input, he'd pouted for days afterward.

Luckily, when I brought it up to Dale later, he thought the same. He waved off the idea, saying it was nice of her to offer, but even if our insurance didn't cover all of it, we'd still take care of it ourselves.

Since we hardly went to the doctor, we opted for the cheaper, crappier insurance plan. That meant we had to fork over $5,000 of our own money before our insurance even thought about paying for anything, even though we paid gobs of money each month in premiums.

In our experience, even when we *had* reached that point, our carrier *still* tried to get out of paying based on some coding or billing technicality. If you ask me, the entire system is rigged and reeks of injustice.

The attack happened in November. And since we didn't use our insurance much, I figured the ER visit alone would be enough to get us up and over our yearly deductible. If there was a positive side to this mess, at least we'd finally get our money's worth out of our insurance plan for a change. Neither Dale nor I thought we'd wind up spending too much out-of-pocket, so it wasn't worth involving her. We just wanted to keep things clean and simple.

74. SEDUCED

About a week after the attack, I was shocked when, out of the blue, I got a call from My Friend's homeowner's insurance company. I had hoped we would keep the incident between us. We'd been friends for a long time. I trusted *her*. I couldn't say the same about insurance companies. Besides, we each had common sense and were reasonably intelligent, so I didn't think we *needed* her insurance company. So far, I thought we'd been doing just fine navigating this situation on our own.

Not to mention, here I'd been busting my ass to keep her and the dogs *out* of trouble. I couldn't see why she'd go blabbing to her insurance carrier and expose herself to the fallout. Involving others was risky. Entities had protocols and procedures, hospitals and insurance companies had rules, and even worse, the police had laws. I hoped I was wrong, but I couldn't help but think she had opened a can of worms by reporting the incident to her insurance provider. As usual, I was right.

Right off the bat, they made it a point to tell me that every call was recorded. I expected to hear a prerecorded message, saying something like, "By the way, we record and monitor our calls to ensure we're serving our precious customers to the best of our abilities because we recognize we wouldn't be here without you." Nope. This was her telling me, in her own regular voice, that the call would be recorded. She then asked if I agreed, and I told her I did. She then said she'd ask me again just before actually recording me, and when she asked the next time, all I needed to say was *yes*, nothing more.

"Sounds simple enough," was my reply.

However, the second time around, she didn't just ask me if I agreed to be recorded as she had seconds earlier. This time, she rambled on for a minute straight, which, and I'm paraphrasing here, essentially amounted to *whatever you say can and will be used against you.*

Being the snarky bitch I am, at the end of her little speech, I didn't just say *yes* as I'd been instructed to do mere seconds before. Oh no, I had to pipe up and throw out some sarcastic comments along the lines of, "I see what you did there, but that's not what you said before. Did you steal that from *Law and Order* last night?"

She then stopped the recording, chastised me, and reminded me that anything other than *yes* wasn't allowed. I reluctantly agreed, and she rattled off her spiel again.

This time around, I did as I was told, even though it felt a bit rapey.

While I had nothing to hide, I'd be lying if I said it didn't feel like an overtly aggressive tactile maneuver on their part. I thought I was playing a friendly game of checkers, but they were clearly playing chess. Their stance immediately put me on the defensive, and from that moment on, I knew My Friend's insurance company wouldn't have my best interests at heart, regardless of what they said.

They told me they'd cover all my medical bills, although "only up to a certain amount." However, I was told I needn't worry. If my bills exceeded that amount, they'd still cover it, but it would just be paid out of "another policy" and "sometime down the road" after I was "done with treatments of any kind." But again, I was not to worry because they would be nice enough to figure all that out for me on their end. Of course, they would.

I'm no attorney, but as a businesswoman, I knew my way around contracts enough to realize it wasn't as cut and dry as they were making it out to be. Some loopholes needed closing, but I was too overwhelmed by my physical limitations, the influx of bills, and the emotional toll this entire ordeal had taken already. Therefore, I was easily seduced when they said, "All you have to do is fill out some forms."

Sold! No problem. That I can do.

75. JUMPING THROUGH HOOPS

It turns out My Friend's insurance company only needed a few things from me. One of those things was my medical history—from birth. On top of that, they required no less than four ways to contact any doctor I had ever seen—in my lifetime. And lastly, they needed an outline of my family tree dating back to the pilgrims—as well as *their* medical histories.

In addition to the forms, they also needed me to upload my medical bills and some photos. In my condition, I didn't appreciate the hoop jumping since typing and pushing small buttons on a scanner were no longer part of my repertoire, but I hoped it would be worth my while for everyone involved, so I sucked it up.

If her insurance company picked up the overage beyond what my insurance company covered, My Friend would be officially off the hook for that portion. Technically, as far as Dale and I were concerned, she was already off the hook, but at least this way, we wouldn't have to fight over it like a dinner check. Plus, it sounded like they might even pick up *my* insurance costs. I didn't care so much if my insurance company saved some bucks, but I liked the idea of not having to deal with them, either, if possible.

I'm not really a follow-directions kind of girl unless pictures or diagrams are involved, so I'll admit I didn't read the emails they sent me in their entirety. I mistakenly assumed I could reply to this insurance representative's email and attach the forms and photos there, but no, it all needed to be uploaded to a particular site and be of a particular size. On top of that, each photo had to be individually named in a particular way that referenced the claim number. However, it's not like she'd voluntarily told me any of this upfront on the phone. It wasn't until weeks later, with more bills rolling in daily, when I called her to check on the status of my claim, that she told me I had done it wrong.

Begrudgingly, I did it the correct and much more time-consuming way. I was already weeks behind in the process and didn't want to delay it further, so after I had it all uploaded, I called to let her know it was done. I was hoping she'd fish it out of the pile and get to work on it so we could finally get the ball rolling. So when she didn't pick up, I left her a message.

It took her over a week to call me back, and when she did, it was to tell me that—wait for it—she never got it. Nope, none of it, because apparently there had been a problem with their internal system.

Because so much time had passed since I uploaded it, I was hopeful my stuff had made it through before the glitch. But when I asked her when the outage had occurred, she changed her story, claiming their system problems had been off and on for weeks.

That's weird.

I expected a Fortune 500 insurance behemoth to have an entire IT force and a slew of backup plans at the ready for situations like this.

As a business owner, I actually felt bad for them, recalling how frustrating it had been whenever technology woes sprung up in my own business. I imagined they had loads of work to catch up on, so to avoid any duplication of effort on both our parts, I probed further. I only wanted to double-check her outage timeline against my upload timeline since I was still hopeful my upload had snuck in the cue when their system was up, not down. But the way she straight-up refused to discuss it any further made me suspect their system had never been down to begin with.

According to this woman, if I wanted to continue moving forward with the process, I would have to resend it all a *third* time. I wanted to lash out at her for being cagey, unhelpful, and indifferent, but I couldn't. Just like I had to be extra nice when trying to get a ride home on the day of the attack, I needed this woman's help.

Man, how I detested that feeling.

The entire process was so damned passive-aggressive it nearly drove me crazy, like, for real.

76. FOOL ME ONCE

I assumed if the hospital removed my stitches, it would wind up costing way more than it should. I'd made that mistake once before when Harry was seven and banged his head in a relative's pool, which required stitches. Like I said before, daredevils.

I thought the emergency room physician was just being thorough when he asked me to bring Harry back a few days later. He'd sold me on the idea by saying I didn't need an actual appointment. I just had to "pop back over" when we had time for a "wound check" so he could take a "quick peek" to ensure it was healing correctly.

I thought it made sense, seeing how it was a head wound and in close proximity to his brain and spinal column. And considering those are both pretty important, I took the hospital up on the offer. Only I got stuck with a bill for $250—and that was *after* my insurance kicked in their part. Even though all I got was a tech who came out to the waiting room to peer at my kid's head for all of three seconds, they billed me for a full-blown ER exam.

I called the hospital to dispute it, but that didn't work. They claimed it was a justifiable exam because they had looked for signs of infection. Duh. I had two boys. When it came to boo-boos, this wasn't my first rodeo. I didn't need somebody to tell me it wasn't infected. So, in protest and as a matter of principle, I refused to pay it.

That is until it came time to close on our new house.

That's when our mortgage broker informed me that my refusal to pay, however righteous, had wreaked havoc on my credit. She said I needed to pay it immediately and in full, including the collection fees, or else we'd end up paying way more in the long run since we no longer qualified for the better interest rate we were initially quoted based on our high credit scores.

Grrrr.

Fool me once, blah blah blah.

This time, there was no way I was going back to the hospital to have the stitches in my butt taken out. Instead, as the hospital initially recommended, I called my primary care doctor to make an appointment for him to do so. Regardless of who ended up paying for it—my insurance, her insurance, or me—I saw no reason for any of us to pay some insane ER markup.

77. REJECTED

I liked our primary care doctor. After all, he passed my initial interview with flying colors when he agreed to give me the pink stuff over the phone for kid number two. He wasn't just a good doctor. I considered him a friend since we had a few things in common. He was a native of our town and had gone to high school with my younger cousin. We also had sons with the same name, and he was a fellow skier, which wasn't easy to find in Florida. He usually skied out West in places we'd never been, so I enjoyed hearing about his trips. Dale and I were starting to travel more, so if my doctor raved about a specific locale, I'd add it to our bucket list.

What I *didn't* like was that my doctor was under the umbrella of a much larger physicians' group. From a marketing standpoint, I was supposed to find value in being able to see any of the seven general practitioners on staff, but I preferred him. The few times one of us had seen another doctor in the group because he hadn't been available, the other doctor had been dismissive. I liked that our doctor knew us. He knew if we were there, it was because we had a bona fide problem, and he took the time to get to the bottom of it.

At my last doctor's office in New York, my doctor's wife had been the receptionist, office manager, and nurse. At this new office, however, being the conglomerate it was, the staff was way more business-oriented than customer service-oriented, like I was used to.

The downside was that because we didn't go to the doctor on a regular basis, I often had to re-fill out stacks of new patient paperwork. Sometimes, the staff claimed it was because they had a new software system. Other times, like when I hadn't seen the doctor in the past year, it was because they sent my file to storage. And if I hadn't been there in three years, it was because they had kicked me out of the system entirely. Penalizing a patient for being healthy and *not* needing to go to the doctor didn't make sense to me, but if I didn't want to find another doctor, that's what I had to do.

I was excited that I wouldn't have to go through any of that this time around since I'd seen him several times the year prior regarding some funky blood test results. My paperwork was current, and I was back in their good graces—or so I thought.

When I called to make the appointment, I was blown away when they flat-out refused to see me. It turned out to be my fault, although I hadn't yet realized my mistake.

When I called, they asked me where I got the stitches. That was easy. "At the hospital." Why did I have stitches? Another easy one. "I got bit by a dog." Her tone then became terse, her speech clipped.

"Dog bite" was apparently synonymous with *Do not touch with a ten-foot pole.*

That's when I started to feel like the rug had been pulled out from underneath me. When the receptionist asked whose dog, and I told her it was My Friend's, the woman nearly hung up on me, leaving me stunned and confused as I struggled to grasp what had just happened and what I could say to undo it.

She claimed they didn't want to get involved in a "third party" situation, but I had no idea what that meant. And when asked, she'd only repeat the same thing over again. So when she finally got around to explaining that they didn't want to get in the middle of a lawsuit, I sighed with relief.

Okay, now I see the problem.

The receptionist had mistakenly jumped to the conclusion that there was a lawsuit. Now, it made sense. That didn't sound like fun to me, either. In my mind, all I had to do was set her straight, explain how that wasn't the case, and we could get back on track, making me that appointment.

I assured her their office would never have to speak to the "third party," explaining that either my insurance would pick up the tab or I would.

I continued to ramble on about how I ran all my medical bills through my insurance first, then whatever they didn't pay, I was stroking checks for. I had learned my lesson with Harry's stitches. I prided myself on a kick-ass credit score and wasn't about to risk it again. These days, I paid every doctor's bill in full, regardless of how outrageous the amount.

It never occurred to me to lie. That's just not me. Although, knowing what I know now, it would've been much easier had I told the receptionist it was *my* dog.

Thinking back to this encounter later that day, I realized I hadn't even told her that My Friend's insurance company had contacted me, let alone been "involved." She'd just assumed they were. But again, being the ridiculously honest and forthright person I am, when she brought it up, I not only admitted they had, I told her everything. Call me naive, but I still couldn't see the problem.

I explained that while My Friend's insurance company was aware of the situation, they were merely waiting in the wings to pay me back once I finished all my treatments.

Still, she refused to make an appointment for me. Still, I couldn't understand why.

I refused to beg. I never begged. Nothing was worth my dignity. Instead, I attempted to win her over with logic. If they were concerned about the money, I told her I'd pay the entire bill right then and there. They wouldn't even have to run it through my insurance first.

Again, she refused.

Frustrated, confused, and embarrassed, I asked her to go find my doctor and ask him. No doubt, my fellow ski buddy could *and would* override all this nonsense. Whether she did or not, I don't know because the answer was still no.

I even threatened to hightail it over there to pick up my records and leave their practice altogether. If they were so business-minded, surely they didn't want to lose a customer, no?

Pfft.

Apparently, they couldn't give a rat's ass about customer retention. Not only did she actually *tell me* they didn't care, she was a smug jerk about it.

As condescendingly as humanly possible, she described the process to me. First, I had to drive to their office to complete a request form. After I'd done so, they'd be *more than happy* to copy any of the file pages I wanted, but I'd have to pay in advance. *Cash, of course.* But lucky for me, they would *only* charge me three dollars per page. Oh, and it wouldn't be ready for me to pick up until two weeks later.

"What time should we expect you—"

I hung up on her midsentence and cursed the stupid doctors in the ER for not using dissolving stitches.

78. DENIED

I couldn't wrap my head around it. I didn't think my doctor could refuse to treat someone, let alone do it so blatantly. Isn't that in the doctor's handbook somewhere? Weren't physicians required to take an oath or at least pinky swear that they'd always help people in need? Hell, I even had to pledge some crap like that, and I was just a Girl Scout.

One of my real estate clients used to be an ER doctor at the hospital downtown, and I remembered him complaining about how he didn't get paid if his patient didn't pay. He'd quit because not only did some patients not pay their bills, but they continued to show up at the hospital expecting to be treated. And guess what? They treated them. I would have thought if doctors had the right to refuse to treat a patient, they would have kicked the non-paying ones to the curb first, not the dog-bite victims.

The crazy thing is, I was totally willing to pay my doctor, as was My Friend *and* each of our insurance companies. My doctor, in essence, had people lined up around the block to pay him, but he still refused to help me. Meanwhile, that other doctor had a line around the block of *unpaying* patients, yet he wasn't allowed to refuse to treat them. I didn't get it.

I then thought about those people who abuse drugs, cigarettes, alcohol, and food. By now, we all know the risks, yet they continue to make bad choices that land them in doctors' offices. Why don't I hear about doctors refusing to treat *them*? If those people don't care about their *own* health, why should any doctor?

Let's take it one step further. How about the people who willingly take illegal drugs in lethal doses. I've got a few friends in the sheriff's department who say they see the same people overdose night after night, yet doctors go to heroic lengths to pump their stomachs and inject them with Narcan to bring them back to life.

When I boiled it down, I was hearing that every human being is worth a doctor's time and attention—unless that person accidentally gets bit by someone else's dog. Yet, unlike the obese smoker who winds up with diabetes and heart disease or the meth addict, I didn't deliberately get myself torn up by three dogs.

I couldn't understand why I was being punished like this. I couldn't comprehend how I could be denied treatment. I thought there had to be some mistake, but no. My insurance company confirmed it. Not only was my doctor not *required* to see me, there was nothing they could do about it. In fact, my insurance company didn't even seem fazed by it.

Confused, pissed off, and in desperate need of a plan B, I set out to find a new doctor. I asked my insurance company and My Friend's insurance company for a list of doctors in my area who participated in their insurance plans. Though I hoped to find one close by, I was willing to travel up to an hour away if I had to. I called each of the twenty-plus offices they gave me, only to be told none could or would see me. I was disgusted.

79. UNHELPFUL

I didn't use our insurance enough to know how it all worked. When I called my insurance company multiple times in the weeks following the attack, most of my questions pertained to their procedures for submitting bills. Or is it a claim? See? I don't even know the lingo.

Though I was no insurance expert, I understood enough to know it was better to submit everything correctly the first time around rather than try to fix it or adjust it after the fact. Then, after My Friend's insurance company got involved, I had even more questions. Since I didn't trust her insurance company, I'd call mine to run any new developments by them, figuring they were more likely to have my back. I was mainly looking for their assurance that I was doing it right so I didn't inadvertently fall into some sort of trap.

Of course, neither of them explained how the process worked entirely, and certainly not voluntarily. When questioned, the insurance people acted like they were on the stand at a congressional hearing. They gave me just enough information to appear cooperative yet gave me nothing of substance I could actually use. Any information they provided was solely dependent on my asking the right questions. Even if I asked lengthy, specific questions, I was still only given short, generic answers in return. Their replies sounded canned, as if they were reading directly out of some training manual.

Since the insurance people only spoke in hypotheticals, I was left to piece together whatever information I did manage to gather from them and guess how it might apply to my specific situation. It was as if their employees were trained to be deliberately unhelpful, only there for show because they were required to be there by law. Again, not unlike Congress.

80. UNEMOTIONAL

As I mentioned before, I'm not overly emotional. Don't get me wrong. It's not like I'm a psychopath who has no feelings whatsoever. I feel all the feelings that everyone else feels. I just prefer to keep mine to a more manageable level—most of the time. I'm a little ashamed to admit that when provoked, I can go from zero to sixty pretty damn quick.

If a fight is what you're looking for, I'm all in. But if I even get a whiff of drama, I'm out of there—especially the crybaby kind. I get it. People aren't robots. They have feelings. I'm not debating that. People can have any feelings they want. All I'm asking is that they keep them to themselves. We all have that voice inside our heads for a reason. Use it.

I'm no Merriam-Webster, but I'd define feelings as sensations or thoughts that rattle around inside a person's brain. However, just because a person thinks something, it doesn't mean they need to act on it, which is why, for me, sensitive has always been synonymous with manipulative.

I'm sure my childhood is to blame for this, too, since both of my parents are what some might call "overreactors." The problem is that feelings change when people put them on display in that "extra" kind of way. I'm talking "extra" in the Urban Dictionary sense: "When you are being over the top, excessive, dramatic, and it's mostly over nothing." See? That's precisely my point. In my house, my parents' feelings were always big, whether the situation warranted it or not. And since their outbursts usually *weren't* justified, it seemed they did so more for attention or to manipulate others into doing something or acting a certain way.

It's no wonder I grew to resent big feelings.

When people parade their feelings around for all the world to see, it's like they're trying to force-feed their feelings to the rest of us. Here's a news flash: some of us don't like how that tastes, and it only makes us want to spit it back in your face.

Consequently, since I have zero interest in playing those kinds of games anymore, you would be hard-pressed to see me get to the point where I'm so worried, scared, or sad that I need to be consoled by someone. It's like this, if I can manage my feelings all by myself, so can everyone else.

That's why my outburst shocked the hell out of me.

81. ROMAN CANDLE

Even if I only count the dog attack itself and not the aftermath, in my mind, I had already endured enough shit to last a lifetime, so from a Karma or Universe payback perspective, I figured I was due for a break. However, every time I turned around, I was handed another big pile of shit I had to figure out what to do with.

I was incredibly overwhelmed by this point and so sick of fighting.

Not only did I not *want* to fight, I was at the point where I didn't think I had any more fight left in me. I would have thought it impossible, but my well of feisty and positivity had run dry, and this was only week two.

When my primary doctor refused to see me, that was the proverbial straw that broke the camel's back. I knew what was coming, and once that fuse was lit, I knew there'd be no stopping it. It set off a reaction in me like one of those Roman candles, where the pressure builds and then sends flaming balls whizzing into the sky systematically, one after the other.

Yet, even in the comfort of my own home, I still didn't want to make a scene. Looking for a hiding place, I ducked inside my bedroom closet and shut the door behind me. I hoped being surrounded by rows of clothes from floor to ceiling would muffle the sound of what was to come.

Each of my frustrations bubbled up, preparing to blow:

> My doctor refused to take my stitches out.
> *Pop! Whoosh! Bang!*
> I can't take a shower on my own.
> *Pop! Whoosh! Bang!*
> I'm forced to eat with my hands.
> *Pop! Whoosh! Bang!*
> My hands and arms hurt constantly.
> *Pop! Whoosh! Bang!*
> I hate having to ask for help all the time.
> *Pop! Whoosh! Bang!*
> My Friend's insurance company is jerking me
> around. *Pop! Whoosh! Bang!*
> My *own* insurance company is jerking me around.
> *Pop! Whoosh! Bang!*
> How can I work if I can't hold a pen and I can't hold
> a phone? *Pop! Whoosh! Bang!*
> Everyone is calling, but I have nothing good to say.
> *Pop! Whoosh! Bang!*
> Will I ever regain full use of my wrists and hands?
> *Pop! Whoosh! Bang!*
> What did I ever do to deserve this?
> *Pop! Whoosh! Bang!*

And unlike the conclusion to the grand finale on the Fourth of July, there were no *oohs* and *ahhs*. Instead, I burst into tears.

This was the first time I cried in . . . I couldn't remember how long. We're talking months, possibly years. Granted, I'd teared up when My Friend came to see me on day one, but those were more sympathy tears, like when you can't help but yawn when somebody else yawns.

Besides, these weren't just tears. This was a full-on meltdown, complete with heaving, sobbing, nonstop waterworks, ugly face, boogers, and all. I'd gotten myself so worked up I was sucking in air, hyperventilating *fa-fa-fa*-like, in between howling like a wounded animal. It was bad. This was something you'd expect from a three-year-old who'd missed their nap, not a nearly fifty-year-old.

I hid in my closet and sobbed. I sat in the shower and sobbed. I sat on my back patio and sobbed. I sobbed until there was nothing left. I swore and cried more in that one day than I had the entire year prior.

82. BANKRUPT

In my twenties, I read where someone described life like a bank account. Their theory was that good experiences, things like fun activities, meaningful moments, time spent with good people, or doing good deeds, add to your bank balance. Meanwhile, negative experiences and dealing with negative people subtract from your bank balance. Then what you're left with, the difference between the two, is what you have available to put forth into the world. This is what you have to "spend" on your attitude, mood, and state of mind. That's why it's so difficult for people to remain positive when everything around them is negative. As they say, garbage in, garbage out.

Prior to the attack, I was content. I was happy with the lovely little life I had built for myself. Granted, I wasn't without problems, but for the most part, I lived my life predominantly "in the black." That's not to say I didn't have to make some drastic changes to get there in the first place.

For starters, I gave up watching the news shortly after September 11th. For someone so unemotional, it's surprising, but I really took any news stories to heart. Of course, it didn't help that they usually only reported on crimes.

I couldn't help but stress out when I thought about how the victims felt and how they'd cope. It unnerved me to wonder what kind of horrible people could commit such heinous acts and how many of them were still running around out there.

I purposely tried to block out negative news whenever possible. I figured if I never let it in to begin with, it couldn't make itself comfortable, and if it wasn't comfortable, it couldn't fester. It was very freeing to discover that I didn't need to know about bombings, shootings, bank robberies, floods, fires, and lying politicians to function in the world.

Speaking of liars, I tried cutting those people out of my life, too. Unfortunately, with certain acquaintances, I still had to deal with complainers, fakes, and drama queens, but I intentionally kept my dealings with them to a minimum. Instead, I strived to surround myself with positive, authentic people who made me smile.

At my gym, I'd made some good friends, and I was happy with my results. There, I got a kick out of trying new things and pushing my body to new limits. Plus, there was a definite correlation between the strength I felt at the gym and the strength I felt within.

While my job could be quite stressful at times, I enjoyed the challenge. Together, I suppose you could say Dale and I made a decent living, but more importantly, we made a conscious effort to live within our means. Neither of us liked worrying about money. Been there, done that. No, thank you.

My husband not only loved me, he understood me. The real me. I didn't have to hide my flaws because he knew everything and loved me anyway. I'd like to say our relationship was fifty-fifty, true partners, with each of us putting in the same effort all the time, but that wasn't the case. Sometimes, I swore I was putting in 90 percent, while Dale only kicked in ten. Yet, admittedly, there were times when I only had 10 percent to give, and Dale was forced to pick up the slack for me. However, I imagine it all averaged out, and along the way, we managed to raise two boys we could be proud of. In later years, to recharge our batteries and regain some of that balance, the hubby and I would take mini vacations every few months or get together with our close-knit group of friends on the weekends.

All in all, life had been good. My life now, though, was one big ball of shit, and I was beyond stressed.

83. POOR ME

It was all so overwhelming. Bombarded with so many hefty hospital bills, I first thought it was a mistake. The initial hospital invoice was so pricey I had presumed it was all-encompassing. So when I received separate invoices from the radiology department and my emergency room physician, I assumed I was being double-billed or, worse, scammed altogether. I mean, come on, who does that?

When I take my car to be fixed, I don't get separate bills from the guy who drives it around back, the one that jacks it up in the air, and the one that rotates the tires. Same with my water bill. The water company pays their meter readers, not me.

After the attack, I couldn't put in the kind of long hours at work like I was used to. And since I owned my own business and worked off commission, there was no paid time off or disability pay. Most of my days were spent at doctor appointments, driving to and from doctor appointments, and sorting out the numerous bills resulting from said doctor appointments. More money was definitely going *out* the door than was coming in. It was scary, and I didn't like it one bit.

I was also spending an inordinate amount of time on the phone. Friends kept calling, and it was emotionally draining having to recount the attack or update them on my injuries.

Then there was my insurance company, who, according to the hospital, had rejected their invoices, so it became this big game of he-said, she-said, with me stuck in the middle. My insurance company either claimed they were never billed by the hospital or that the hospital hadn't coded the invoices correctly. Yet, even after I got all that straightened out and sent them bills that *were* coded correctly, they still didn't pay them because no matter what it was for, it turned out not to be covered by my insurance. It figures.

Since My Friend's insurance company was also being a dick by making me resend all those forms, photos, and invoices multiple times, it didn't take long for me to realize that they were jerking me around on purpose. With that, any hope of them helping me went out the window. This only made me feel dumb for ever trusting them in the first place and wasting all that time jumping through their fake hoops.

Frankly, I expected that from the insurance companies. I didn't expect that from my own doctor because I thought he had vowed to help people. And since we never reached our insurance deductible for our insurance to kick in, I also thought I'd paid him enough money out of our pockets over the years, whereby I was at least owed some courtesy. I'd considered him a friend and literally trusted him with my life and my children's lives. But when I really needed him, he told me, not with his words but with his actions, *Screw you. You're not worth the hassle.* As if I *chose* to be attacked by someone else's dogs.

It was bad enough I had to endure the terror of being bitten, shaken, and almost killed by three dogs. Now, getting doors slammed in my face as if nobody cared if I got the treatment I needed left me feeling desperate and hopeless. Needless to say, I never did find a doctor to take out my stitches, and while I could have gone back to the hospital, I still didn't want to stick anybody with an unnecessarily hefty bill.

My meltdown wasn't about being sad. It was about being frustrated beyond what I had ever felt in my entire life. My positivity bank account, where I'd been making regular deposits for the last twenty-five years, had been wiped out in one week. It was as if three armed dogs in ski masks had barged in and made off with every last cent.

84. DR. DALE

Though my tears were more out of frustration and, considering the circumstances, totally understandable, I was still ashamed. I wasn't a crier, and I definitely wasn't someone who worked herself up into a tizzy like that.

My go-to method of slapping on big girl panties or pulling myself up by my bootstraps was no longer an option. I simply wasn't that girl anymore. I was like one of those toddlers throwing a tantrum face down on the floor in the middle of Target, and I wasn't budging unless somebody dragged me out to the car.

That somebody was Dale.

I'd been trying to cry in private, but considering I wasn't particularly quiet or dainty about it, it was no shocker when he eventually tracked me down in my closet. No doubt in search of whatever large rodent had somehow gotten itself trapped between our walls. Relieved I hadn't chewed through our electrical wires, he patiently listened as I blurted out my long list of Roman candle rounds.

Dale admitted that my future was uncertain. There was no denying I had some valid points, but he also reminded me that the attack had only been the week before. While I might have been in the thick of it now, Dale assured me my situation would improve with time. He acknowledged that he had no magic wand for my pain or mobility issues, but he did offer to take my stitches out.

I appreciated the offer but almost didn't go along with it since Dale's strategy for taking out slivers was horrendous. Mine were usually cactus-induced, so they were those pesky clear ones that were tough to see—even by someone with good eyes. His eyes were a year and a half older than mine, so they were just as damaged, if not more, by computer rays, ultraviolet rays, gamma rays, and whatever other rays. However, since his pride was light years ahead of mine, he refused to use the cheater reading glasses I stashed all over our house. Instead, he "found" slivers by dragging the tweezers sideways back and forth over the area. Then, when I'd wince and recoil, he knew he'd "found" it.

This man has an MBA, yet he couldn't seem to grasp the concept that my *feeling it* did not equate to him *seeing it*. As you'd expect, all his dragging would eventually cause the sliver to break off, leaving only the part under the skin, so he'd then resort to digging at it. Of course, he couldn't see that, either, so he'd just repeatedly stab me with the fattest, bluntest needle he could find until it started to bleed. Then he'd get all frustrated and call it quits as if implying it was all my fault for bleeding and the reason he couldn't see it, though we both knew *he never saw it in the freaking first place!* I'm pretty sure, as we speak, there are still seventeen slivers in my body decomposing ever so slowly.

Nevertheless, I had no better options.

So later that day, he sterilized some scissors and tweezers and got to work snipping and pulling each stitch out. Like that positivity bank account, I felt I'd already used up all my for-better-or-worse credits. Wasn't bathing me, wiping my netherlands, and waiting on me hand and foot enough?

I should have felt relieved after he took my stitches out, but instead, I felt guilty. At this rate of 100 percent effort on Dale's part and zero percent effort on my part, I didn't think we'd ever get back to our fifty-fifty batting average.

85. COMMENTARY

I'd been through all kinds of shit in my life, but I've never considered myself a victim. I hate to say it, but I've always considered victims weak. I'm sorry. I realize that's unfair, and please know I'm cringing as I write it.

I didn't see it at first. It took days, weeks, months, and years of looking inward to understand why I utterly loathed all the questions and unsolicited commentary from people around me. Talk of how I found myself in this horrible situation made me feel like a victim—a dumb, weak victim.

Truth be told, I had a chip on my shoulder from the get-go regarding any commentary. Usually, I don't give a shit what other people think. I mean that. We can have totally opposite opinions, and so long as you don't try to shove your opinion down my throat, I'm cool with that. After all, that's what makes the world spin. Kumbaya and all that crap.

Everyone wanted to hear about the attack and my injuries. In return, a few even felt compelled to share their own stories of how they, too, had been bitten by a dog. It didn't matter that they had been nipped by their grandma's shih tzu when they were eight—or so their mom told them. They were so *not* traumatized by the ordeal that they couldn't even remember the incident themselves. Yet, in their minds, we had been through the same thing. Therefore, they expected me to find comfort and inspiration in how they overcame such adversity. *You have exactly five seconds to get out of my face.*

Only a few crass people wanted to assign blame and debate the fate of the dogs in those first few days, but they were immediately shot down as I made it clear that neither topic was up for discussion. I was amazed that so many people, having not lived through this themselves, would feel such outrage over the incident and, even worse, project that onto me, claiming that I should be outraged, too.

I was outraged, all right. Who the hell were they to tell me how to feel? I struggled enough with sorting out my own thoughts. I didn't need them dumping their opinions on bad friends and dead dogs on me. Whatever happened to *If I wanted your opinion, fuckwad, I'd ask for it?*

86. PRIMPING

Though I was going stir-crazy at home, preparing to go out was too much of an ordeal. I couldn't blow dry my hair because the blow dryer was too heavy to hold. And even if I could lift it, I didn't have the wrist moves to wiggle it back and forth so as not to set my scalp on fire. Since that same wrist flexion problem also made it impossible to brush my hair or put it up in a ponytail, my hair did whatever it damn well pleased. I had zero say in the matter. Think Nick Nolte's DUI mugshot.

Makeup was out of the question, too. Anything requiring fine motor skills was unthinkable, to the point it made me too sad and angry to even try. Not that it mattered. Even on a good day, my look would have been considered more "presentable" than "dolled up." Despite being inundated with makeup tutorial ads on social media, I'd yet to master the smokey eye. Even before the attack, any attempts made me look more like a member of Kiss or an extra on *The Walking Dead* than a sultry Kardashian.

Looking crappy was one thing, but smelling crappy was another. Putting deodorant on required me to put pressure on my hands and move them around in ways they couldn't bend anymore. Lucky for me, Dale had severe allergies, which left him with little sense of smell.

Brushing my teeth was just as bad. Since I couldn't take the vibration from my electric toothbrush, I had to use a regular one. However, because I couldn't hold it properly, I had little control over it. I'm embarrassed to say, ultimately, I did more sucking the toothpaste off the toothbrush than actual brushing. My apologies to my kids for giving them crap for doing the same when they were four—and to my dentist.

The number of everyday tasks I'd once taken for granted was astounding.

Before, I never would've thought twice about ripping hangers off the bar in my closet. On a typical day, while deciding what to wear, I'd whip twenty things out and onto the bed (which may or may not have eventually wound up on the floor). It was demeaning enough I had to ask for help putting on deodorant. So rather than ask for help finagling hangers, I opted for clothes folded in drawers or on shelves.

I was fortunate that, thanks to Kate Hudson and Lululemon, athleisure wear was all the rage in my

Stepford-esque town. Even though I wasn't one of those mommies who spent her days at Starbucks, Sephora, and Sak's, at least now I had an excuse to look like one—minus the Range Rover. The trouble was my workout clothes were too tight and, therefore, too tricky to get on, even with assistance. If you've ever stuffed an uncooperative, squirmy, chubby baby into a onesie, you get the idea. Hence, most days, "getting dressed" consisted of slapping on a fresh pair of jammies.

87. VETERAN'S DAY

The first time I left the house was only a few days after the attack. There was a luncheon scheduled for Veteran's Day, where my stepdad, a World War II vet, was to be honored with another award. Unfortunately, the last time, when a local congressman awarded him a flag that had been flown over the capitol for him, Dale and I had been out of town and unable to attend.

This time, we wanted to be there. Not only to show our love, support, and appreciation for all he did for our country but also for our family. Before the attack, we'd already RSVP'd that we'd attend, and we didn't want to disappoint him by not being there again. But because I was still heavily bandaged, I thought I might do more harm than good by being too much of a distraction. Not wanting to take the focus off him, I debated not going, although I really wanted to be there.

My mother-was one of those "extra" people I tried to avoid in situations like this, so I hadn't spoken to her since the attack, but I knew Dale had been keeping her in the loop. Since my mom liked Dale more than she liked me, I made *him* call her to go over the ground rules.

This award ceremony needed to be all about Chuck, so if I did go, she had to promise to pretend there was nothing unusual about my appearance and that nothing had happened to me. There would also be no gasping, crying, or fussing over me whatsoever. Begrudgingly, she agreed, so we went.

That day, my mother greeted me with the biggest, fakest smile she could muster, and we hugged awkwardly. What can I say? I learned from the best. I'd taken my sling off for the occasion, so unlike when My Friend had tried to hug me, I could lift my arms this time. However, it was still only the hug version of an air kiss as I desperately tried not to bump any part of my upper extremities on any part of her.

There was no denying I was in rough shape, but I downplayed it the best I could, deflecting remarks and concerns from others with a phony smile and casual replies like "It's no big deal," "It's nothing," and "I'm fine." Then I'd quickly redirect the conversation back to Chuck, how nice it was for everyone to come out for him that day or to his upcoming book.

Fortunately, Dale and I were seated with my stepsister and a few cousins. We were all middle-aged, but compared to my stepfather's friends, it felt like we were at the kids' table again. In order to blend in and not appear helpless, I attempted to serve myself in the buffet line—only my wrists thought otherwise. We all giggled when I nearly had to do a back bend trying to ladle dressing onto my salad, and again when I chased my fruit salad around the plate with my fork.

88. WORKING

I can honestly say I didn't miss much work since we were approaching Thanksgiving, which tends to be a slower time of year for the real estate market. Sure, the snowbirds and tourists are in town, and they love to tour pretty homes, but most are just in it for fun and not necessarily looking to buy. Meanwhile, locals are usually preoccupied with holiday decorating, shopping, and parties, so most would prefer not to deal with showings on top of all that—that is if they don't have to.

While I couldn't necessarily pursue new business laid up on my couch, I could maintain what I had in the works. I just pushed the noncritical to-dos to a time when I felt more up to it. Since I worked for myself, all I needed to keep up with my business was my cell phone and laptop. For typing, I had to resort to the good old hunt-and-peck method, just one finger for all the keys, but I managed. While it took me forever to complete even the simplest tasks, working helped me feel normal again.

I didn't want my customers to know what had happened to me. While I considered my customers my friends, the incident seemed too personal to be discussed in professional circles. I had always been a full-service kind of gal, and I didn't want them to think I wasn't up for the job or that they'd be better off taking their business elsewhere—I worked on commission, after all. Besides that, I really wasn't thrilled to have to discuss it at all, no matter who the person was. I never lied, but when my clients assumed I was busy with other appointments, I didn't correct them.

Whenever I had to go somewhere for work, I'd always schedule it in the evenings. Since I didn't have the wrist strength and hand mobility to grasp or turn the steering wheel, I needed William to get home from work so he could drive me around town—like Miss Daisy. He wasn't thrilled to be helping, but just like bitchy Miss Daisy, I reminded him I wasn't thrilled when he put me through two days of contractions and an emergency C-section. Call it payback.

89. DRIVING

I gave driving a whirl only five days after the attack under the pretense of going to get groceries, but more than anything, I was in it for the change of scenery.

Before the attack, I was always on the go, racing from one end of town to the other, always late for something. Now, I felt like a cheetah at the zoo. Granted, I wasn't trapped in a cage per se. But like the elaborate habitats and enclosures at modern zoos, loaded with features that are supposed to amuse a cheetah, my house didn't compare to being out there, running in the wild.

I still couldn't make a fist, but I could make the okay sign with each hand, so I planned on holding the steering wheel in the okay holes.

The store was less than two miles from our house, and I assured Dale I'd take the back roads on the way there— less traffic. Plus, this way, I'd only have to make right turns, which required less steering. Then, on the way home, I'd take the usual route, a busier road, but again, it would allow me to avoid any left turns. He wasn't crazy about the idea, but if being married to me had taught him one thing, he knew that telling me no would only make me want to do it more.

I then reminded him we had a reasonably low auto insurance deductible, which I think did more harm than good in persuading him—and rightly so, considering my little adventure didn't go so hot.

Backing out of the garage and down the driveway, I was all *See? I've got this.*

In my mind, I was Mario Andretti, yet in reality, I was pretty much just idling in reverse. Gravity and inertia essentially rolled me down the drive. Then, as soon as I hit the street and was required to do something other than check my mirrors, I realized I'd *way* underestimated the strength needed to turn the wheel. However, being a glass-half-full kind of girl and not wanting to admit to Dale that he was right, I ventured on.

As John Quincy Adams once told me via the *SkyMall* catalog, "Try and fail, but don't fail to try."

Besides, if I had the strength in high school, back when I was a scrawny little thing, to drive a friend's Ford EXP with rack-and-pinion steering, I could certainly drive myself two miles to the grocery store. They don't call it power steering for nothing.

Unfortunately, I also hadn't given any thought to turn signals. The wrist flexion in my left hand and the wounds on my right prevented me from flipping them on in the usual way. I say in the usual way, but let's be real; I barely used them before the attack. I wasn't alone. This was Florida, after all. Half our drivers took their road tests back in the Eisenhower era. Our whole state sucked at driving.

However, realizing my injuries probably made me more of a menace on the road than usual, I decided to play it safe and use my turn signals. Only I had a devil of a time trying to remember to use the tops of my thumbs to turn them on. Thinking before doing was not one of my special gifts, so I kept doing it the old way, which was now the new wrong way, and each time, I winced.

When I returned home, and Dale asked how it went, I puffed up my chest and proudly proclaimed I hadn't crashed. To ease the tension, I also made a wisecrack about how I was no worse than the average senior citizen out there. I also sheepishly admitted it was trickier than I thought and vowed not to do it again until I could drive better—which was apparently the next day. Insert face palm emoji. And more on that to come.

90. DATE NIGHT

Aside from our Veteran's Day luncheon excursion and that one trip to the store, I didn't leave the house. I was sick of lying on my couch, being in constant pain, and stressing over my injuries. I felt like I'd fallen into a pit of despair. My so-called life now revolved around the attack's aftermath, and I was over it.

Since the day it happened, I'd wanted nothing more than to put it all behind me, but by this time, I *needed* to put it behind me. I was afraid if I fell any further into that pit, I'd never able to crawl back out, so I was eager to make that mental shift, like flipping a switch from off to on, from dark to light.

I wanted to be out there living my life, and I needed to start making some hefty deposits into my positivity account. Determined to counteract all the negativity that had enveloped my life, I decided to purposefully seek out more positive experiences.

For our first date night out, the hubs made plans for us to go to dinner with another couple. I was excited but also apprehensive—considering how my grocery run had gone the day before.

In deciding where to go, I knew a steak house was out of the question since it was downright impossible to maneuver a knife. The whole purpose of this little escapade was to help me feel normal, so a husband cutting a grown-ass woman's meat as if she were a child was definitely *not* what I had in mind. I also had to put the kibosh on pasta joints or noodle houses since my fork-twirling days were over, at least for the time being.

Since the attack, my table manners were straight out of Disney's *Beauty and the Beast,* with me being the Beast. However, the dancing silverware definitely would have come in handy.

While I didn't have the coordination to properly hold an eating utensil, I *could* fist a spoon like nobody's business. Granted, I probably looked like the Jungle Boy, but if I thrust my bent elbow high in the air, I found I could land more *in* my pie hole than not. Feeling proud of myself, these were the kind of small progress notes I reported to family and friends: *I held a spoon like a two-year-old today. Woo-Hoo.*

Whenever possible, I ate without using my hands at all. Picture a pie-eating contest at a Midwestern State Fair with the contestants' hands tied behind their backs. That was me. If I could slurp it out of a bowl or slide it off my plate straight into my mouth, I was as happy as a pig in poop. Otherwise, I'd fist a fork, stab the whole thing horror movie-style, hold it up in front of me like an ice cream cone, and nibble at the edges. However, I couldn't pull off any of these moves in an actual restaurant, not if I had any chance of feeling like a civilized person.

91. THIS LITTLE PIGGY

The other couple lived closer to the restaurant, so we met at their house to visit a bit over drinks beforehand. That's when I realized my master plan of acting like a regular person didn't stand a chance. The conversation started out as one would expect. There was the obligatory "Good to see you out and about," then we talked a little about the restaurant and mixed in some chitchat about the upcoming holidays.

What took me by surprise was how they looked at me. Our friends, whom we'd known for fifteen-plus years, would not make eye contact with me—like, at all. Here I was, looking at their faces—because that's what *normal* people did—but their eyes were darting all over my body.

My first thought was this must be how pigs feel when they're auctioned off at the county fair. We had other friends whose kids raised pigs for their high school 4-H program, and each January, we'd sit in the stands of the arena and wait for their pig to come by so we could cheer for it. Or maybe it was the kid we were supposed to be cheering for? Regardless, there were probably a hundred pigs to get through, so we were usually there for an hour or two.

As we waited for their pig's turn, to kill time, we'd size the other pigs up and down and try to figure out why some sold for a higher price than others. As with most things, we assumed bigger meant better, but we didn't know how bigger translated on the flip side. Did that mean fattier bacon or more bacon? I preferred lean bacon, but I could definitely see the value in having *more* bacon.

I knew how this ended for the pig, so in the grand scheme of things, I didn't see why it mattered if the kids could make their pigs walk a straight line, but it was still fun to watch.

Our friends continued to eye me like I was This Little Piggy who went to market. Being a November evening, it was a tad chilly, so I wasn't showing much skin. Therefore, they should have only needed to perform a quick scan to see all there was to see and get it out of their system. I also thought the few times they *did* glance at my face, they'd see me staring back at them, realize they'd been busted, and would knock it off. No such luck.

It was almost funny. This couple was so distracted that they actually had a hard time following the conversation. In fact, sometimes, they forgot what they were saying midsentence and would stumble over their words as if they were having a seizure. So, in an attempt to address the elephant in the room, I asked if they wanted a closer look.

Like a magician, I pushed up my sleeves and rolled my hands and arms around in front of them, allowing them to get a good look for as long as they liked. I even took it one step further and strategically hiked up my skirt and top to show them what the dogs had done to my thigh, calf, and stomach. And no, I didn't show them the one on my butt cheek, lest they lose their appetites.

I then offered to answer any questions so we could set this aside and move on to the ordinary and fun portion of the evening that I had been so looking forward to. This was one of the couples Dale had been texting from the hospital the day of the attack. They were good friends who were concerned and curious. I got that, so I tried not to mind. But so far, it didn't feel like a fun night out, so much as it did one of my many doctor's visits.

Not to sound self-centered, but I really wanted this to go well. Cancel that. I *needed* this to go well since I'd had a rough day, which I'll get into a little later. The purpose of dinner wasn't the nice meal or the catching up with friends. It was a chance to recharge my batteries and bank some positivity. This date night was supposed to take my mind off everything. That is, as much as was humanly possible.

I thought I had done what *I* was supposed to do. I had psyched myself up. I had mentally flipped that switch, and I was pretending I was normal. Now I was counting on others to do their part. This was supposed to be my first day back as Old Me. However, being gawked at wasn't my idea of a fun and positive experience.

Though I was committed to putting it behind me, I kept getting dragged back to that wounded and weak place, a victim of a shitty experience that my life continued to revolve around. I was resentful, but again, to protect those around me from feeling bad, I reassured everyone that I was fine and cinched the deal with a plastered smile. Any feelings of being cheated or let down, yet again, I kept to myself. All this, and we hadn't even left the house.

92. CAR TROUBLE

It wasn't just other peoples' curiosity that was frustrating. Being out and about that night brought new challenges I didn't expect. Things like putting on a sweater without making a spectacle of myself or getting a seatbelt on fast enough before the incessant dinging made everyone in the car want to punch me in the throat.

When we got to the restaurant, the other husband, who drove, stopped in front of the restaurant to let us ladies out. When I didn't hop out of the backseat, he must have assumed the doors were locked because he flipped the power lock switch a few times. *Ka-klunk, ka-klunk.* Only, I still didn't get out. Since his wife had managed to get out, he probably thought I was one of those *special* people who continuously paw at the door handle when someone flips the switch. So, for good measure, he flipped it a few more times. *Ka-klunk, ka-klunk, ka-klunk.*

The doors weren't locked. It turns out I *was*, in fact, one of those people who manhandled door handles when they weren't supposed to. But not because I didn't grasp the concept. I'd been trying to open it all along but was having difficulty maneuvering my fingers in the small space. I couldn't get that middle finger, the one missing all the skin, into the opening without bumping or dragging it along the casing surrounding the handle.

If I'd been playing that kids' game, Operation, the buzzer would have been blaring, and the dude's nose would have lit up the entire car. To avoid the pain and injuring it further, I tried to hook the handle with just my pointer finger, but I lacked the mobility and strength to pull it all the way.

Riding shotgun, Dale was oblivious to all this. But thankfully, the driver's sweet wife could see me struggling through the window on her side. When she walked around to my side to let me out, she gave me a pitiful look. Then she came to my rescue again when she deflected the blame, claiming it wasn't me. Instead, she announced to the group that the child safety lock was probably on.

It's too bad their youngest was twenty-three years old, had his own car, and didn't live at home, so it was safe to say he was no longer at risk of jumping out of their backseat while traveling at a high rate of speed.

93. SELF-RESPECT

Mealtime was no better.

For starters, who would've thought drinking water could be so complicated? I couldn't open my hands wide enough to grasp the heavy crystal water glass, nor did I have the strength to lift it with one hand—or the wrist mobility to tilt it, for that matter. I had no choice but to hold it in front of me with two hands like the Holy Grail and throw my elbows up in the air as if I were the Pope himself.

Having given up Catholicism shortly after making his first communion, Dale, uninterested in playing church that night, quickly rustled me up a straw. However, when it arrived, he was engrossed in the conversation. Not wanting to interrupt, I attempted to do it myself, even if it meant chewing the wrapper off. Motor skills, shmotor skills.

Having to lead with my elbows every time I moved my arms, I looked like I was doing the Chicken Dance, that not-so-distant cousin to the polka and a fan favorite at weddings—just ask any great aunt. All my flapping meant placing my water glass within easy reach was out of the question out of fear I'd dump it. Now, thanks to the straw, all I had to do was lift my ass up out of my seat and lean my body over half the table to take a drink.

It seemed I was one step away from becoming one of those toddlers that crotchety fancy people complain about in fine-dining establishments. *Mind your business, Buffy.*

I ordered the salmon, which was flakey and cooperative. The rice was fairly agreeable, too—at least while it was still in a big enough pile where I could scoop it onto my fork head-on. My salad, on the other hand, was like one of those Chinese puzzles. The kind that gives your fingers *and* your brain a good workout.

First, I'd lock in on a target: tomato, cucumber, piece of lettuce, or, God forbid, a crouton. Then, I'd formulate my strategy. Had I remembered anything from physics—that is, had I actually *taken* physics—this would have been the time to apply it. Could it be stabbed, or would it prove stronger than I was? Could it be scooped, or would it just flop off?

What made things worse was, on top of doing all that, I had to simultaneously make polite conversation in an attempt to divert their attention from the fact that I wasn't just playing with my food; I was full-on fighting with my salad—and the tomato was clearly winning.

After dinner, when it was time to drive home, I had to stand at the back door of their big black SUV, incapable of opening the door, like some helpless celebrity or a 1950s housewife—so much for self-respect.

94. FEELINGS BOUNCER

A little background: If it's not obvious by now, I'm not a super feely person. Spoiler alert: this is the crux of the matter come therapy time. However, I think what I lack emotionally, I make up for in practicality.

Practical Me acts like the playground bully, bossing the feelings around in my brain. As feelings pop up, my bully stands like a bouncer at a Canadian nightclub door, holding a flashlight up to my chalked-up high school driver's license. Any feelings that don't serve me well, like sadness, jealousy, disappointment, and hate, get turned away.

Only, like my tenacious sixteen-year-old self, those feelings don't go away away. They just go to the back of the line and try again. The next time around, they try to sneak in by disguising themselves as "lesson learned," "shit happens," "that's okay," "it's no big deal," or "forgive and forget" because those are the kinds of feelings my bouncer can work with.

Okay, technically, those aren't feelings, although it took me a year of therapy after the attack to figure that out. Remember, I'm a doer, not a feeler. I've always considered picking myself up by the bootstraps, putting on big girl panties, thinking up a plan B, or cutting people out of my life to be far more productive than crying or giving myself an ulcer.

Outrage, frustration, and disbelief served me no purpose in those early weeks after the attack. I thought I was better off focusing on healing, forgetting, and moving on.

95. NEWSFLASH

As I started getting out of the house more often, unfortunately, I found I had to talk about the attack more often. And it wasn't limited to only the people who had heard about it but hadn't seen me since. It was also friends at the gym, our pest control guy, strangers in line next to me at the grocery store, and even some random guy pumping gas twenty feet away.

I was left with a giant bruise that took up the entire back of my leg from my knee to my ankle, which people could see from far away. And apparently, they thought nothing of walking up to me to ask what had happened.

Umm. Hello?

I'm all for being extroverted and direct, but when did it become socially acceptable to ask an acquaintance or a perfect stranger about a physical imperfection?

Sure, I'll tell you about my bruise if you tell me what's up with that giant wort on your face, and while we're at it, let's talk about your saddlebags. Oh, so that's not okay to ask? My bad.

Everyone wanted to know why I looked the way I did, but like a gateway drug, it didn't end there. Telling them I was attacked by dogs only spun them into a frenzy of awe and more questions.

I get it. It was a freakish thing that didn't happen that often, but they all wanted specifics, which was more than I was willing to share. My initial solution was to minimize it. I'd say dog instead of dogs and bitten instead of attacked, but that didn't help, either. They always wanted to know how I'd found myself in that situation, whose dog it was, and what happened to the dog, none of which could be easily summarized in the time it took for me to tap my credit card in a checkout line.

No matter what fifteen-second elevator speech I threw out there, it was never good enough.

People always had lots more questions and wouldn't let up until they got their answers, regardless of how uncomfortable it made me. All anybody wanted to do was talk about the attack, but I was so damn tired of talking about it. Yet, had I been brave enough to tell them that, they would have considered *me* the rude one.

I knew better than to come right out and tell them all to fuck off, even though that's precisely what I wanted to do. Contrary to what my family and friends might think, I really do have a filter. But why was I expected to be the bigger person? It's not like that had ever been my strong suit before. I counted on others to pick up on my one-word answers or my more civilized nonverbal signals like rolling my eyes or sighing. I hoped they would get the picture that I didn't want to discuss it, but most were too dense to notice.

I couldn't help but feel these people should've known better. How did they *not* realize I was being forced to recall and relive the attack with every stupid question? Plus, I was still struggling to process it all myself. No wonder I couldn't move past it when I was made to rehash it day after day after day.

Eventually, I posted the story on Facebook in a desperate attempt to spread the word in one fell swoop. As was my go-to by now, I covered the basics of who, what, where, when, why, and how. I also assured everyone I'd be fine, but considering I had to type all that out with one finger, I let them know I wouldn't be commenting further. I thanked them for their understanding in helping to put this behind me and asked everyone to please drop it.

It did help get the word out to friends, though not as much as I'd hoped since I wasn't one of those people who was Facebook friends with every person they had ever met in their entire life.

96. GYMMING AGAIN

Just as I was gearing up to quit physical therapy, I learned from the therapists that stretching the tendons and muscles in my hands, wrists, and forearms was the next step in trying to get everything working in the ways they used to. They wouldn't go so far as to say gymming was approved or even good for me, but I got the feeling it would be tolerated.

Not only had I been used to working out six or seven days a week, I missed my friends. I called my coach and confided in him how frustrated I was with my injuries and how much I was dying to get back to my version of normal. I also confessed that I was somewhat wary about coming back since my orthopedist had warned me it was best to wait a little longer. The doctor wanted me to be able to move my hands and wrists better before returning to any old routines.

Knowing I didn't like being told no and that I'd most likely do it anyway on my own, my coach assured me if I really wanted to come back, he'd find exercises for me to do that didn't involve using my wrists. His thinking was, at least that way, I'd be supervised. Needless to say, I was back in the gym the next day.

At first, I couldn't bend my wrists to maneuver a barbell correctly, but I could handle light dumbbells. Floor exercises were also tricky since I couldn't put any weight on my wrists for very long. For instance, if I did push-ups, I could only manage to do a few, and if I planked, I could usually only go for fifteen seconds before I'd have to lift my arms up in the air and shake out my wrists to relieve the intense pressure and pain. It felt good to be back at it, but it was equally discouraging. For every one thing I could do, I discovered there were even more things I couldn't.

I eventually graduated to holding an empty barbell in what's called the front rack position: standing, barbell across your chest just under your chin, hands shoulder-width apart, palms facing forward with the bar resting where your fingers meet your palms. The weight of the forty-five-pound bar forced my wrists to bend back further than I could ever get on my own or even at physical therapy, for that matter. As I stretched my wrists, it felt like they were old rubber bands, still stretchy, but if pushed too far, they'd break and snap back to bite me.

The stretching made me anxious. With injuries like mine, we didn't know what was happening inside. That in itself was a big problem. While the orthopedist's initial MRI showed the swelling, it hadn't detected the scar tissue, so everyone had a hard time trying to determine its impact. Over and over, the orthopedists, physical therapists, and my gym coach left it up to me to explain to them what was happening—on my insides.

The problem was, I had no idea. I didn't go to college for this crap, so how the hell would I know? Let's not forget, I'm basically the house version of a used car salesman. Even if I did have X-ray vision, I lacked the medical vocabulary necessary to explain it in a way that made sense.

The only bones I knew the names of were the big ones. The ones that looked like the kind Fred Flintstone hurled out the kitchen window for Dino to fetch. If someone asked me to point out an appendix on an anatomy chart, they might as well slap a blindfold on me and spin me around in circles first.

I didn't know the difference between a tendon and a ligament, so I sure as hell couldn't tell anyone what either of them happened to be doing deep inside my wrists at any given moment in time. I would have been more qualified to tell Monty Hall whether there was a tropical vacation or a geriatric dairy cow behind door number 3.

That's why I honestly didn't know whether I was doing more harm than good and had no real sense of how far was too far. I just knew I could only take the intense pressure for a minute or so before I'd have to rerack the bar and shake my wrists around up in the air to get them to fully release from that cramped bent back position.

I stuck with it because the feeling that followed the stretch was freaking amazing. That is, after the blood started recirculating in my wrists again. They felt alive afterward, nothing like the immobile tree limbs I'd had to contend with for the last month or so.

It was a race against the sticky scar tissue. I knew I had to get my wrists moving properly again—and soon, if I wanted to make a full recovery. So, each day, I'd hold that barbell for as long as I could in the hopes of adding more weight every few days. At least it was a start.

PART SIX

DOGS AND ME BEFORE

97. ANIMAL LOVER

I've always been an animal lover. Growing up, we camped—a bunch. I'm not talking cabin or camper camping. No, no, no silly goose. I'm talking about the kind of camping where we threw all our shit into a canoe, then paddled a few miles, yes miles, to the other side of a lake. There we'd unload it all, making no less than ten trips back and forth carrying all said shit, including the canoe, through a forest infested with giant mosquitos that probably hadn't seen a human in weeks, only to pop out on the other side and load it all back into our canoe.

We'd then canoe a few more miles, yes miles, to wind up on what we hoped was a deserted island. But on the off chance we weren't alone in the woods, to play it safe, we'd hang our food in a tree and dig individual holes to bury our poop some twenty yards away from our tent. Are we having fun yet? Oh, and did I mention I was only seven?

While I despised camping, I'll admit the nature hikes were cool. It would have been even more enjoyable if my father hadn't felt it necessary to scream at his daughter (who probably had ADD but hadn't been diagnosed because it hadn't been invented yet) to shut up and walk in complete silence so as not to scare away any wildlife. Yup, I'm still bitter. But I did get to see bears, moose, wolves, and all the other random camping critters you'd expect.

My dad was a nature freak. According to my grandma, he and his kid brother were always bringing home stray or injured animals; though, Gram spoke way more fondly of the birds and bunnies than the snakes, mice, rats, and bats. As an adult, he still brought home animals, including a young gray squirrel after it had fallen from its nest and broken its leg, as well as an entire litter of red squirrels after their mom was killed in a tree-cutting incident at my dad's friend's house. I wanted to keep every one of them as pets, but they were quickly rehabilitated and returned to the wild.

Growing up, in my house, bugs weren't squished. They were relocated back outside. Even the occasional groundhog or rat that feasted on my parents' backyard garden was caught in a humane trap rented from the local SPCA and rehomed elsewhere.

I was taught every animal's life was valuable as they all served a purpose in the circle of life. And while my interpretation was a wee looser now that I was an adult (I'm talking to *you*, spiders in my shower), I could never bring myself to hurt another living thing.

I was primarily a sucker for anything drowning. When I say drowning, I mean anything my kid-sized brain didn't think was supposed to be swimming or wasn't swimming up to my standards. Things like butterflies, toads, and beetles—any insects, really. I'd gently scoop them up, careful not to damage their delicate wings or legs, and set them back on solid ground, feeling quite proud of myself.

However, that feeling was often short-lived when saving a bee or wasp. Those ungrateful assholes left me coated in a baking soda and vinegar paste, my family's home remedy for stings, more times than I could count. Seriously, where was the parental supervision when I needed it?

98. NO DOGS ALLOWED

I didn't grow up with a dog, though certainly not from any lack of begging, wishing, and praying on my part. That's probably why I forbade myself from begging now. Like crying, clearly, that shit didn't work, either.

My parents had said since they both worked, it wouldn't be fair to leave a dog home alone all day. It's funny how that rule didn't apply to their only child because, apparently, having an eight-year-old latchkey kid was perfectly acceptable.

Even though I swore up and down and vowed to do everything and anything that had to be done to take care of a dog, they still said no. As with most things, my parents blamed me. Since I was what my parents called a "quitter," they feared they would wind up having to take care of it, and they didn't want the added responsibility. It wasn't until years later that I eventually realized my parents probably never wanted the responsibility of taking care of a kid, either.

Their marriage had been tumultuous from the get-go, so I always felt like I had to tiptoe around them, never knowing when the next bomb would go off and which combatant would light the fuse. As I grew older, I conceded a dog would be one more source of stress for my parents and one more reason for them to lash out at me, so eventually, I quit asking. However, I'd be lying if I said I stopped secretly hoping for a dog of my own.

99. CINDY

My dad's best friend, my godfather, whom I called my uncle, had a cinnamon-colored mutt named Cindy. She was on the big side, a high-energy breed, probably an Irish setter-golden retriever-Lab mix. What I loved most about her were her silky, floppy, moppy ears. Oodles of endorphins immediately flooded your entire body when you ruffled them.

Our favorite game was fetch, although nobody would know it from how hard I had to work to wrestle the slobbery tennis ball out of her mouth as she fake growled at me. To get her to drop it, I'd stick my nose right up to her nose and urge her to let me have it in my breathy, sing-songy who's-a-good-girl voice. Inevitably, she wouldn't be able to resist talking back to me, little howls and yelps, sing-songy in their own right, and would loosen her grip on the ball just enough that I could snatch it from her mouth. If I was lucky, she'd drop it altogether when she could no longer fight the urge to lick my face, which was pressed up against her own.

When playing in the house, my uncle made us take it down a notch. Inside was more for petting, butt scratching, belly rubbing, and slipping her table scraps. I was basically a sucker for anything that made her tail wag. We were also content to curl up on the floor together, with either her in my lap or her as my pillow. My uncle didn't have kids of his own then, so when we visited, Cindy was my playmate and vice versa.

My uncle's girlfriend, who moved in with him years later, often banished Cindy to the basement even though the dog never did anything bad. I think the girlfriend just didn't like Cindy underfoot. As I mentioned, she was a big girl, and the table scraps didn't help.

It hurt my feelings when Cindy was sent to the basement. I imagine it hurt Cindy's feelings, too, because she'd always hesitate at the open door at the top of the stairs, so ultimately, the girlfriend would use her foot to nudge Cindy down.

It was hard to watch Cindy scramble to get her footing before the momentum propelled her big body down the steps, probably faster than she would have liked. The sound of her long nails sliding and scraping on the painted wooden steps, like nails on a chalkboard, made me shudder.

As one might expect, Cindy would bark the entire time she was down there, and the girlfriend would shout for her to stop. Even as a kid, the whole ordeal made me uncomfortable. I don't know if I would go so far as to say the girlfriend abused the dog, but that's not how I'd ever treat *my* dog.

100. TIMMY

Around that same time, my cousins adopted a gray cockapoo named Timmy from a local shelter. He was full-grown, but his facial characteristics and small size made him appear more puppy-like. However, we could tell from his somewhat crusty disposition he had probably not been treated kindly in the past. Like most shelter dogs, he came with baggage.

Me too, Timmy, me too.

Timmy seemed to reserve his ornery side for older men who shuffled their feet, but for the most part, he was all bark and no bite. However, occasionally, Timmy nipped at the pant legs or tops of the shuffler's shoes. He also snapped at a toddler once after she accidentally fell on top of him, and while he may have even broken the skin, we chalked it up to him defending himself the only way he knew how. Regardless, from then on, to be on the safe side, all little kids were instructed to stay far away from Timmy.

I often hung out at their house, so I grew to love this little doggo, and he loved me—I think. Put it this way, I think you need to love me to put up with my bullshit, and this little guy sure did.

Timmy's bed was just some oval fleecy or velour-covered thingy, nothing like the elaborate and luxuriously fluffy dog beds they sell nowadays.

I can't count the number of times I've been at HomeGoods thinking I'd scored the fluffiest pillow on the planet, only to realize, a little farther down the aisle, amid the cutesy, artsy pet bowls, that I was hugging and rubbing a dog bed on my face.

After being duped several times, I exercised my phone-a-friend option, telling my friend Jennifer that she had up until the time it took me to walk to the checkout to give me three good reasons why I shouldn't buy it anyway and try to pawn it off as an actual pillow. She, being just as smartassy as me, which is probably why we remain such good friends, agreed that I would *definitely* benefit from a calming, plush pet cushion and maybe even a thunder vest to boot. But she came at me with: "How about because it's a dog bed, it's meant for dogs, and you're not a dog? That's three."

Bummer.

I assure you, Timmy's bed was nothing like this, certainly nothing worth getting worked up over, yet he was still super protective of it. Nobody could touch that bed without him running over to defend it. He might have been scrappy, but he was a small dog. He knew his place, and he didn't push his luck. Again, it was usually more bark than bite.

I was around a lot, so when Timmy needed medicine, I was often recruited to either hold him, pry his mouth open, or shove the spoonful of peanut butter with the pill hiding somewhere in the mix into his mouth. I bring this up because, testy as he was, I never thought twice about sticking my fingers in his mouth, even if it meant forcing him to do something he didn't want to do.

When visiting, I'd start by petting him all nice-nice, but it always morphed into me tugging at his bed or some toy he was lying on just to rile him up. What can I say? I like crazy, rambunctious dogs. Maybe because I'm a little crazy and rambunctious myself—*and* a bit of an instigator.

Timmy not only tolerated it, I think he liked it. So much so that we eventually got to the point where he'd allow me to lie on the floor and use his precious bed as a pillow. However, still reluctant to let me have it all to myself, he'd squeeze in, too, and curl up next to my head, even on top of my face if he had to. Then he'd look up at my aunt or cousins with his sad little cocker spaniel-esque eyes as if to say, *Do you see this? A little help, please.*

101. MORE DOGGOS

As a kid, most of my friends had dogs, too. My friend Chris had a German Shepherd named Fraulein. *Technically,* she wasn't a trained K-9, but Chris' dad was a police officer, so we'd all pretend she was. When I was in elementary school, her dad would have us hide outside and then order the dog to go find us. He'd also strap a giant foam contraption on our arm, then give the dog a command in German from across the yard, and on cue, Fraulein would charge toward us and drag us to the ground. Keep in mind, this is what we did for fun.

As long as I've known her, Chris has always had German shepherds, and none of them ever gave me a problem—unless you count covering me from head to toe in dog hair.

Later, around the time I got married, my friend Jennifer and her husband got a white boxer they named Zeke. When they discovered he was deaf, they opted for sign language obedience school. There, the couple learned how to stomp the floor with their feet and give hand signals to Zeke. At the same time, Zeke learned to turn toward the stomping vibration and what each of the hand signals meant.

Boxers are rambunctious as hell. If you don't know, they will literally stand on their hind legs and swing their front paws at you like they're trying to box you. This is just how they play—I think. Let's just say that's how Zeke and I played, which totally pissed off Jennifer. She collected expensive Oriental vases, but they were the expensive kind; therefore, we had to pronounce them vazzes, and we couldn't wrestle in the house. However, since she was one of my best friends, I'd just blow her off by saying things like, "Chill out. We're just having fun. Don't worry, we're not gonna break anything." Eventually, when she realized *I* wasn't going to listen, she'd then try to convince the dog to knock it off. You know, the *deaf* dog.

That crazy, adorable dog didn't want to stop playing, either. Zeke told her to chill out, too, but in his own way. As Jennifer stomped the ground to get his attention, he'd purposefully turn his head the opposite way so he couldn't see her trying to give him commands. No wonder I loved that dog.

Picture Zeke all riled up, bounding all over the place, and Jennifer trying to jump in his line of sight while stomping the ground feverishly and flailing her arms around. She looked like a country line dancer. And a bad one at that. Eventually, the dog and I would settle down, but mostly just so we could watch her jump around like an idiot while Zeke and I laughed our asses off. And yes, surprisingly, to this day, Jennifer is still one of my closest friends.

Kathy, another cousin, had two big shelter dogs. Both were mixed breeds. One was a German shepherd Lab mix, and the other they thought was a Weimaraner, Great Dane, Rhodesian ridgeback, pit bull combo. When I traveled back to my hometown, I'd often stay at her house, so I'd help her take them for their evening walks. Who am I kidding? Since we practically had to jog to keep up with them, it was more like they took *us* for walks.

At night, when the dogs piled in bed with me, their panting shook the entire bed. The following morning, we'd joke about it being like one of those beds people feed quarters into at a cheap no-tell motel. *Cough, cough.* Not that any of us would know anything about that.

However, the truth is, we'd lived close to Niagara Falls, the mid-century honeymoon capital of the world. An era also known for the tremendous technological breakthrough, the vibrating bed. The addition of heart-shaped tubs and mirrored ceilings made these older motels legendary, as anyone who attended a prom within a twenty-mile radius can attest to.

Throughout my life, it seemed everyone I knew had a dog. Other friends had huskies, Dobermans, dalmatians, Great Danes, mastiffs, and pit bulls.

Our current neighborhood is loaded with dogs, which makes sense considering we have not one but two dog parks. However, most of my neighbors still walked their dogs, presumably so everyone involved could socialize while the dogs tended to business. If I was outside, it wasn't uncommon for some doggo to come strolling up my driveway and flop on his back for a belly rub while I chitchatted with their mom or dad.

Though I'd never had a dog myself, I'd been surrounded by dogs my entire life. Little yappy dogs or great big dogs, I didn't care. I loved them all. This is why I didn't think it was a big deal when My Friend asked me to feed her dogs.

102. JUNKYARD DOG

All this talk of my love for dogs is not to say I'd never had a bad encounter with one. I did. For example, I remember the time we wound up off the dedicated hiking trail on one of our camping trips when I was a kid, though now

I can't recall why. I imagine we either got lost or had to cut it short because it was too long. Both seem probable as my parents didn't excel at planning—family planning included. Case in point: I was a whoopsie, and they never failed to remind me.

Whatever the reason, my dad had us cut through a massive junkyard, and, as one might guess, said junkyard came with its very own junkyard dog. Let's stop right there.

What I want to know is why the hell didn't my dad assume there would be a dog? If *Name something you'd find in a junkyard* is a *Family Feud* question, and the top five answers are on the board, I'd bet my ass *dog* is going to be up there.

Being big, black, and mean-looking, the dog fit the stereotype to a tee, but thankfully, it didn't instantly attack us. Instead, I got a crash course in Mean Dogs 101 from my dad, who apparently *did* know a thing or two about junkyard dogs.

First, I was instructed not to panic. There was also to be no running, no acting afraid, and no looking the dog directly in the eye. Which is all way easier said than done when you're eight years old.

Looking back, I can't recall if the owner called off the dog, if we continued walking while ignoring the dog, or if we immediately walked out the same way we'd walked in. Again, my mom and dad weren't the best at this parenting thing, but I hope it was the latter. All I know is nobody got bitten.

103. CRASHING

Until my attack, I'd never been maliciously bitten by a dog. Sure, there were times when I'd been roughhousing and had gotten bruised or scratched by a tooth, but nothing I'd characterize as an actual bite. However, if we're talking about being injured by a dog, that's another story.

About ten years before my attack, our family went to another family's house for dinner. As soon as we arrived, our kids ran inside to join our friends' son in doing what adolescent boys do best—play video games. Dale only made it as far as the garage. The other husband was restoring a classic car, so the two of them huddled under the hood to discuss his progress and whatever technicalities. Meanwhile, I headed to the kitchen to say hello to the wife and see if there was anything I could do to help with dinner.

I found her in the laundry room with the washing machine repairman. Neither she nor the repair guy could get a complete sentence out because their yellow Lab, Jake, was barking nonstop and lunging at the guy. I imagine Jake just wanted to lick every square inch of the guy's skin that wasn't covered by his uniform, butt crack included.

The mom looked disheveled and exhausted, bent over and peering into the front load washer. Thrusting out her arms and legs wildly, she reminded me of a hockey goalie as she simultaneously tried to fend off the dog.

Between juggling dinner and playing defense on a power play, she had her hands full. Not to mention, she was going to make us all deaf in the process of scream-splaining the problem to the repair guy over the barking dog. To help, I offered to take Jake for a walk to get him out of their hair.

We'd only made it to the end of their street before Jake took off after a squirrel. Like a typical Floridian, without signaling, he made an immediate left turn from essentially the far-right lane, causing me to trip over the leash and crash to the ground.

Jake, unfazed, continued booking it down the street, dragging me behind. When forced to choose between the squirrel or my shoulder socket, I was like *Sayonara, tree rat!* and finally dropped the leash. Even though I ended up with a hole in my jeans, some road rash, and an absurdly sore shoulder, I didn't hold it against him.

Come to think of it, that might explain how I tore my rotator cuff.

I'd had another run-in with a dog when taking photos of a house I was selling. I was standing on the property line in the backyard, but since none of the homes in the area had fences, it was all wide open.

The next thing I knew, I heard a couple yelling, "Precious! Precious! Come back!" Turning toward the commotion, I saw a white pit bull charging straight at me. A second later, she threw her meaty body up against mine, leaning into me, hard. She caused my leg to buckle, and I stumbled into the side of the house. Instinctively, I had picked up my arms and covered my face, so I hadn't prepared for the impact, at least nothing to that degree.

Precious didn't bite me, so I imagine she only wanted attention. However, I'd never know since she made a speedy U-turn to return to her family, leaving me with a chipped camera lens and a scraped-up hand, thanks to the rough shaker-style siding—just a victim of a hit-and-run.

104. FUR BABIES

Pets are meant to be petted. It's right there in the word. It used to be where if a dog came within ten yards of me, I'd march up to the owner and ask if it was okay to pet them. And if I'm being completely honest, I didn't always wait for an answer. I know you dog owners hate that, but frankly, you need to be quicker if you want a say in the matter because when your dog dances in place, frantically wagging his tail, he's basically answering for you with a resounding *Yes, please!*

However, I wasn't *that* bad. I didn't run around petting the ones sniffing my crotch in the customs line at the airport or those service dogs wearing the "Do not pet" vests. I'm not an idiot.

Don't get me wrong, I still *wanted* to pet those dogs, too, but I *didn't* want to get wrestled to the ground, arrested, or miss my flight either.

Long before the concept of a "fur baby," I was a member of the camp where dogs were considered one of the family. With that, I thought they were entitled to people food or, at the very least, something a person would eat mixed in with their dog food. I also thought, and still do, that they're entitled to sleep in cozy beds. Not in a dog bed or crate. I'm talking people beds. That means a doghouse outside or tied up in the yard is most definitely out of the question. Wait. It gets worse.

I also believe dogs have feelings. The whole gamut of feelings—happy, sad, mad, scared, lonely, jealous, confused, embarrassed, anxious, you name it. When a person purchases or adopts a dog (PSA: Adopt, don't shop!), they should have to sign something whereby they swear to feed it, give it shelter, play with it, and love it— like wedding vows, but for pets.

If dogs have to rely on their owners for 100 percent of their needs, it makes sense that owners would then be 100 percent responsible for their dog's feelings.

Taking it a step further, since a dog is entirely dependent on its person, some say the dog will love them unconditionally, but I think it's a tad more complicated than that. I believe a dog will show loyalty and affection to whoever fulfills its needs, *with the caveat* that they're treated with love and respect.

I've known several dogs that, even though they found loving homes after being rescued from a bad situation, continued to carry that burden by acting out in some way when they felt fearful. Duh. Half the people in prison probably wouldn't be there if they'd been treated right. I think the same goes for dogs. I've said it before, garbage in, garbage out.

105. STRESSED OUT

As a working mom and business owner, I've had more than my fair share of stress. Like most people, when I'm overworked, underappreciated, or hungry, my fuse is a little shorter than usual, and it doesn't take much to set me off. I don't see why dogs would be any different.

Years passed, and my uncle married that girlfriend of his. It may have been a combination of my parents not getting along with his wife or my uncle now being preoccupied with two little kids. Regardless, we didn't see as much of them as we used to.

My parents divorced around the time I started high school, and I wound up living with my mom in the house I grew up in. Shortly thereafter, for reasons unknown, my uncle asked my dad to take his dog Cindy. Since my dad lived in an apartment, he couldn't keep her, but he agreed anyway and brought her to my mom's house because we had a big backyard. Without my mom's permission, of course.

I was thrilled—my mom, not so much. Considering she wasn't keen on anything that required extra effort or nurturing on her part, I wasn't surprised when the dog wasn't allowed inside.

I wasn't privy to the behind-the-scenes conversations, but I got the impression my uncle's wife wanted Cindy gone. I presume my uncle didn't want to rock what might have been an already rocky boat on the home front, nor could he bring himself to put her down. The dog, not the wife. I thought it best to clarify since Cindy had been his significant other for longer than my uncle had even *known* his wife.

I assumed our house was meant to be a temporary solution. Knowing my uncle, he was probably trying to buy some time until his wife calmed down or until he could make other arrangements. Then again, perhaps he hoped his goddaughter, who once adored his dog, would be happy to just pick up where he'd left off.

Of course, I jumped at the chance. My dream had finally come true. I had a dog of my own!

The problem was everyone was on edge. Cindy wasn't the same dog I remembered. She was old by then, less playful, and crankier. I imagined I'd be, too, if I'd been banished to the basement for the majority of the last seven years. Remember, my mom never wanted a dog in the first place, so she definitely wasn't happy. Even I was stressed out. Not because I didn't want Cindy there but because she was tied up in the backyard day and night, which, per the preceding chapters, expressly conflicted with my dog-rearing ideology.

During a thunderstorm, Cindy's howling and barking were so intense it felt like my heart was on the verge of breaking. Eventually, unable to take it anymore, I brought her inside despite my mother's wrath and curled up with her beside our back door. My mother, always thinking of herself, was probably thrilled she could finally get some sleep since she pretended not to notice I'd snuck the dog in.

But when the skies cleared the following morning, my mother tied Cindy outside again. This continued for a few more days while we anxiously awaited word from either my dad or my uncle about a better plan.

Of course, my mother wanted to be rid of the dog. But I wanted a better life for Cindy. She deserved more than being alone in our yard all day—no matter how big it was.

Once, when I got home from school, Cindy growled at me and wouldn't let me anywhere near her *or* our back door. I didn't blame her for being confused and angry. I should have been her advocate. I should have tried to do more for her. I was just as angry with myself, but standing up for Cindy would have meant standing up to my parents, which, in the past, had always made matters worse for me.

I didn't want to tattle on Cindy. I figured our house had been the last resort, and I was afraid my uncle was out of options. I didn't want to consider the alternative even though, in my heart, I knew none of us could help her. The damage had already been done.

Someone picked her up the next day while I was at school, and we never spoke of it again.

Seeing how time heals all wounds, in writing this, I asked my parents how it had all gone down, thinking surely there'd be no need to shield me from the truth now. Only my dad's memory isn't what it used to be, so he didn't recall anything of the sort, and my mother paints a far rosier picture of our involvement. I'd ask my uncle, but he's unavailable. He's busy throwing drooly tennis balls for Cindy—up in Heaven.

My point in all this is that I had a pretty conventional relationship with dogs. I wasn't dumb, inexperienced, or oblivious about how to interact with a dog. I also wasn't naive from having only had good experiences with dogs or not knowing my way around big, scary dogs.

I thought I was prepared when I walked into My Friend's house that morning. I thought I knew enough.

106. WELCOME WAGON

For as long as I've known them, My Friend and her family have always had dogs, scrappy mixed breed types with varying degrees of pit bull. Granted, I never tested their DNA, but I'd been around enough pitties to tell from their size, physical characteristics, and attitude. Think high school jocks.

Before their divorce, their property was gated with a long dirt driveway that ended in a circle in front of the house. As soon as I'd drive through the gate, all the dogs would appear out of nowhere from various directions. The way they always slowly meandered, all cool and calm, made me think they'd just awoken from their naps. They'd eventually surround the vehicle on all sides, walking next to, in front of, and behind as they ushered the car and me toward the house, like a dog version of a welcome wagon.

To ensure I didn't hit one, I'd drive with my head sticking out the open window or craning my neck to see all the way over the hood, going only as fast as the dog in front walked.

My Friend would be waiting for me outside, and as soon as I was within earshot, she'd start mocking me for driving so slow. She'd motion for me to hurry up, joking that the dogs may be dumb, but they weren't dumb enough to get themselves run over.

By the time she called to ask me to feed the dogs in question, I'd known her dogs for some time. Granted, the dogs and I weren't BFFs, but I'd been around them enough and had heard enough stories about them to know what I was getting myself into.

107. RAT PACK

Not only did I see firsthand how they worked as a team to herd my car, My Friend blatantly referred to them as a pack. However, her stories mostly consisted of them messing with critters in their yard. They wouldn't swoop in with all their might and kill the critter right off the bat. Instead, they preferred to play with it, each taking turns smacking it around or nipping at it. Like a barn cat whose job it is to catch mice, I saw nothing wrong with her dogs policing their own yard, and I never suspected they would dare to mess with a human.

For the most part, My Friend only intervened when she had to put a critter out of its misery or when they were messing with a deadly snake. Sadly, they'd lost a few dogs to snake bites over the years. Hence, the rattles in jelly jars, tanning snake skins during hockey tournaments, and my hang-up with getting murdered on accident by danger noodles, which is how some country folks referred to the many venomous snakes around town.

From time to time, I'd hear stories about one of the dogs escaping and chasing some neighborhood chickens or spooking a neighbor's horse. But only once did I hear about one of their dogs having a questionable interaction with a human.

It involved a contractor who had been working on their home addition. I assumed he and the dogs had gotten to know each other since he'd been working on the project for a few months. So, at the time, I filed it away as just an encounter rather than a full-blown incident.

However, truth be told, now I can't recall if Red had merely bothered him, come after him, or actually bit him. Regardless, according to the contractor, he'd had no choice but to whack the dog with a board, implying he did so to show Red who was boss. He bragged that Red had gotten the picture and left him alone after that.

My Friend, on the other hand, made it sound like the contractor had somehow instigated or provoked Red, causing the dog to react the way he did. Coincidentally, the contractor was one of the hockey dads, so I knew him, too. Since both he *and* the dog could be confrontational and domineering, I assumed the truth lay somewhere in the middle, as it most often does.

Looking back now, most of My Friend's stories seemed to involve Red more than any of their other dogs, including Kaya. That is until Hank showed up.

108. HANKERS

Hank was originally her son's dog, but they quickly learned his apartment was too small, and he was too busy with college and bartending to train a high-energy pup. When everyone came to see that it wasn't fair to Hank, either, My Friend took him in.

When My Friend ran errands, Hank rode shotgun. As far as I knew, this was the first time they'd babied one of their dogs like this, and I liked it. Because he was freaking adorable, I couldn't help wanting to touch him, but from the get-go, he preferred eating and sleeping to being held or petted. My boys had gone through a similar phase during their adolescent growth spurts, so I didn't think much of it.

Even when he was full grown, Hank was still My Friend's sidekick. She even brought him to our kickball game once. Yes, a bunch of us middle-aged hockey parents and some other friends got together at a local park every Thursday evening to play in a kickball league. Let's just say middle-age kickball was way harder, and the other teams took it way more seriously than I remembered as a kid. In other words, we mostly lost.

At the park, Hank turned heads. It was hard not to notice the big dog, with the big bark, who stared down every other dog as if daring them to throw the first punch. As My Friend's petite pre-teen daughter tugged at his leash to hold Hank back, I overheard one of the guys on our team comment on how it was crazy to bring a dog "like that" to our game. He made *like that* sound prejudiced—judgmental at best—and I considered both unfair since he didn't even know the dog. I understood why people didn't like pits, but I always thought it was a matter of a few bad apples spoiling the bunch.

Before I could defend Hank, he continued, "If that dog took off, there's no way that girl would be able to control him."

Oof. That hit hard. I had to admit my teammate wasn't wrong. So, instead of jumping in as planned, I let it slide.

109. THE APPRAISAL

When My Friend and her husband decided to officially divorce, they asked me to help them sell their house, the big one on the seven acres. As was customary, when I received a request to show the property, I always checked with each of them to ensure nobody would be home during the requested time. This way, potential buyers wouldn't feel rushed. I hated to refuse a showing due to scheduling issues on my end, so the few times the family wasn't home to wrangle their doggos, I volunteered to do so myself, although it never came down to that.

After the house was under contract, the appraiser requested access to the property. Again, My Friend and her soon-to-be-ex were both out of town, but since everyone was eager to close, rather than delay the appraisal, I met him out there myself. For security reasons, I wasn't comfortable handing out their gate code to a stranger, so we parked our cars outside the gate and entered the property together via the pedestrian gate that ran alongside it.

Immediately, the dogs trotted up to surround us. Despite all the barking, I assured him they wouldn't hurt him. However, out of an abundance of caution, I said it was best not to try to pet them but to instead keep walking. And so we did, all 320 feet to the front door, with no problem.

While the appraiser did his thing inside, I took in the pretty view, admiring their expansive yard out the sliding glass doors in the great room. Since the sellers hadn't been expecting the appraiser, the house wasn't as tidy as it had been during showings, so scattered about the porch were dog beds, a few food and water bowls, and some miscellaneous dog toys.

Two toys, a feathery stuffed bird and a squeaky rat, were lying on one of the beds. My first thought was, *Awe, they must sleep with them like teddy bears . . . how cute.*

However, upon further inspection, I noticed the "stuffing" hanging out of the bird looked nothing like white polyester fiberfill. And while the rat might have squeaked at one time, its squeaky days were definitely a thing of the past.

I wasn't shocked, nor was I grossed out. Years of watching *Mutual of Omaha's Wild Kingdom* had taught me all about the circle of life. And even though our cats are the indoor kind, they still catch and maim enough bugs, lizards, and snakes on our lanai, which they proudly drop at our feet or in their water bowl. I quickly realized the bird and rat weren't friends to snuggle with; they were trophies they'd stashed in their beds for safekeeping.

I couldn't help but snap a few photos, which I texted to the sellers, along with the sarcastic comment: Don't you feed your dogs? LOL

I knew the dogs were intimidating, especially after our not-so-warm welcome, so when it was time for the appraiser to do his thing on the outside, I thought it best to put the dogs away so they wouldn't bother him.

My Friend assured me their son would be home shortly to let them back out, so I filled up their food and water bowls in the garage, led them from the back porch into the garage, and shut the door behind them, all without incident.

110. RULES AND REGULATIONS

While selling My Friend's existing house, I was simultaneously trying to find an investment property for her sister, who was eager to take advantage of our hot real estate market. Meanwhile, My Friend, who wasn't sure about her long-term plans and wasn't looking for a lengthy housing commitment, agreed to be her sister's first tenant—win-win.

Even though her family was going through a significant change, with the divorce and all, My Friend was adamant about minimizing the disruption for her kids' sake. That meant keeping the kids in the same school district, near their friends, and somewhere that would accommodate their dogs. It wasn't easy.

For starters, in Florida, we love us some homeowners associations (HOAs)—and all the stupid rules that go along with them. Neighborhoods think nothing of dictating how many dogs a person can have, how many total pets they can have, and which dog breeds are permissible. Some communities say no "dangerous" breeds, some say no "aggressive" breeds, while others specifically list which breeds aren't allowed. Usually, the no-no list includes some, if not all, of the following: Siberian husky, Doberman pinscher, Rottweiler, Akita, German shepherd, bullmastiff, and Chow Chow. Oh, and let's not forget everyone's favorite dog to hate: the Staffordshire bull terrier, sometimes also referred to as an American pit bull terrier.

Some HOAs go so far as to specify the size of the dogs someone can have, whether by height or by weight. On top of that, I also had to verify whether fencing was permitted and, if so, the specifications of such a fence to ensure My Friend could contain the dogs. You can see now why this was hard.

There was no getting around that there were three of them, how much they each weighed, and how tall they were, as those were verifiable stats. However, when it came to which breed they were, well, that's where things got a little fuzzy.

111. BREEDS

Like most mixed-breed dogs or dogs that get adopted from shelters, their histories are often unknown, so their paperwork can be sketchy. While DNA tests are an option, they're also expensive, so they aren't standard procedure for animal shelters that are already underfunded. Instead, staff members just use some combination of their judgment, past experience, or a breed book to essentially guess the breed. Most stocky, short-haired, block-headed dogs are lumped into the pit bull category by overworked and underpaid employees, especially if the intake form used by the shelter doesn't list a variety of better options.

On the flip side, pit bulls have gotten such a bad reputation that some of their proponents will purposefully err on the contrary and *not* label the dog a pit bull even though it very well may be. They fear that by doing so, they're assigning those dogs a label that might not only make their lives more complicated but one which could possibly sentence them to death.

As adoptees, My Friend's dogs didn't have the proper paperwork. Clearly, they were all mixed breeds, but nobody could say for certain which breeds they were or which they weren't. Hank, the one that looked the most pittie, had paperwork from a veterinarian saying he was a Lab, golden retriever, or some other mundane All-American breed. I suspected the breeder or vet did her son a favor so he could get Hankers approved by his apartment complex since there was no way in hell anyone in their right mind would've labeled that dog as anything other than a pit bull. As I recall, we all thought it was funny at the time.

As a licensed real estate broker, I could never allow clients to rely on false paperwork, nor would I ever let them presume they could lie to a homeowners association. Nobody wants to go to war with their HOA, incur fines, have to hide their dogs from their neighbors, or worse, have to move or rehome their dogs when the HOA finds out they lied—because they *will* find out.

I made it one of my top priorities to find My Friend and her sister a neighborhood that would welcome all three dogs regardless of their pedigree and one which allowed fences so the dogs could run around in the yard. It wasn't easy, but that's what we did, and in July 2019, they moved in.

112. UNNEIGHBORLY

The new backyard was less than a quarter acre, a far cry from the seven everyone was used to and the privacy it had allotted them. On several occasions, My Friend's elderly new neighbor cornered her to express her concern over the dogs and how they had "bark attacked" her. That wasn't all. This woman also had an issue with their poop.

Let's digress: The dogs were pooping in their own fenced-in yard. My Friend, or her kids, were then scooping said poop in their yard and throwing it away every day, in a trash bag, in a trash can. A trash can that sat in My Friend's garage until the county came—twice a week, mind you—to pick it up.

It's not like My Friend could very well prevent the dogs from barking—or pooping, for that matter. Frankly, if I had to summarize a dog's entire life in a nutshell, it would be barking and pooping. My Friend tried kindly explaining this to the elderly know-it-all; however, the old biddy still didn't get it.

This carried on for months, with the neighbor growing even more demanding.

The cranky woman then requested that My Friend pay for a service to come to her house daily to scoop the poop and take it with them. Seeing how this woman was so unreasonable about the poop, we assumed she'd been exaggerating about the barking, too. Besides, we never quite knew what to make of "bark attacked" anyway.

Even though My Friend was well within her rights, she eventually caved from the stress. When the woman threatened to file formal complaints with the neighborhood association *and* the police, she simply decided to keep the dogs in her garage more often. If anything, to spare her sister, the actual property owner, any aggravation that might result from this woman's threats.

Apparently, Red hadn't been thrilled with the new living situation, either, since he began digging holes under the aluminum fence and chewing through their underground electric fence. He didn't do it to go out into the world and attack innocent bystanders—at least not that we know of. He'd simply disappear for the day, a mini vacation, if you will, considering he always returned by the end of the day or the next morning.

That certainly wasn't the norm for him, but he hadn't been feeling himself lately. He'd had a few seizures back at the old house, although the underlying cause was never determined. There had only been a few, and he always seemed to bounce back, so I think everyone, their vet included, just attributed it to old age.

PART SEVEN

THE WHY

113. SEARCHING FOR IT

I believe everything happens for a reason. God hands us lessons and opportunities, but what we ultimately do with those and make of it all is up to us.

In writing this book, my intention wasn't to be all "Poor me," but I thought I had to cover the back story before tackling this next part. While this book may be about mental fortitude, healing, and overcoming—and yes, it was very cathartic getting it all down on paper—that wasn't my original purpose. What had been resting most heavily on my heart, still is, and I presume always will be, were the dogs.

I knew I'd continue to struggle to sleep at night until I knew why this had happened. Ever since I hopped that fence to safety, questions like that had been swirling in my brain, although more so in the background.

If somebody asks me what happened, what do I say? Shit. What did *actually happen? How did it go so wrong?*

I knew I didn't want to get My Friend in trouble, but was there actually trouble to be had? Was somebody at fault? If someone had been at fault, I figured it was me. My Friend's family managed to live with the dogs for years and none of them got attacked, so I must be the one to have brought this on.

Okay, there's one more thing you need to know about me: I'm not the mom who defends her kids no matter what. Granted, I'll *love* my kids no matter what, but if they do something wrong, I'll be the first to serve their asses on a silver platter so they can face the consequences and learn from their mistakes. Some might call it tough love. Some might call me a bitch. To each his own.

Having said that, let's remember we had two boys.

With boys, everything's a quest for world dominance. They're physical, and they play rough. Being a tomboy myself, I had no problem with that—for the most part. I'm not saying it didn't drive me crazy. It absolutely did, but I quickly learned it came with the territory and when to pick my battles.

If my boys were fighting, and nobody was bleeding, I'd let it slide. I preferred that they work it out themselves. Because Lord knows those problem-solving, conflict-management, and bullshit-tolerance skills would serve them well later in life. But of course, they had no way of comprehending that back then and didn't see it for the favor it was.

On the other hand, the rules were vastly different if we weren't at home. At birthday parties, restaurants, playdates, and the like, I had a zero-tolerance policy for acting out, and they knew it. If shit went down, and they were anywhere in the vicinity, they would be in trouble. There was no investigative process. It was pure guilt by association. I didn't care if so-and-so did it too or if so-and-so started it. They knew better, period.

While I might have been tough on them, I also held myself to that same standard. This is why I desperately wanted to know what I did wrong—me, not the dogs. Whether My Friend might have played a role in all this never occurred to me.

I probably replayed that horrible morning in my mind a thousand times, trying to spot *it*, the thing I'd done wrong. I was sure I'd fucked up somehow, that I knew, but for the life of me, I couldn't pinpoint how.

114. THE TALK

That first day, the day of the attack, talking about it was like reliving it all over again, but I was still eager to share my side of the story and discuss it at length with My

Friend. Similar to how one might bounce a problem off a friend or partner to get their take. I didn't get far when analyzing it myself, so I assumed I was too close to the situation to see it from any angle other than my own. Having raised and lived with the dogs, I hoped she'd bring the insight needed to help fill in the blanks. Surely, if anyone was going to spot the thing that went wrong, it would be her.

I wanted to know what I did wrong, what I should have done differently, what signs I had missed, or how I could have avoided it altogether. I always assumed it was me. I had never owned a dog; therefore, it must have been my lack of dog experience that led to the attack. Granted, I thought I had known what I was doing, but I guess not. Apparently, I had done something wrong, and that something unintentionally provoked the dogs and made them do this. And I needed to know what that something was.

My Friend, it turns out, chose to come at it from the same angle. We both wanted to know why it happened, but while I thought the answers lay in what *I* had done wrong, she looked to the dogs for answers. She was in it to learn why her family pets suddenly turned vicious.

No wonder we were friends—we thought the same way. Neither of us considered blaming the other, and this was the best place we could hope to begin—starting from neutral and heading toward the same goal, wanting to know why.

Talking about it was laborious, so I stopped often, taking long pauses. Sometimes, it was to give my heart rate a chance to slow or for my breathing to catch up. Other times, when it got to be too much, I'd take longer pauses and shake my head. I did it subconsciously as if the shaking was a fast-forward button or like the beeps they inserted over the swear words on television. It's probably another one of those built-in self-preservation features we're born with. All I know is that it worked.

The head shaking bought me some time, which I used to shove those really shitty parts to the back of my brain. I didn't want those memories to inadvertently come flying out of my mouth and upset either of us any more than we already were.

I also paused to allow My Friend time to regroup after one of her crying bouts. Fearful she'd want to quit if it got too painful, and since we still hadn't gotten to the why, I tried to keep the conversation light enough to keep it moving. I'd even toss in a funny comment when things got too doomy and gloomy because I didn't want to stop until we'd found the answer. However, it was hard to find momentum with all the starting and stopping.

As we slowly made our way through our discussion, we asked each other questions in a desperate attempt to fill in any gaps. If we had a complete picture, we thought whatever had gone wrong would then become glaringly obvious.

115. A LIFE RAFT

As one would imagine, we covered everything:

> How often did My Friend keep the dogs in the laundry room?
> In what instances were they put in the laundry room?
> What time did she put them in the laundry room?
> Would they have peed in the laundry room if they really had to go?

Did I do something to make them think I was
    there to hurt them?
Could they have thought I'd done something to
    hurt her and her family?
What did I say to them?
How did I say it?
What did her family usually say to them?
How did they say it?
Had the dogs ever been left alone with a non-
    family member?
What kind of chemicals did she have in the
    laundry room?
Which dog was the first out of the laundry
    room?
Which dog took the first bite?
Did all the dogs bite me?
Did one dog bite harder than the others?
Why didn't I shoot them?

We rehashed these questions and more for days.
Sometimes, even several times a day. We did it in person,
and we did it by phone. Whenever one of us would think
of another possible factor or plausible reason, we'd call
each other to talk about our latest theory, no matter the
time, day, or night. It was that important.

Still, we came up with nothing. Honestly, we tried, but
neither of us could pinpoint the one thing that had gone
wrong to send us down this dreadful path.

The truth is, nobody had done anything wrong.
Nobody could have prevented it. It was, as they say, a
perfect storm. Who knows? Maybe we were looking for
something to cling to, an easy way out, like a life raft, and
calling it a freak accident was our best option. Even if it
was a cop-out, was that such a bad thing?

116. SHOULD HAVES

I continued to play it back in my mind. In the beginning, the physical pain kept me awake, and no matter how much I tried to distract myself, there was no getting around thinking about the attack. I was still trying to imagine how this whole thing could have been avoided, still looking for what I had done wrong.

I had so many *should haves*, and I mapped each one out in my head like an old-fashioned flow chart, the kind with the various colored shapes and arrows working their way around and down the page. If this, then that. If that, then this. Think 1980s policy and procedures manual.

For starters, I wondered if I should have brought someone with me. But to do what? That's the kind of stuff bad dad jokes are made of. How many people does it take to open a sliding glass door and throw food in a bowl?

I never would have thought feeding a few dogs would be a two-person job. Besides, what if I *had* brought someone along? Where would that person be right now? I find it hard to believe the dogs would have bitten just one of us and allowed the other to escape scot-free. And if that other person *did* get attacked, I don't think I could've handled that kind of guilt on top of everything else I had going on. So, no, bringing another person would not have helped. If anything, it would have made matters worse.

117. DRESSING FOR SUCCESS

Should I have changed out of my gym clothes before showing up to feed the dogs? True, my shorts were shorter than the ones I typically wore. I'd bought them for our gym's annual "Murph" workout to honor the service sacrifice made by fallen Navy SEAL Lieutenant Michael

P. Murphy. The workout consisted of a one-mile run, 100 pull-ups, 200 push-ups, 300 squats, and another one-mile run. I picked them not only because they were red to go with my commemorative blue and white tank, but also because they were guaranteed not to ride up. And since they weren't cheap, I'd been trying to get more use out of them. While I bet the manufacturer never had *this* in mind, I had to give them credit; those shorts had stayed put. However, if I'd been wearing longer shorts or, better yet, leggings, I might have avoided that hefty bite on my rear.

When I go to the gym, I'm there to work. I'm not there to merely look the part, and I'm most definitely not there to pick up dudes by parading my tits around in a skin-tight, low-cut, midriff-baring spaghetti strap sports bra.

I prefer billowy tank tops made of cotton because I need to be able to lift them up over my face so I can mop sweat out of my eyes. Sexy, huh? And to drive home my "unapproachable" look, I always wear tanks with sarcastic gym sayings. Things like "Thick thighs, thin patience," "Nobody cares, work harder," and "Not fragile like a flower, fragile like a bomb."

Looking back, I suppose a thick sweatshirt would have been a better choice, but come on. Who's working out in a heavy hoodie in humid Florida?

Then I got to thinking that maybe I got the dogs all riled up because I smelled like sweat. I didn't think I stunk, but I'm guessing most people who stink don't think they stink; otherwise, they wouldn't stink. Because, let's face it, nobody wants to stink.

Then again, maybe I *had* peed in that pad a little when jumping rope that morning, and perhaps the smell is what pissed off the dogs. Pun intended. I know it pisses me off when I smell it in subway stations, outside bars, or within half a mile of one of those tent cities that seem to be cropping up all over the country these days. I wouldn't have thought they could detect a drip, but then again, dogs do mark their territory with pee. I could see why that might make them mad, but let's be real, it's not like I'd peed all over their house in an attempt to claim it as my own.

Going home to change first meant I would have taken more time. If the dogs were angry because they really had to go to the bathroom, presumably, they would have been even more furious if I'd shown up later. Then I shuddered, thinking what the attack would have looked like if the dogs had been even more upset.

Maybe I should have worn protective gear? Seriously? Why would that have ever crossed my mind? For me to have even considered gearing up, I would've had to have known I'd be attacked. And if I'd known that, I wouldn't have gone in the first place. Duh.

Besides, what does protective gear for feeding dogs even look like? Is it similar to what professional paintballers or dirt bike racers wear? Sure, I mean, who doesn't have that kind of equipment just lying around? (shaking my head)

Okay, I'll admit mittens would have been awesome. Preferably, the big, thick subzero ones used by researchers in Antarctica, where it's so cold that people can die of exposure within minutes. But let's not forget I would have had to remove them to mess with those pesky sliding door locks, and that was before they started biting. Was I supposed to be all "Hold up, let me put these back on first"?

When it came to pants, a part of me thought the dogs would have been repulsed by the feel of the material in their mouths and quit after the first bite since that always made me gag, too. However, now I can't recall why on Earth I had ever bit fabric in the first place. On the other hand, since most dog toys are made of cloth, maybe they don't have the same gag reflux as humans—well, at least *this* human.

Jeans definitely would have protected me better, but who am I kidding? My jeans are so damn tight I have to unbutton my top button just to sit down, so there was no way in hell I was running or hopping fences in jeans.

If I went with pants, I supposed leggings would have made the most sense as I imagined their teeth gliding and sliding over the slippery, thin spandex. Then again, if the material was too thin, it would have been no match for their sharp teeth.

I got my sweater snagged on a wild raspberry bush once, and after Dale painstakingly extricated me (and himself after he became entangled, too), everyone was scratched to hell and pretty ticked off. So, having three dogs stuck to my pants like Velcro probably wouldn't have worked out well either.

I couldn't help but think some different clothes would have made counting the bites easier. Not to sound morbid, but I'd be curious to see what those clothes would have looked like afterward. Swiss cheese? Aside from my scars and memories, I didn't have any tangible . . . *What? Souvenir? Do you really want a memento from the absolute worst day of your life? Oh my God! What is wrong with you?*

118. HOW YOU SAY IT

I questioned whether calling out to them when I walked in had been the best idea, even though I imagined surprising the dogs would have been much worse. I knew three other people lived in my house, but I still jumped when I closed the refrigerator door and saw someone standing in my kitchen.

It occurred to me that perhaps I should have waited to call out to them until I was nearer to the laundry room rather than from the kitchen, thus giving them less time to stew about it. That is, if we think the problem was that they'd gotten themselves too worked up in the time it took me to walk back there.

I liken it to when a toddler falls, and you have approximately four seconds to either laugh in their face or distract them before all hell breaks loose. The process is slow but inevitable. First, their face reddens, their forehead wrinkles, and their eyes get squinty. Then their mouth opens, but no sound comes out—like how the water recedes before a powerful tsunami wave rolls in. Once that kiddo starts sucking air, there's no stopping them. They're going to scream. Similarly, maybe the dogs had *too much* warning and worked themselves up to the point that no matter what I did, they were still going to blow.

I also wondered if I should have spoken to the dogs more forcefully. Not all people treat their dogs like baby humans. I imagined serious working dogs, like police dogs, search dogs, and drug-sniffing dogs, with their intimidating "Do not pet" vests, were housed in kennels or crates and given commands using commanding voices.

As far as I knew, My Friend's dogs weren't formally trained to respond to specific commands or specific voices. But if I had to guess, since they were more outside dogs than inside dogs, I had to assume they didn't get much baby talk. So maybe her dogs saw me as a pushover because of my less-than-commanding voice. Even though I wouldn't have thought they were smart enough to recognize that, let alone use it against me. Then again, maybe my cheery who's-a-good-doggy voice automatically told them I was a stranger since everyone else they knew used low, deep, bossy voices. In that case, perhaps they attacked me in the name of good ol' stranger danger.

The internet says yelling at kids makes them more aggressive, both physically and verbally. *Huh* . . . Maybe the dogs were bossed around too much, and that's what turned them into assholes. I then made a mental note to unpack that a little later for myself, as it sounded a lot like my own generational trauma.

So if my usual dog voice is bad, and a too-bossy voice is bad, my only other option would have been sticky-sweet. On the surface, that sounds good, but I'm a soprano. My normal voice is high, to begin with. Kicking up the "nice" would only make it go higher. At least, that's what happens when I'm meeting someone new and trying to sound friendlier than I really am.

I think I'd have difficulty pulling off super sweet without sounding like a sarcastic bitch. Like when a southern belle says, *Bless your heart,* and some people think they're being prayed over, but she's actually saying *You stupid idiot.* If my voice got any higher and I came at the dogs sounding like Karen from *Will and Grace,* I'd bite me, too.

More than likely, it wasn't that what I had said was too bossy or sweet, but more so that I screamed it. As any of my old teachers will tell you, I don't have an indoor voice. Instead, I'm what you would call a "projector."

Since My Friend is more soft-spoken than I am, I probably just scared the shit out of the dogs, and because they're dogs and can't use their words, they were probably just telling me to shut up the only way they knew how. I swear, if I'd known all this, I would have gladly found my indoor voice real quick, and we could have skipped all that biting and shaking.

I know they say dogs have sensitive ears, but I always thought it was more due to pitch, not volume. While some might say my voice is shrill, it's not as irritating as a dog whistle. However, Dale says that's debatable.

Maybe I had it all wrong. Perhaps it wasn't quality but quantity. I wouldn't be surprised if I'd said too much. It's not like I hadn't heard that before. Technically, I suppose I didn't have to have said anything to the dogs, but it's not like I rambled on and on. I struggle to think of things to say at mixers, so you better believe I wasn't trying to entertain the dogs with small talk. That wasn't it.

119. WHO YOU GONNA CALL

Looking back, I knew something was up the minute they showed their teeth, but I was already surrounded by them, instantly in the thick of it. Where was I supposed to go from there? I couldn't very well pick them up and put them back in the laundry room, and it's not like I'd stashed pieces of cheese in my booty shorts that I could've thrown into the garage for them to chase before slamming the door behind them. If only I could have blown my whistle, made a big *T* with my hands, and called a time-out like a sideline referee.

In hindsight, jumping onto the counter and calling someone might have been a good idea, but who would I have called? My Friend was a three-hour car ride away, so there wasn't much she could have done from there. I suppose I could've put her on speakerphone so she could tell the dogs to back the fuck off, but I doubt that would've worked.

Should I have called my husband, who doesn't even like dogs, and asked him to save me like some damsel in distress? And how exactly does one save another person stuck on a kitchen counter surrounded by vicious dogs?

It's not like fixing the garbage disposal. I don't think there's a YouTube how-to video for that.

Of course, I could have called 911, but what would I have said? *My Friend's doggies are barking and looking at me funny*? Because up until Red sunk his teeth into me for the first time, there had been nothing outlandish to report, certainly nothing that warranted the police or constituted a crime. Remember, while I knew the dogs were unhappy from the get-go, I had no idea they would attack me until they did—and once they did, it didn't stop. By the time I realized the situation was serious, the attack was already in full swing, and I had no access to my phone or use of my hands.

DOGS AND ME AFTER

120. ABNORMAL

Earlier, I wrote how this couldn't have happened to a better person because I was tough and fit. But in other ways, this couldn't have happened to a worse person. My entire mindset had changed literally overnight, and I *hated* the person I'd become.

The day after the attack, lying on my couch, I heard my neighbor's older schnauzery dogs barking while out for their evening stroll. Barking was their way of greeting their dog friends or of luring nearby humans to come pet their big bellies.

Before the attack, I was the lady that petted everybody's dog. If I was outside and any dog walked down the sidewalk past our house, it would automatically meander up my driveway, knowing I was always down for a belly rub or a good butt scratch.

Yet the day after the attack, hearing the familiar barking, I was frozen in place, staring at our front door, my heart beating wildly. Even though I was inside our house, my first thought was, *I hope the front door is locked.*

Locked! It wasn't enough that the door was closed. It had to be locked, as well. In my psycho mind, I believed the dogs would race to my front door and turn the doorknob on their own accord, so the only thing preventing them from entering my home was a deadbolt. Even if that could happen, and we all know it couldn't, what was I so afraid of? Did I actually think these arthritic, half-blind, overweight pooches with five-inch legs would come bounding up onto my couch and somehow "get me?"

What the hell was wrong with me?

I chalked this newfound fear of mine up to a lack of sleep or something like PTSD. I didn't give myself permission to think it might be *actual* PTSD. In my mind, that was reserved for soldiers who had laid their lives on the line fighting for our country and who had witnessed way more horrific things than a few dog bites.

I assumed it was only natural that there would be some fallout from the attack, but not to the extent I was feeling. Clearly, I was overreacting. Although I imagined it was nothing a little tough love couldn't cure.

I got this . . .

Listen up, you idiot. Don't be ridiculous. There's no way those dogs can let themselves into your house. Besides, even if they could, it's not like Abby and Gabby are going to maul you to death. For Christ's sake, girl, get your shit together.

There. Problem solved. Or so I thought. Little did I know this was just the beginning.

121. PET STORE PROBLEMS

A month or so after the attack, I was at the pet store to buy cat food when I passed a few small dogs on leashes shopping with their owners. Normally, I would have asked if I could pet them, and most likely, without even waiting for an answer, I'd have gone in for a good scratch behind the ears. But since the attack, I wouldn't dream of petting a stranger's dog, even with permission.

I suspected bumping into dogs would be problematic, but I figured the more I did it, the easier it would get. That day, recognizing I wasn't ready, I cut myself some slack and didn't even consider petting them. I strode right past them, the self-talk in my head reminding me that not everyone has to pet every dog they see.

I rationalized with myself: *It's not that I'm not petting those dogs because I'm afraid. I'm just one of those people who don't pet strange dogs. Yeah, that's it.*

Taking it one step further, I told myself it didn't bother me. I was in a hurry, anyway. I didn't have time to pet dogs, I reminded myself. Only it *did* bother me.

I absolutely wanted to pet those dogs, but I was too afraid to do so and too ashamed to admit it. Instead, I made up a bullshit cover story to tell myself to shut up the pouty, angry, and disappointed Old Me deep within. I knew it was a farce. I wasn't fooling anyone, especially myself. Still, I played along.

I was scouring the shelves for the costly grain-free, salmon-flavored kibble we got suckered into buying to help prevent our one cat with allergies from licking the fur off her legs when I heard barking. I froze in place, my heart beating a mile a minute. Freezing seemed to be my new immediate response to anything dog-related. I then listened intently for anything that might indicate what was happening a few aisles over and how it might impact me.

The longer I stood frozen in place, the angrier I got. I knew my reaction was stupid. Two dogs barking in a different part of the store had nothing to do with me, and at no point was I at risk.

What pissed me off the most was I had zero control over any of this. Believe me when I say, there's nothing a control freak loathes more than *not* being in control. Especially when it comes to her own damned feelings!

This made no sense to me. I consider myself to be an extremely logical person. I have a college education. Granted, I'd majored in legal and environmental studies, so I was far from a math whiz. Still, I was reasonably sure 99 percent of the dogs out there were friendly. That meant, statistically speaking, my chances of being attacked again, and in the same brutal manner, were not only improbable but highly unlikely. Yet there I was, petrified of another attack *and* berating myself for worrying about it. I couldn't win.

122. IRRATIONAL

The paralyzing fear, or whatever it was, continued for months. Just when I thought enough time had passed for me to finally come to my senses, it would happen again.

Like the time I was working out at a park with my gym crew. A German shepherd was playing fetch with its owner, and even though it was off in the distance, I couldn't take my eyes off the dog. I had to be able to see it the instant it decided to come running across the field to attack me. Not *if* but *when* it attacked me. In my mind, those few extra seconds I'd gain from watching it the whole time would aid my eventual getaway and ultimately determine whether I lived or died.

Before the attack, it seemed there were selfie-worthy dogs everywhere I turned. Now, it seemed I was a magnet for only the scary kind, like the security dog at the airport. Every passenger, including myself, had to take turns sauntering past the dog while the officer trainer led the dog back and forth across the passenger's path. I suppose it was there to sniff out drugs or forbidden fruit. (I'd gotten busted in Hawaii with an illegal apple in my backpack once. Who knew?)

Even though the dog wore a muzzle, or maybe *because* it wore a muzzle, my insides were jumping.

Seriously, you wacko?

The freaking muzzle was practically bolted around its snout, and some mountainous dude hung off the other end of the leash less than a foot away. It was basically the Hannibal Lecter equivalent for dogs, yet I was so freaked out it was *me* who was panting. I'm not sure how *actual* drug smugglers behave in instances like this, but I doubt they'd look as guilty as *I* did.

There I was, twisting my head from side to side, frantically watching the dog's every move, just in case.

Just in case, what? Just in case the muzzle, and *the leash,* and *the dude all failed at the exact same time to do the one and only job they were there to do? And then what? Would the dog drag me to the ground and tear me apart limb from limb in the middle of the security line while two hundred other travelers whipped out their cell phones to record it, with nobody jumping in to help? Sure, Cheryl, because that's plausible. Again, you're an idiot.*

I swear, I don't know which was causing more damage to my psyche, my initial crazy thoughts or the brutal self-deprecating talk that always followed.

On that same trip, walking down a city street, I saw a woman with a pit bull on a leash. Rather, I noticed the *pit bull,* then the woman—who had whom on the leash was up for debate. The dog stood within three or four feet of her, but she was engrossed in conversation with another woman and facing the opposite direction. Neither woman seemed to notice that the dog had taken an aggressive stance and was staring at something up ahead. We were walking away from the group, but I refused to take my eyes off the dog. I was positive that, at any second, the dog would bolt after whatever it had locked in its sights. And since the owner wasn't paying attention and appeared to have a loose grip on the leash, I assumed it would take her by surprise, causing her to drop the leash, leaving the dog running loose, its sole mission being to kill me—of course.

I even resorted to walking backward until we were at what I considered a safe distance away, although I wasn't gauging that distance based on a specific number of feet. Because, let's face it, Logical Me wasn't calling the shots. Instead, I waited for Crazy Me to give me the all-clear before turning back around.

My inner scaredy-cat needed time to analyze my surroundings and work through each possible scenario. I couldn't turn around and walk like a normal person until she, Crazy Me, was convinced the dog would get distracted by closer or easier prey before it got to me. Same with bear attacks. They say you don't have to be the fastest so long as you're not the slowest.

This new version of me had wildly irrational, dark thoughts about dogs. I loved dogs. I didn't want to think like that, but I had no idea how to stop it.

After I tore up my shoulder and again when I busted my knee, the doctor had said the first step in healing was to quit doing anything that aggravated it. Similarly, I assumed if I avoided all dogs for a certain amount of time, whatever was causing me to freak out would eventually heal on its own.

123. GRACE

My ART therapist, whom I'd been seeing regularly to break up those lumps of scar tissue, always brought his two Labrador retrievers to work with him. I suppose if I'd asked him to keep the dogs away from me, he would have. But I was trying to keep my newfound crazy under wraps. Since I always petted the heck out of his dogs when I saw them in the gym pre-attack, he probably didn't think anything of it, so he never offered.

I figured I could handle being in the big gym with them, but I definitely wasn't seeking any form of interaction with them. Besides, I was preoccupied. Trying to decipher my therapist's uber-cool South African accent and carry on a conversation while simultaneously trying to stifle the bloody-murder screams building inside me as he stabbed me with his plastic scraper required more effort than you might think.

Before I knew it, one of the dogs had her nose in my face, and the other had her fanny pressed against my hand, which had been lying at my side. It was their way of letting me know they wanted to be petted, just like old times. Their gestures were sweet and familiar, yet my heart couldn't help but thump wildly.

Even though I knew my therapist's dogs would never bite me, Crazy Me wasn't taking any chances. I constantly scanned my surroundings, always on the lookout for any odd behavior that might lead to an attack. Despite them being well-behaved and good listeners, I still couldn't turn off my new hypervigilant dog radar.

One time, after one of our sessions, I was absentmindedly petting one of the dogs on her back. That is, until she barked. Although it was only one bark and meant for another dog outside the thick glass window, I jumped back from where I'd been standing. Embarrassed, I immediately glanced back at my therapist to see if he'd noticed. It was a big jump, so he had, but he was a kind man who knew my story, so he just shot me a small sympathetic smile.

At that moment, a wave of assurance swept over me. My therapist didn't judge me; he understood. Of course, I'd have weird lingering feelings about dogs. Who wouldn't?

But that thought quickly faded, and I seethed with self-disgust. How was it that this acquaintance could offer me grace, yet I was so full of contempt for myself?

124. EXPOSURE

This new dog aversion was driving me crazy, literally, but I had no idea how to overcome my apprehension. I only knew avoidance had proved unrealistic since dogs were apparently everywhere and more than ever before.

While I'm no psychologist, I knew a thing or two about facing my fears from my experiences jumping out of planes and swimming with sharks.

My core philosophy mirrored that of Nike—just do it. Surprisingly, Dr. Google agreed. As it turns out, from a medical standpoint, exposure therapy is supposedly an effective tool for overcoming fear.

By December, I was already petting Sharon and Robert's dogs without incident—the small ones I used to walk and feed when they were out of town. However, my CrossFit mentality told me I needed more dogs, bigger dogs, and badder dogs—and the sooner the better since, in my mind, the more dogs I petted, the faster I'd be "cured."

So, like that famous boxing announcer who, before every big fight, bellowed something about a rumble all drawn out–like, I was all *Bring on the puppers and let the pettingggg beginnnnn!*

125. SERGEANT

My experiment worked to some degree. I was still leery of big dogs, so I couldn't bring myself to *pet* all dogs. But at least I was no longer *petrified* of all dogs.

On New Year's Eve, we planned to hang out with friends at the two house parties we'd been invited to. All three of our homes were within a two-mile radius. Since holidays are notorious for having more drunks on the road than usual, we preferred to stick close to home.

Tom and Mary, our first stop, had a German shepherd named Sergeant. Though I'd known this dog for five-plus years, I spent days psyching myself up to see him.

Being back in the saddle felt both nerve-wracking and exciting. I looked forward to interacting with a bigger, more "aggressive" breed like I used to. I thought if I petted and played with some big dogs and they didn't attack me, I'd retrain my brain not to freak out on me every time I saw a big dog. That's what Logical Me thought. Crazy Me still thought we were going to die, hence my trepidation.

When we arrived, Dale and I walked around to the backyard, where Tom was adding wood to the log teepee in the fire pit. Sergeant, who was also out back, moseyed up to us, and I pet the side of him using short, gentle strokes. So soft, in fact, I didn't even make contact with his body, just that top layer of thick fur above his ribs. It didn't matter; my heart still raced. Even though it wasn't much to be proud of, it still felt like an accomplishment to me. Baby steps.

A few minutes later, before my confidence had a chance to take hold, I found myself alone with Sergeant. Outside. In the dark.

They lived on a small ranch with no nearby houses or streetlights, only the fire's flickering light, which was creepy in itself. I could hear their horses making noises in the barn and muffled voices inside the house, but what I heard most was the silence, so much so it made my ears ring.

Dale had hurried inside to set down the potluck dish I'd made, and Tom followed behind to fix them some drinks. Sergeant stood between me and the back door to the house, his eyes locked expectantly on mine.

When I say I was paralyzed with fear, I'm not kidding. I couldn't move.

In retrospect, I doubt he blocked me on purpose, but in my mind, it was as if he had shouted at me like an actual sergeant, *Freeze motherfucker! Don't you dare take another step toward my house or my people!*

In reality, Sergeant wasn't that tough. In fact, he's a little lazy and not the brightest, so he was probably standing there trying to decide if it was worth the effort to follow everyone inside or whether he'd be better off parking his fanny on the deck and waiting for everyone to venture back outside.

I called out to Dale, careful not to call out too loudly or too panicky. I didn't want to anger the dog, and I didn't want him to sense my fear. Yeah, right. As if it wasn't already oozing from my pores.

The problem was I had to call Dale repeatedly. Like most couples, after almost thirty years together, he had a knack for tuning me out. Therefore, I've found if I *don't* call him loudly or panicky, he's libel to ignore me altogether.

Remembering my dad's number one rule on how not to get attacked by a junkyard dog, I refused to look at Sergeant. Unfortunately, that meant I had no way of knowing what he was doing or what he was thinking. If he was snarling, inching towards me, or getting ready to pounce, I had no idea. And unrealistic fears don't help when you're trying not to panic.

Dale eventually showed up, but by then, we were both ticked off. Me, because it took him so damn long to come to my rescue. Him, because he didn't think leading a dumb dog four feet to the right so I could escape some imaginary life-or-death situation two months after my attack necessitated rescuing in the first place.

Okay, when he puts it that way, maybe I *can* see why he doesn't come running every time I call.

126. SYBIL

My life had become a goddamned Chutes and Ladders game. One step forward and two steps back. There I was, proud of myself for touching a big dog again, only to discover a new fear.

Apparently, on top of everything else, it looked like I could no longer be left alone with a dog, either.

Greeeaat.

Only, for the rest of the night, I wasn't great. I was super on edge but pretended not to be. Others seemed to notice when I flat-out ignored the dog, so I tried to interact with him in minute ways. A friendly word here, a tiny pet there, but always way behind his head, far away from his teeth. And only with plenty of other people around to help get the dog off me or help me get away if need be.

I tried to rationalize with myselves. I told Logical Me I really *wasn't* being a big baby. I had lumped being alone with a dog into the same bucket as not liking it when owners didn't appear to have control over their dogs, which is, in fact, logical. Therefore, I was just being practical. I wasn't overreacting. It was no biggie, certainly nothing for her to be upset over.

I then told Crazy Me that she had to stop hijacking my brain like that—but I was nice about it. I let her down easy, telling her I understood. She and I had been through a lot. However, it wasn't like I was *trying* to get us killed. I promised her the attack had been strictly a one-time-only deal. If she didn't like me being alone with dogs, I assured her that was something we could work on, even though I wasn't thrilled about adding one more thing to my 101-things-to-do-to-get-over-a-dog-attack list. I was already bogged down with physical therapy and trying to find random small dogs to pet. Buuuut, if she needed me to ease back into being alone with dogs to shut her the hell up, so be it.

127. PARTY POOPER

When we got to the second party, I could see through the glass front door that everyone was gathered in the kitchen down the hall. I didn't think they'd hear the doorbell over the loud music, and since I'd already texted them to let them know we were on our way, I just walked in. Dale followed close behind, carrying the nibbles we'd brought.

I'd only made it a few feet down the hall before two dogs bounded up to me, one being a spaniel of some sort and the other, I found out later, was a vizsla. No surprise, as soon as I saw the vizsla, I froze.

Our neighbor Sharon, who was also there, rushed over to give me a Happy New Year hug, and I buried my face in her chest. The coloring of the vizsla and the shape of his snout were so much like Red's I couldn't even bear to look at him. She tried introducing the dogs to show they were friendly, but I couldn't bring myself to look up. She ended up just holding me until somebody led the dogs out of the room.

Thanks to Sergeant, these dogs had sniffed my legs extra hard, but they minded their own business for the most part.

It didn't matter. I was hot, shaking, and practically hyperventilating. I wasn't just embarrassed for being a dumb baby. I was mad at myself for turning this into a thing when, in actuality, I was desperately trying to avoid any "things" whatsoever. I threw out some quick apologies along the lines of "It's not you, it's me, and by the way, Happy New Year" and bolted out the door.

I could see Dale and Sharon were beyond disappointed in me. They'd been looking forward to a fun evening, and I knew I'd just ruined it. This only made me feel worse.

My inability to act normal wasn't just affecting my own happiness. It was now affecting others around me, and that wasn't fair to them.

I was also frustrated because as time passed, instead of overcoming my fears, I kept uncovering new ones.

This started out as just a fear of being attacked by a gang of pit bulls again, and rightfully so. However, now I felt like the Universe was toying with me, mocking me. I envisioned some higher power ticking off my list of fears on their fingers: big dogs, aggressive dogs, being alone with dogs, same-color dogs, and just for giggles, let's make her afraid of same-shaped dogs. With that last one, we were suddenly talking about all dogs because, let's face it, dogs are going to be shaped like, like, well . . . like *dogs*!

I was fed up and *so* angry.

Why was this still happening to me?

Had I not been punished enough?

Was God trying to teach me a lesson, but I couldn't get it through my thick skull? No doubt, another notion I'd picked up from my parents. It's not like I'd *chosen* to react that way. I had no idea that would happen. My body and mind, which I was once so proud of, betrayed me over and over again even though I told them repeatedly to knock it the hell off.

Dale wanted to go home. I certainly wasn't in the mood for any more parties, or any more dogs, for that matter, but I also didn't want my panic attack to completely ruin the evening. I explained how, at home, I'd only beat myself up more, and in doing so, I convinced Dale to take us back to Tom and Mary's. But who was I kidding? Of course, I still beat myself up over it. The only difference was I did so sitting around a fire pit with ten other people and a fake smile plastered on my face instead of lying in bed staring at the ceiling or watching some ball drop on the tube.

Though Dale would never say so, he was no longer in the party mood, either. Although, I could tell he was trying hard to rekindle that festive feeling by how fast he was sucking down his Captain and Cokes. Meanwhile, I replayed that last scene again and again in my mind, wondering what I could've done differently, and I begged God to make me stop overreacting.

I'm not going to lie. I've had *way* better New Year's Eves. A few even included sleeping with my face on the edge of a toilet seat. Without a doubt, I knew this year's resolution had to be to get myself some professional help.

128. WITCH HUNT

From day one, My Friend's dogs was the subject people were most interested in. I was shocked how everyone in my world, whether it be family, friends, neighbors, coworkers, old high school classmates, or medical practitioners, was so intent on blaming the dogs before they even knew the whole story. I honestly didn't blame My Friend or the dogs, but these people were like a Salem mob parading through my life, pitchforks and torches in hand. But how could I give up a witch when one didn't exist? Yet, when I attempted to explain that, they acted like I was holding out on them— and I couldn't help but feel they might burn *me* at the stake instead.

If I didn't care about these people's political beliefs, you better believe I didn't give a shit about how they felt about My Friend or her dogs. Yet years of spewing their unsolicited opinions all over social media compelled them to tell me, anyway.

As far as My Friend was concerned, it wasn't like she *made* the dogs attack me. She didn't yell *Sic 'em*! Hell, she wasn't even home at the time, so as far as I was concerned, she had zero culpability. As for the dogs—and let me make this crystal clear—this was between them and me. *Only* them and me.

I didn't understand how these random people in my life could have such a strong opinion about something they knew little about. It was infuriating how they could be so flippant about whether an animal, a living, breathing creature, not to mention a freaking family pet, lived or died. Let alone that they had the nerve to lecture me about it.

They'd dramatically list the various reasons why they were right, and I was wrong, pressuring me to agree with them the whole while. Some acted as if they were auditioning for a nationally televised debate, but instead, they reminded me of those bad actors in after-school specials. They came at me with arguments so incredibly one-sided I could tell they hadn't even *considered* the other side. I imagine they thought highly of themselves, the way they passed their opinions down from on high as if they were the sole voice of logic, smarter than me, who knew better than me. Instead, they came across as ignorant, smug, and arrogant. Some even had the gall to get nasty with me when I refused to see things their way.

Oh, hell no!

These discussions did little to persuade me. If anything, they only made me despise the person for assuming or implying that I hadn't lain awake most nights, pondering every imaginable reason on my own. I swear, I poured over those reasons repeatedly every day and every night. Yet, despite it all, I couldn't bring myself to concede that the dogs should die.

129. LIFE OR DEATH

As I mentioned before, beginning the day of the attack and every day that followed, My Friend and I analyzed every aspect of the incident from every angle. We discussed our days leading up to the attack—hers, the dogs', and mine. We looked at it from her perspective, and we looked at it from mine. We even tried to imagine what the dogs had been thinking.

Knowing how or why it happened was vital because we knew that would ultimately determine the fate of the dogs.

The first few days after the attack, still stunned and confused, I didn't allow myself to voice my opinion. To make an educated decision, I needed the whole story. Even though I was an animal lover, I wasn't so stubborn and biased to not consider all the options, and I urged my friend to do the same. But to make an educated decision, we needed the whole story.

On the day I was attacked, she asked me why I hadn't shot the dogs. At the time, it didn't surprise me because, I honestly didn't take her question seriously. In our discussions, we each tossed far-fetched what-if scenarios around. And while shooting the dogs *could* have been an option, it was an option in the same way I *could* win the lotto—with both being equally as unlikely.

In the spirit of *There are no stupid questions,* I didn't tell her she was nuts. Instead, I told her matter-of-factly that I didn't have my gun in my purse at the time, nor could I have reached my purse even if I did have it with me. Both were true. Seeing how it wasn't possible in the logistical sense, we never progressed to discussing it any further in the moral sense.

I missed it at first, but thinking back, she may have been subconsciously planting that seed or taking my temperature on the idea of it all. She wasn't asking my permission, per se. Like me, I don't think she felt she required anyone's permission for anything. However, she may have been looking for some affirmation from me that it wouldn't have been out of the question, if not okay.

Though I wasn't there for Dale and My Friend's conversations, I pieced together that they had spoken a few times by phone and in our driveway before she came to see me that first day. However, as I overanalyzed their driveway encounter, like I overanalyzed everything having to do with the attack these days, I wondered if he just happened to be there when she pulled in, or if he'd planted himself there on purpose so they could speak privately beforehand.

A part of me could see Dale preparing her for what I looked like and allowing her some time to get her emotions under control. Another part could see him giving her a piece of his mind. But while I knew he'd been pissed when Mr. BMW had dropped me off, I thought Dale had let that go by the time we got home from the hospital.

I found out later that My Friend had told my husband in the driveway that day, if he wanted to go back to her house to shoot the dogs, she'd understand. But neither of us has a vengeful bone in our bodies, so of course, he'd never agree to something like that. According to him, he merely dismissed her suggestion, chalking it up to the fact that everyone's emotions were running hot that day.

I mentioned it before, but it bears repeating. My Friend was *very* distraught over the entire thing and *very* apologetic. I didn't think she was serious when she'd made those comments. I took it as more of a nod to *I'm so sorry this happened. I don't know what I can do to make you feel better or how I could begin to apologize, but if this were to make you feel better, I wouldn't be happy, but I wouldn't blame you, either.* However, and again, I'm just hypothesizing here, she may have thought if he took her up on it, it would've made things a lot easier for her.

130. NOT HANK

I'm no dummy. During all our early discussions about the attack, when My Friend and I were trying to determine the big "why," she was also fishing for culpability. Her questions revolved around which did what. She wanted specifics, so I laid it out for her bite by bite the best I could.

Not only was it essential to know the details so we could determine what went wrong that day, she needed to know for her own family's safety. Her primary concern was the role Hank, the youngest of the three dogs and, I suspect, the family favorite, had played in all this. She even took it one step further, asking if I was 100 percent certain it was him.

It pained me to say it, but there was no denying it was him since Hank and I had shared that moment I will remember for the rest of my life.

Nobody can imagine the immense guilt I felt as I explained how her beloved pet almost killed me, how I, too, was in disbelief as I pleaded with him, face-to-face, to let me go, and when he didn't, how I'd been forced to contemplate my own death. I didn't want to make her cry, but this was no time for sugarcoating.

Some say I could have easily lied, but I'd never do that. Growing up, I was lied to and forced to lie to back up other people's lies, so I decided long ago that I wouldn't play those games. Besides, if I lied to save Hank and someone else got hurt, I'd never be able to forgive myself.

However, that didn't mean I had to tell her *everything*. I chose to leave out the part about how I considered Hank the worst offender because, of the three of them, I'd trusted him the most. I viewed the other two as basic, one-dimensional yard dogs, but Hank was different. They'd had him since he was a pup, and I'd watched him grow up. He'd been socialized. He had a personality. I got the feeling everyone in her family considered him their buddy, not just their dog. So, having spent so much time doing people stuff, I honestly thought he would've known better than to cross that line. And the fact that he did, made me wonder what else he might be capable of.

When she started crying, I had a flash of recognition. I immediately realized she had already decided to put the other two dogs down before she came to see me, and this latest visit had been to determine what would happen to Hank.

Shit.

131. THE DECISION

Until then, I'd left the dog decision up to her and told her so repeatedly. They were her dogs, not mine. It felt weird, cruel, and almost blasphemous to openly discuss their fate, but we did so every day. It wasn't because we wanted to; we had to. And while I didn't offer her my opinion, I felt it my obligation, as her friend, to help her process all that goes into deciding something of that magnitude. I played the role of a high school debate coach, listing all the reasons for and against that I could think of, leaving her to decide which resonated with her and her family the most.

On the one hand, they weren't attack dogs. She'd owned them for a long time without incident. Those dogs had been around her kids when they were little, her kids' friends, and everyone in her big family, yet they'd never had a problem. Even when she got home on the day of the attack, she said the dogs had acted completely normal, as if nothing had happened.

We all know someone who has made a big dumb mistake, but that doesn't make them a bad person, and we certainly don't "put them down." So why are we holding dogs to a standard that isn't even fair to judge rational human beings?

I'm pretty sure those dogs didn't wake up that morning and set out to kill someone. I'm no dog psychologist, but I'm fairly certain dogs can't think premeditative thoughts. I think they're just operating from moment to moment.

I know we want to believe that our dogs think of us as their best friends, but does anyone know for sure if a dog is capable of actual thoughts, or are they running solely on instinct? How can we judge a dog as we would a person if they aren't equipped to think or behave like one?

On the other hand, My Friend and I weren't oblivious. I was left with injuries, pain, and horrific memories to remind me of what those dogs were capable of. Meanwhile, she was left with a house that, in her words, "looked like a crime scene" to remind *her*.

132. THE CRIME SCENE

Crime Scene. Until My Friend said that, it hadn't even occurred to me, but it made sense. With all the blood dripping from my deep puncture wounds, my arms dangling well below my heart, my heart beating wildly, and the dogs flinging my arms all around; naturally, there'd be blood spatter.

And she had *nice* furniture. Of course, her sofa couldn't have been an ancient dark-red scratchy plaid hand-me-down from her grandma. It was one of those Pottery Barn-esque slipcover sofas, although probably a better-made one than that. And cream, no less.

Her ottoman was covered in horsehide or cowhide. Maybe it was zebrahide. Whatever it was, it looked expensive, like a one-of-a-kind piece they sold in furniture galleries in Austin, Aspen, or Albuquerque.

Then I wondered how someone goes about getting blood stains out of animal skin. More importantly, who would even know that? It's not like people go around laundering farm animals. All *I know* is that it's not written on the stain stick, that's for sure.

I was going to say at least she had tile floors, but they were the fake wood plank style. The kind that's textured to look like wood grain, with lots of cracks and crevices, therefore lots of places for blood to settle into. In addition, the fluffy cream rug that had once graced her living room would probably now be classified as a biohazard and would no doubt have to be trashed.

Ugh.

I'd traveled all over her living room and kitchen while trying to escape, so I wondered how much other damage I had done.

How did the rustic wood coffee table that looked like an antique fare?

What about the throw I tried to wrap around my arm and the throw pillow I pondered grabbing? I bet I'd dripped blood over all of those, too.

Shit.

No doubt I'd gotten it on those damn bulky curtains when I struggled with the sliding door locks. But at least they were brown, though if I'm not mistaken, they were velvet, so not at all easy to clean. Lord knows they'd never fit in a washing machine, so she'd be looking at a hefty dry-cleaning bill, for sure. I knew there was no chance she'd just pitch them. She'd liked them so much I had to go to battle with the other real estate agent when the buyers of her old house tried insisting she leave them.

I felt so bad.

Even the cream paint on the wall was that flat builder-grade paint. The kind that, when wiped with a damp cloth, ninety percent of the paint comes off on the rag. That meant My Friend probably had to repaint the whole damn wall.

Good grief.

The movie of me being attacked, which had been on repeat in my mind, now became a double feature. The bonus clip starred My Friend as she cleaned her home for hours on end, on her hands and knees, Cinderella-style, while contemplating whether the family pets lived or died. I'd give that movie two thumbs down for sure.

In actuality, I don't know when she got around to cleaning since she wouldn't let me over to see it. She was afraid being in her house again might somehow trigger me. However, knowing how distressed she must have been to see the mess, how much it traumatized her daughter, and what a good housekeeper she was, she probably took care of it immediately.

All of this was my fault. I was the reason My Friend had to cut her vacation short. I was the cause of everyone's emotional trauma—hers, her kids', Dale's, and mine. It was also my fault that the dogs were in, what I knew deep down in my soul to be, immeasurable trouble.

Just when I thought I couldn't feel any worse, I now had to picture My Friend frantically cleaning the bloody crime scene on top of checking in on me multiple times a day, making me her yummy homemade chicken chili, caring for her own family, and pondering the lives of her dogs.

The whole thing sucked.

133. THE FATE OF THE DOGS

In discussing the fate of the dogs, I can't recall if she ever asked me flat-out what I thought she should do. Again, she wasn't an ask-permission kind of person, so I never would have expected her to do so, but early on, I'd let her know that I could not and would not make that decision for her. These were her dogs, her pets, and from a legal perspective, they were her property.

I didn't necessarily agree with the dogs as property juxtaposition, but it was one I'd learned long ago as a prelaw major in college. It had also come up recently in our last neighborhood, where the residents had an ongoing heated debate regarding what was deemed safe and unsafe for dogs riding around in golf carts. Talk about first-world problems. Yeesh.

After the attack, my thinking was warped, and understandably so. Since I was afraid little yappy neighborhood dogs would break into my house, I thought that would have made me the last person someone would go to for advice about what to do with the dogs. But I suppose, if anybody had *earned* that right, it was me. Yet no matter how hurt, sad, frustrated, devastated, or angry I felt, I *never* wanted My Friend's dogs to die.

134. NATURE OR NURTURE

I'm not known for my grace. In fact, I've been known to hold a grudge here and there, but for whatever reason, I gave those dogs a pass on day one. Even before we knew the whole story, I reassured My Friend it was all just a freak accident that nobody could have predicted; therefore, nobody was to blame, and nobody had to be sorry.

I'll even take it one step further and say, technically, the dogs didn't really do anything wrong. I imagine in their minds, they were just defending their family and their home from an intruder. So why would I hold that against them? If anything, they should be applauded because they did their job with unrelenting precision. These were just big dumb dogs doing what big dumb dogs do.

Nature had gifted them with protective instincts, so how naive were we to be surprised when they acted on them? I suppose if we had to name the one thing that went wrong and caused this shitty mess, it would be that we underestimated them. We should have assumed an attack was possible.

All dogs have the potential to attack a human, and we're fools to think otherwise. I'm not saying all dogs *will* attack. I'm just saying that the average Fluffy or Fido isn't immune to biting someone, and who's to say how severely, so why not play it safe.

Even if the dog owner thinks of themselves as Cesar Millan, the dog whisperer, or the dog has the equivalent of a doctorate in obedience training, I think we all need to consider the possibility of an attack. We owe it to those around us. The cold truth is there's a fine line between instinct and training, and nobody can say for sure where one ends and the other begins.

Slapping a tutu on a dog does not instantly make it nicer, and socialization isn't the be-all and end-all, especially when instinct is so unpredictable.

My Friend and I should have expected—and been prepared for—an attack. Dogs do stupid shit. Period.

People can't control a dog any more than they can control another human being. If a dog decides to attack, it will be happening before you even realize what hit you.

135. THE SURRENDER

The attack happened on the Saturday before Veteran's Day 2019. On Monday, My Friend took the dogs to the only open veterinarian's office she could find because her usual vet, like most others, was closed for the holiday. Even though our county had a population of almost

400,000, we all joked about it being a small hick town because everybody seemed to know everybody, like that six degrees of separation thing. Sometimes, this came in handy.

My friend Kellie's daughter, Samantha, worked for a vet's office, which just so happened to be the same office where My Friend brought her dogs that day. This fell on the one weekend a month Sam had to work. Then, just when My Friend was explaining the situation to the girl at the front desk, Sam, who had been working in the back, coincidentally walked up front at that very moment.

Tell me again that God doesn't have a plan.

I heard about it the following day from Kellie. My Friend obviously didn't give anyone my name, but Samantha, having heard my story from her mom, asked My Friend, "Are those Cheryl's dogs?"

My Friend had gone there to have the dogs put to sleep, but they refused her.

It sounds cruel, but the Centers for Disease Control mandates that in an attack situation, the offending dog, cat, or ferret must be quarantined for a ten-day observation period prior to being euthanized. Even though it may appear healthy, they do this to ensure the animal doesn't have rabies.

Instead, Sam's vet office suggested that My Friend take them to her usual vet, where she and the dogs might feel more comfortable when they reopened the following day.

I can't remember if it was that same day or the day after. But rather than taking them to her usual vet, she took them to our County Animal Services Shelter. It is there that they spent the remainder of their ten-day quarantine.

I found out a week later that she could have held them herself for the ten days, but for whatever reason, she'd chosen not to. Once she'd made that difficult decision, it was full steam ahead.

With the vet offices being closed or short-staffed for the holiday, I thought she would have taken it as a sign that someone was trying to tell her not to put them down. I know I would have. Then again, I'm a spiritual pushover like that, always looking for a sign from God or the Universe, even when making small decisions.

My Friend may not be super religious, but she is practical. I consider myself practical, too, so it's one of the many things I like about her. She said the decision itself had been hard enough, so once it was made, there was no going back. She couldn't waffle like that on her family. So, after it was decided, she gathered all the dogs' stuff and donated it to a nearby pet rescue center. There wasn't a single dog bed, bowl, or toy left in their house. She said it was important to her and her kids that they didn't have those kinds of reminders popping up after the fact. Her family dealt with what had to be dealt with, and she ripped that Band-Aid off with one fell swoop.

136. NOW OR NEVER

Once I realized My Friend was serious about her decision and had taken that first step, I decided to kick my plan into high gear and make my opinion known. I couldn't have lived with myself if I thought she was having them euthanized for me. Yet, ironically, that's exactly what I was doing now—only now, I was hoping she'd reverse her decision for me.

I pressed upon her that it was all just a big mistake, that ultimately, it wasn't that big of a deal, and this was the dogs' first offense. To drive it home, I even added how unlikely it was that the dogs would attack someone again. However, speaking those words out loud, I suddenly felt like I had tempted fate or dared God.

Quickly, I backtracked a little, adding the caveat: "So long as you never leave another non-family member alone with the three of them." Then, feeling as if I might have lost what little ground I'd worked so hard to gain, I added, "Just to be on the safe side."

I pushed, but I'll be the first to admit, not that hard. It's not because I didn't feel that strongly about saving the dogs—I did—but there was no denying these were *her* dogs, and it was *her* family at risk.

Just like I didn't like people vomiting their opinions on the subject all over me, I had to respect that it was her decision. It wasn't within the bounds of our friendship for me to push any harder than I did.

My heart ached for so many reasons. After the decision had been made, bombarded by emotions, I felt tremendous guilt because if we boiled it down, the dogs wouldn't be in the boat they were in if it wasn't for me. I also felt so sorry and so sad for My Friend and her family. I couldn't imagine having to mourn the loss of three pets all at once. We'd recently lost one of our cats to kidney disease, and I swore the sun hadn't shone as bright since.

I also felt immensely conflicted since, truth be told, I also felt relief. If these dogs never attacked another person, nobody would have to go through what I'd gone through, and My Friend would be spared any additional pain, guilt, and stress.

God, please forgive me.

137. UNFINISHED BUSINESS

I couldn't escape the feeling that the dogs and I had some unfinished business. I felt cheated and disappointed. Like the feeling you get when someone leaves your party without saying goodbye or when you don't get a chance to say everything you wanted to say in an argument before the other person hangs up or storms off.

It wasn't like I had anything in particular to say to them. I just couldn't let our last encounter be my last memory of them. The attack was so fresh and vivid that I found it impossible to conjure any memories of them from before the attack. I thought seeing the dogs again would give me a new, better memory, which I could swap out for the shitty one, or so I hoped.

I mentioned my plan to Dale, and I got: "That sounds like a horrible idea. Why do you care? You don't have to do that. I don't know why you'd want to see them. They aren't your dogs. It's already been decided. They probably won't let you see them, anyway."

Whoa. That's not at all how I expected that to go.

I presume, in his mind, he'd given me a long enough list of good reasons not to go. So when I never asked him for a ride to Animal Services, I imagine he just assumed I'd changed my mind. *Silly Dale.*

I immediately recognized that we were way too far apart on this issue. And after spending that entire first week getting beat up by insurance companies and doctors, I didn't have the mental strength to try and convince him otherwise. I mentioned my wanting to see the dogs to a few others, and each of them voiced concerns similar to Dale's.

Too bad, I'm going anyway.

138. NOT THE BOSS OF ME

Why are people so quick to tell others how to live their lives? It's everywhere you turn. Don't date that person. Don't take that job. Don't buy that. Don't say that. Don't do that. We're all individuals. We all have different personalities, values, beliefs, strengths, challenges, opinions, and experiences.

What may or may not work for one person may or may not work for another. Can I get an Amen?

While I may have been *curious* about what other people thought, that wasn't to be confused with requiring anyone's permission. I was totally capable of making this decision on my own. I knew this was something I had to do. And for me, there was no way around it.

I've spent my entire life tuning out other people's opinions and disassociating, so I'll be the first to admit I've built a bit of a reputation for doing the exact opposite of what someone tells me to do. I can't help it. I think I do it out of principle. Having grown up with strict, authoritative parents, as an adult, if there's any inkling or suggestion of "control," I'm automatically bombarded with thoughts of *You're not the boss of me!* However, visiting the dogs wasn't one of those instances—at least not entirely.

139. ON A MISSION

On Friday, six days after the attack, I drove to where My Friend had surrendered the dogs several days earlier, our County Animal Services Shelter. I would have gone sooner, but it took me that long to be able to drive. Although, if I'm being honest, I still sucked at it. Since the attack I'd only driven once. That was the day before when I'd gone to the grocery store, and it had only gone so-so.

Nevertheless, I wasn't in the mood for another lecture about wanting to see the dogs, so I drove myself and told no one where I was headed. Let me rephrase. I didn't tell anyone where I was *really* headed.

I snuck past my live-in security guard when he was on an overseas conference call. Later, when he called to ask me where I'd gone, I told him I went to the grocery store or was swinging by the gym to talk to the therapist. Neither had been on my agenda, but to avoid lying, I vowed to make an extra stop. Only it would have to wait until I was on my way home. I was a woman on a mission.

140. MID-SHIT

The whole dog visiting experience was way more emotionally grueling than I expected.

Even with my windows rolled up, driving up the long entrance road, I could hear barking—lots of big, deep, agitated barking coming from all directions. It was nerve-wracking to hear dogs but not be able to see them. Having never been there before, I didn't know the lay of the land—like whether the dogs were kept inside or outside and where the administrative offices might be. All the massive live oak trees with their dangly Spanish moss blocking my view weren't helping.

Immobilized by fear, I sat in my car, trying to mentally map out where all these dogs were based on where the sounds were coming from. At first, I tried to be smooth about it, glancing around via the reflections in my car mirrors, but that wasn't good enough.

So, to get the full picture, I'd stare intently in each direction for a long while, afraid of what I might miss if I blinked or looked away in another direction, even if only for a second. If I *did* glance away, I was sure one of the dogs would see I wasn't paying attention and use that opportunity to pounce. Similar to how a lion moves swiftly when its prey isn't looking but then crouches low in the grass again when her soon-to-be dinner picks its head up to sniff the air. I was slowly taking it all in, unable to get out of my car—at least not until I was sure of what I was getting myself into. I was convinced if I stared long enough, I'd eventually catch some dog looking to kill me.

I didn't know what to make of the several volunteers walking dogs in the area. By my estimation, they weren't close enough to count on in an emergency. And since they all appeared to be petite retired women, I doubted whether they were strong enough to control their dog if it decided to come after me.

I watched closely, trying to anticipate how far they would go on their walks before turning around. I wanted my stroll from the parking lot to the entrance to coincide with when all three volunteers and their dogs would be the farthest away and headed in the opposite direction. That way, I'd have a greater chance of exiting my car unnoticed. However, if they *did* notice, I figured I'd be far enough away that they wouldn't see me as a threat. And if they did charge me, at least I'd have more time to make it to safety. I remember thinking how perfect it would be if I could catch one of them mid-shit.

I regretted parking in the row facing the woods instead of the closer row facing the building, but I'd had no choice since my wrists still only allowed me to make right turns. Since my car was only fifty feet from the door, if worse came to worse, I figured I could run back and jump on top of it, even in a dress.

I didn't have the hand and wrist strength nor the mobility to wrestle pants yet, so I wore dresses in public and baggy drawstring pajama pants at home.

141. ENTER HERE

The front doors to the shelter were flanked by two pens. They were big. I'd say thirty feet by fifteen feet with a six-foot-tall chain link fence surrounding them. As luck would have it, every dog in there appeared to be a pit bull mix.

Walking past, I didn't allow myself to look directly inside the pens or at any of the dogs being walked on the property. I only stole a few quick glances here and there. I wanted to watch the dogs—this way, if they made a run at me, I'd have some warning. But I was too scared of making eye contact with them, even accidentally.

In trying to decipher what had gone wrong that horrible day, I'd been reading up on dog behavior and recently learned that dogs might see eye contact as a challenge, threat, or an act of aggression on my part. Since that was the last thing I wanted, I made my way quickly and without looking around. However, I listened uncontrollably for the sound of panting, toenails on asphalt, shouting from volunteers, or anything that would indicate one of the dogs had gotten loose.

In the spirit of "Fake it until you make it," I strutted confidently and chanted in my head some bullshit like *Everything's fine. This is no big deal. I'm calm. You're calm. I come in peace*, as if I were Obi-Wan Kenobi, and could will the dogs to ignore me. I was convinced they could sense my fear, but I'd yet to figure out what that meant to the dogs and how their behavior might change as a result.

There was this back-and-forth in my brain, a volley of thoughts. I tried acting all confident in an attempt to convince myself I wasn't afraid. But with no logical reasons to support my fears, I felt more silly, irrational, and not the slightest bit confident. So basically, I wasn't fooling anyone with my strutty walk and steely, forward gaze, especially myself.

142. SHELTER ANGEL

When I got to the reception desk, I signed in per the instructions noted on the counter. I then told the two employees in the lobby that I had an odd request, so it was probably best if I spoke directly with the manager.

It had been less than a week since the attack, so my injuries were very apparent—swelling, big bruises, scabs, and a whole bunch of surgical tape. I definitely had a "problematic" air about me, so the two workers seemed to sigh with relief, more than happy to pawn me off on someone else.

As they called the manager over the walkie-talkie, I paced around a little in search of something other than the two employees to look at. They were sizing me up and down. And like the dogs out front, I was desperate not to make eye contact with them as I didn't want to have to field any questions if they made an attempt at small talk.

It hadn't gone well when I surveyed Dale and a few friends about my intent on coming here. So, I didn't want to risk being shot down if these two pieced together what I was up to before I had a chance to plead my case to the final decision-maker.

I briefly explained my situation to Ms. Manager and was so grateful when she agreed to let me see the dogs. She was clearly busy, yet rather than coming across as frazzled, she radiated an easygoing attitude, which told me I could trust her. So, as we slowly walked back outside toward the building where the dogs were being held, I proceeded to tell her the whole story.

Being in charge of a big facility like that, I knew Ms. Manager had to be somewhat of a dog expert. But after seeing that their typical "clientele" mainly consisted of pit bulls, it only upped her street cred even more. So, by the time I found out she was there the day My Friend had brought the dogs in, I was practically in love with this woman. She wasn't just super knowledgeable about big scary dogs in general; she actually had firsthand knowledge of *my* big scary dogs. I was so thankful I trusted my instincts to go there when everyone else thought I was crazy. Again, this was God in action.

She said that while none of My Friend's dogs had given her a problem since they arrived, she did say Red had shown signs of being "unstable," "on edge," and "agitated."

We talked at length, and Ms. Manager surmised that the move, particularly the transition from seven acres to a small lot, had been traumatic for him, especially now that he was older and probably more set in his ways. She also thought the dogs most likely weren't thrilled with their new routine of being kept inside or in the garage, considering that, back at the old house, they could roam the entire property as they pleased.

Ms. Manager thought Red may have also been stressed out, either from being cooped up overnight in the laundry room with the other two or because My Friend had been going out of town most weekends for the past few months. Plus, he was probably just old and cranky.

Of course, there was no way to know for sure what had been bugging Red. These were just some possible contributing factors, and any combination could have led to that perfect storm, just as we all suspected.

143. SAYING GOODBYE

When we entered the kennel, the noise was almost unbearable. Any barking freaked me out these days, so this whole experience was pushing me way beyond my newfound boundaries. Intense and loud, it was as if the dogs were trying to outdo each other, each begging for help, each vying for our attention in some game that clearly had no winner.

As we made our way down the hallway, I steered clear of the fencing that separated the kennels from the walkway. Even though it was five feet wide, I was still careful to walk down the center and keep my arms straight down at my sides. As ludicrous as it sounds, I was afraid one of the dogs might latch onto me and try to pull me through the holes in the fencing.

Most of the dogs jumped up as we approached, thrusting their front paws on the kennel gates. The sound of banging metal echoed as every inch of the building appeared to be constructed of either concrete or metal fencing. Walking past, I couldn't help but take notice of all the gate latches, making certain each was secure. If some dog came flying out a kennel door, even if by accident, I thought I'd die of a panic attack on the spot.

"My" three dogs were in a shared kennel, and they looked the same as the last time I'd seen them. Kaya barked and barked while moving around in loose circles. Hank sat next to the gate, and it sounded like he was growling and whining at the same time. Meanwhile, Red jumped up in one place, lifting his front paws off the ground and pointing his nose at the ceiling while barking continuously.

My first instinct when greeting a dog used to be to offer it my hand to sniff, but not today. I didn't dare. I was afraid the dogs would remember my smell, and it would trigger another attack. I also feared the smell of my scabs would make them think I was easy prey.

Too self-conscious to say all I needed to say out loud in front of Ms. Manager, I crouched down in the hopes that if I were closer to the dogs, they could somehow hear my thoughts or feel how sorry I was, how I forgave them, and how much I needed them to forgive me. When their barking grew more intense, it scared me, and teetering there just on the balls of my feet, I lost my balance a little. Scared that this position would hinder a life-saving getaway if need be, I quickly stood again.

Such big emotions were flooding my brain all at once. So much sadness, frustration, guilt, fear, and shame. I was beside myself with thoughts about what the dogs were going through. I couldn't imagine how confused they must have felt, wondering how they wound up there, why they'd been deserted, and what had happened to the family that loved them. I bet they missed their soft beds, missed the warm sunshine.

I'd already forgiven the dogs days ago, but seeing them like this, I felt a surge of renewal, and I vowed to do everything I could to try to save them.

144. EVALUATIONS

Back outside again, where we could hear each other over all the barking, Ms. Manager and I talked some more.

Since the dogs were now involved in "the system," they had to make their way through the formal process, though I learned it wasn't as unyielding as I'd originally thought. While the attack *did* have to be noted on each of their records and recorded with the county, they didn't *have* to be euthanized. The system only mandated they be held for ten days after an attack. Whatever happened to them after that was up to the dog's owner.

Ms. Manager, a true dog lover, believed there were no bad dogs, only bad dog owners. I cringed. That was harsh. I reminded her she was talking about my friend, yet I also understood and appreciated where she was coming from.

Ms. Manager said she couldn't condone putting any dog down unless it was in pain. Of course, that all sounded good in theory, but we needed to come up with an actual plan—and fast since we only had a few days before they were scheduled to be euthanized. So, standing in the courtyard, we analyzed each of the dogs as I made mental notes, which I intended to use as ammunition in my battle to convince My Friend to change her mind.

Red clearly wasn't happy. Being older, he most likely had a lower tolerance for change. She could see him being a problem in the future unless My Friend took a very active interest in managing him and learned to recognize his stress signals. We surmised he would always be a handful, and we didn't think My Friend, having no formal dog training, would be up for what would be required to keep him happy and healthy. He was already slipping, as evident by the seizures.

Kaya wasn't exhibiting any stress symptoms out of the ordinary, at least nothing more than what was typical for being in a shelter. Ms. Manager suspected Kaya had some difficulty dealing with the changes herself but felt more than likely she'd just been feeding off Red's stress on the day of the attack. Ms. Manager felt Kaya would do okay back home, but she'd need to be closely monitored.

If My Friend decided she could only handle one dog in her new house, Ms. Manager and I agreed that Hank would make the most sense. She said he seemed more confused and sad about being in the shelter than aggressive or angry. Ms. Manager thought Hank would do fine if My Friend took precautions in the future, like no strangers over to the house, and set schedules for food, bedtime, and playtime.

Neither Ms. Manager nor I wanted any of My Friends' dogs to die, but we knew we had an uphill battle—make that *I* had an uphill battle since apparently Ms. Manager was forbidden by her employment agreement to make any formal recommendations. She wasn't even allowed to call My Friend to discuss her decision. Ms. Manager *did* say, however, that if My Friend wanted to call *her*, she would be happy to tell her what she and I discussed today regarding the disposition of each of the dogs. Still, My Friend had to be the one to initiate the conversation.

Ms. Manager's last request rocked me to my soul. She said My Friend had indicated when she dropped them off that she didn't want to be there when the dogs were euthanized on Tuesday. If I couldn't convince My Friend to pick up the dogs and take them home, Ms. Manager asked me to plead with My Friend to come to the shelter to be with them in their final moments. She said that was the most heartbreaking part for the employees, seeing the dogs go through the most harrowing day of their lives all by themselves.

I was now more motivated than ever to get My Friend to change her mind.

145. POSSIBLE ALLY

As soon as I was safely back in my car, I called My Friend's sister, the one who owned the house and with whom My Friend was visiting in New York. I figured since I was working with a limited time frame, I needed all the help I could get.

Here's how I saw it playing out: She and I would essentially gang up on My Friend. We'd basically take turns bombarding My Friend with all the reasons she should keep the dogs while the other agreed and enthusiastically reiterated what a good point the other one had just made.

Only that's not at all how it happened. Not even close. Her sister refused to even broach the subject with My Friend. She said My Friend was still having a tough time coping with almost losing me, and her sister didn't think My Friend could handle it if the dogs wound up hurting someone else she cared about or, God forbid, something worse.

I knew My Friend had recently gone through a lot—packing, moving, the divorce, the attack, surrendering the dogs—and she desperately needed a break from all that. Being close to her family was probably helping her to relax and cope, and I loved her, so I wasn't about to wreck that for her by calling her while she was on vacation. Besides, I needed time to rethink my strategy. She would be home again on Monday. That gave me two more days. We could rehash all of this then.

146. SECOND CHANCES

Well, it turns out my super thought-out strategy was nothing more than just shy of pleading. At first, I asked My Friend to keep all three. When that didn't work, then two. Then one. And then just to be there on Tuesday.

I usually considered my negotiation skills to be Middle East nuclear arms crisis-worthy, but I couldn't play her like that. Knowing how much it pained me to have the people around me cramming their opinions down my throat, I couldn't bring myself to do that to her. I had valid arguments, but so did she.

She said they'd already decided that letting the dogs go was for the best and had come to terms with it as a family. I told her Ms. Manager hoped she would return to the shelter to be with the dogs in their final moments, but My Friend feared it would be too traumatic. Having just gone through the same with our cat not that long ago, unfortunately, I knew precisely how heart-wrenching it was.

It's not that she didn't care. My Friend was downright distraught over losing her dogs, but she said the attack was too much for her to ever have to bear again. *No fucking kidding.* I was living the same nightmare, convinced if another dog ever sank its teeth into me, my brain would initiate an instant heart attack just to avoid the horror of it all a second time. So I couldn't very well argue with that.

PART NINE

THE ROAD
BACK

147. HOCUS POCUS

I've always gravitated toward that old saying, "What doesn't kill you makes you stronger." And not just because it's a catchy Kelly Clarkson song; although, can I get a *Yes, Queen!*?

Over the years, I've used it as a big fat paintbrush to whitewash over parts of my childhood. It's a good one-liner to throw out when people get too nosy about my past. Much like Forrest Gump's "That's all I have to say about that." I originally thought I'd use it to deflect talk of the dog attack, but it didn't feel right.

The problem is, I'd also heard it used in the gym after a particularly tough workout and by a divorcee after another one of her boyfriends dumped her, so somewhere along the line, Nietzsche's once powerful sentiment had lost its oomph. Using it in this instance would have made it sound more like a crutch or an excuse than a victory cheer.

Besides, after all of my failed dog encounters thus far, New Year's in particular, I realized I needed more help than some catchy positivity mantra I hoped to brainwash myself with. This is why I decided to seek out a referral to a clinical psychologist sometime in January.

You always hear of people who swear by therapy. Some even attend religiously their entire lives. Yet the idea had never appealed to me.

I'll admit I wasn't super confident a professional could cure me. I just knew my feelings were on the upper end of abnormal, and I had to do something to make them stop, even if that meant toying with something way outside my comfort zone.

148. GROUP THERAPY

The only other time I'd participated in therapy was back in the early eighties when my parents were going through their divorce. My dad had signed the two of us up for some good old-fashioned group family counseling, whereby the adults went off in one direction, the kids went off in the other, and then we all came together at the end. I'm inclined to say it had been court-ordered, but I think it was more along the lines that his attorney had highly recommended my dad do so to give himself a boost in the eyes of the judge.

What could be worse than talking about my feelings out loud, you might ask? How about doing so with a gaggle of strangers as spectators every Thursday night? I would have preferred to shove sticks in my eyes.

Therapy was traumatic, but not because discussing my feelings about their divorce was difficult or painful. Their marital demise had been a long time coming, and frankly, things on the home front had been much quieter since their trial separation. Being the summer before my first year of high school, I couldn't have given a crap what my parents did. For most of my life, but especially at that age, I only wanted to be as far away from them as possible.

What made it torturous was sitting in a community rec room surrounded by a flock of sobbing seven-to-twelve-year-olds.

Even though my dad dragged me there under false pretenses to please the court, we ended up sticking with it because it had worked out nicely—*for him*. Having a group of lonely, vulnerable women in search of a shoulder to cry on was like fishing in a barrel for my father. He was basically speed dating, although technically, it hadn't been invented yet.

It didn't take him long to settle on one, whom he more or less moved in with, leaving me home alone most of the time. If I had cared that he had practically abandoned me to play house with this woman and her kids, it was only for a short time since I quickly learned having no parents around had its advantages. It was far easier to stay out late, skip school, and tango with trouble if nobody was around to notice or care.

149. ROUND ONE

Someone gave me the number of a therapist, claiming, "You're going to love her. She's so nice."

Fact: I don't care how nice anybody is. In my personal life, I'd much rather somebody be fun, intelligent, authentic, or interesting than nice. And when it comes to business, my only requirement is that they be effective at what they do. That's all. If I'm looking for a home inspector, I want them to be good at inspecting. In the same way I need an accountant who's good at accounting and a lawyer who's good at lawyering. I need people to perform specific tasks for me; it's not a casting call for *The Mickey Mouse Club.*

Don't get me wrong, this therapist was a good person and well-credentialed. She immediately recognized that I was struggling with post-traumatic stress disorder and anxiety. A diagnosis that left me surprised and disappointed. Somehow, I'd wound up with not one but *two* psychological problems due to the attack. One being a particularly nasty one, which I thought only military veterans owned the rights to.

Though I wasn't thrilled with her findings, I was relieved to have an actual medical condition—if only to google the hell out of it for days on end. Regardless, I supposed it was better than calling myself "crazy" as I had been.

Our weekly sessions consisted of me rehashing my story and talking about my feelings and her telling me it was all normal, considering what I'd been through. While it was encouraging to know I wasn't broken in some way for feeling the way I had been, I didn't enroll in therapy in search of *permission* to feel that way. I was there because I wanted those feelings to *go away*.

She proposed medication as an option, but I dismissed it entirely. Given my recent history with the pain meds, I was back to adhering to my no-medication-no-matter-what policy, not even an aspirin. Besides, I wasn't looking to mask what I had going on. I was looking to fix it entirely. I also didn't want to delve into any of my childhood shit. I'd made peace with that ages ago and decided I could live with being a little defective in that department. I just wanted to go back to being the me I'd been before all this happened. Was that too much to ask?

I saw her every week for a couple of months and learned some good stuff along the way. I began to understand why this was happening to me, and I learned breathing techniques to help me cope when I'd inevitably beat myself up over those the-dog-is-going-to-eat-me thoughts—no matter how irrational I now knew them to be. However, our visits did little to stop me from freaking out around dogs.

150. THERAPY DOGS

My therapist and I agreed I needed more dogs to practice on, but unfortunately, I didn't organically run into many dogs working as a real estate broker. I spent most of my time on the phone or the computer in my home office, and when I showed properties to buyers, the sellers had usually left the house taking their dogs with them.

At $175 an hour, the sooner I could fix myself and nip this therapy crap in the bud, the better, so I became dead set on bumping into as many dogs as possible. One, I needed something other than my feelings to discuss in these shrink sessions. And two, I hoped by doing so, I'd become desensitized and prove to myself that dogs weren't as scary as I was imagining these days.

My thoughts on fear were like those of most feelings—useless. I lumped fear into the same category as worry, as neither was likely to come true. I thought doing the scary thing anyway would prove my fear had been irrational, and *voilà!* I'd be cured of my phobia. At least, that's what my zero years of medical training had taught me.

This was why I struggled so much with my new dog aversion. I had experienced some tough times and had done some scary shit, so this wasn't new to me. On top of that, I'd made plenty of bad decisions throughout my life and have had to deal with all kinds of repercussions and ramifications as a result. I'd handled all of that myself and came out the other side relatively unscathed—no therapy required.

Seeing or petting a dog didn't sound challenging, but if that's what my therapist wanted me to do, so be it. Then my CrossFit gym rat split personality decided to throw her two cents in, telling me I needed to confront more dogs, bigger dogs, scarier dogs, and I needed to do it a lot.

Bring on the funky feelings! We're gonna work through this shit, exorcism-style! Let's goooo!

I started by calling my closest friends and inviting myself over to play with their dogs. When I say play, what I really mean is petting them while staring at them intently and desperately trying to interpret their body language and predict their next move. I couldn't read lips if my life depended on it, but now, I thought I could read some damn dog's mind if I tried hard enough. I deserved to be in therapy. Clearly, I *was* crazy.

Luckily, Kellie's daughter, Sam, who worked for the vet's office, had volunteered to work with me. Then again, maybe her mom had volunteered her, or I guilted her into it, I forget which.

Coincidentally, she and her friend Katie had dog park play dates near my house on their days off. Samantha brought Chief, whom I'd known since he was a pup, and Katie brought her one-year-old vizsla, Porter. I was excited to practice on both. Chief was a pit bull mix, and the vizsla was the same breed that had made me wig out on New Year's Eve.

I formulated a mental checklist for selecting which dogs would be best to practice on: rambunctious, big, jumper, barker, mixed breed, looks like a pit bull, any so-called aggressive breed, tugs on its leash, or better yet, *not* on a leash. The more boxes I could check, the worse the dog scored on my scary scale, but the better the choice for my highly unscientific let's-try-to-freak-Cheryl-the-fuck-out-but-not-kill-her-in-the-process experiment.

151. PRACTICING

I don't know who was more excited about going to the park, the dogs or me. The first time we met, Sam, Katie, and the dogs were already there by the time I arrived, so I caught up with them at the pavilion. The first thing I noticed was that Katie had Porter on one of those leashes where the strap wraps around the upper part of the snout. Seeing how fixated I was on it, Samantha explained that it was merely a tool for teaching high-energy pups leash manners. However, my warped brain saw it as a muzzle and kept referring to it as such. Sam corrected me, although a little less patiently each time.

Overall, our visit was uneventful. While I struggled to not be hyperfocused on where their mouths were at all times and the proximity of my hands to their mouths, I did manage to pat some backs and butts. This was easier said than done, considering they were practically bouncing off the walls, eager to run and play.

We met another time, and again, I was the last one to get there—which anyone who knows me knows is to be expected. This time, their little group stood beyond the pavilion in the grassy area, approximately forty feet from the park entrance. Spotting them, I called out a cheery hello, at which point Sam bent over and unhooked Chief's leash. I now had a pit bull barreling toward me.

Here we go. Game on.

Old Cheryl, Normal Cheryl, would have dropped to her knees and let him knock me backward and cover my face with slobber. New Cheryl was super freaked out but tried to play it cool. I bent forward and, tapping my thighs with my palms, called out in an overly friendly voice, "Come 'ere! Come see meee!"

We had done this dance many times before, so I expected he'd wiggle his way between my legs and stop midway through with only his rear remaining in front, perfectly positioning himself to have his fanny scratched while he shifted his weight from side to side to let me know I was doing it right. Instead, it was like Lucy had pulled the football out from Charlie Brown. At the last second, I stood straight up, pulled my arms in tight to my chest, and turned my entire body to the side, including my face, so I wouldn't see what was about to happen.

What happened was nothing. Somewhere along the line, Chief had made a U-turn and headed straight back to Sam, where he looked up at her expectantly.

My heart sank. I was so confused and disappointed in myself. Whatever had just happened was certainly not on purpose. Those were definitely not the instructions my body had been given. It was as if I was a marionette, like Pinocchio, and someone else had pulled the strings. In *my* mind, I'd been ready. I didn't think I'd been scared. In fact, I had envisioned the whole thing going rather well.

Evidently, sheer will, positive self-talk, and all the deliberate muscle movements in the world were no match for my PTSD-riddled brain. I'd prepared for this. My brain and my body, we'd had a deal. But at the last minute, my dumb brain reneged and turned my body against me. It was a dick move, straight out of a backstabby-tweenage-girl playbook.

I felt embarrassed, silly, ashamed, and angry, and I confided as much to Sam and Katie. Katie took the high road, telling me it was okay and to be expected. Having known Sam since the day she was born, she told me like it was. My hesitation, the stiffening and turning away, had sent a message to Chief, loud and clear, that I didn't want him, so he shouldn't approach me. However, since I initially called him over, he was confused. Not knowing what to do and looking for reassurance and comfort, he returned to Sam.

For the rest of our visit that day, I tried to earn Chief's trust again, but I couldn't get him to warm up to me. In fact, he mostly ignored me, preferring to hang with his buddy Porter. In trying to be kinder to myself like the therapist taught me, I told myself it wasn't me. Porter was simply more fun than me. *No kidding.*

I continued to meet the four of them at the park. A few times, I even managed to take the ball from a dog's mouth and toss it to them. Once, in particular, when we girls were sitting on a bench, with Porter lying underneath it, I reached under to grab the ball from him. But because I couldn't see him, I felt around for it blindly, bumping into his teeth and practically poking him in the eyeballs. Since neither one of us freaked out, I'd call that a win. Porter, probably not so much.

152. NOT MY NORMAL

I'd report my dog encounters to my doctor, and each week, no matter how it went, she'd tell me that my results were normal. I suppose for some, but we still hadn't worked our way back to *my* version of normal.

So it was no surprise when, a month or two into my sessions, I got the inevitable—and by now all too familiar—doctor cop-out: "This is probably as good as it's going to get."

I didn't understand. Don't doctors have to go to school for like fifteen years? I would have thought that took perseverance, yet I had never met a bigger bunch of quitters.

Nobody goes to the doctor wanting to feel somewhat better or wanting to be a little cured, so I didn't think I was asking too much. For God's sake, I was only bitten by a dog. Okay, it was a few dogs, but my point is it wasn't jungle warfare, so my PTSD shouldn't have been *that* difficult to fix. I wanted more. I needed more out of this treatment plan if I planned on living my life the way I had been before the attack.

Buckle up, Buttercup. Looks like we're gonna be playing with a helluva lot more dogs!

153. JAX

Between meeting up with Sam and Katie, I also hooked up with other dogs, like Kellie's Jax. He was another rescue dog—because what can I say, my friends rock like that.

Technically, Jax was a mutt, but he reminded me of a Jack Russell: small, smart, and spazzy. Energetic and unpredictable, I thought he'd make a great test candidate, especially since he was at that stage where he chewed on everything, my hand included. However, since he was still a puppy, he'd yet to grasp the difference between playful and owie.

When he bit down so hard I could feel the pressure on the bone in my hand, I thought I'd faint. I hadn't felt that feeling since the day of the attack, and I'd forgotten what that specifically felt like. Immediately, neurons in my brain started firing big-time, and like fireworks, they lit up those forbidden dark corners of my mind.

While I was playing with the dog, Kellie and I had been talking, but I stopped mid-sentence, suddenly unable to speak and unable to breathe. It was as if she could hear my brain yelling, *Bite! Help! Please! Do something! WTF!*

Kellie called Jax off right away, but I motioned with my free hand for her not to. It would be good for me to learn that a dog's teeth on my skin didn't necessarily mean the dog would eat me alive, and sure enough, each time he bit down, it was a little easier to tolerate. Maybe there *was* something to this exposure therapy.

I was far from curing myself, but I felt I was making progress. I was learning how to read a dog's body language, what interactions I could handle, what my limits were, and what I still needed to work on.

Feeling like I'd gotten the most I could out of Chief and Porter, I decided I needed to up my game.

154. NEW RECRUITS

In search of new recruits to pet, I visited a nearby animal rescue center. I'd attended their rigorous volunteer training program a few years before but never got around to volunteering like I'd hoped—something to do with scheduling issues, I think. This time, I went there to see about participating in supervised playtime—if that was even a thing. But the day I showed up, they told me they were too busy helping "actual customers" to help me. *Alrighty then,* I thought, a bit taken aback by their frankness.

Part of me was disappointed I wouldn't get to interact with their bigger dogs, seeing how I needed the practice. But being a huge proponent of the "Adopt, Don't Shop" movement, I was happy so many people were adopting.

Pit bulls or mixed breeds, whatever people prefer to call them, were definitely proving harder to get over, so I was feeling discouraged. Again, Sam offered to help. One of her friends had two pit bulls, and she planned to ask if she could borrow them on our next visit to the park.

Remembering how our County Animal Services had a surplus of pit bulls, I called and left a message for Ms. Manager, who happened to be on vacation. I reminded her who I was and asked if she had some nice ones I could play with as I worked through whatever lingering crap I had going on.

When the world started talking about shutting down in March 2020, out of caution, my therapist cut back on her hours. Meanwhile, I took off on a cruise, even though the State Department had expressly advised people against it.

I told you I was an adrenaline junkie—and crazy.

Seeing how this was before everyone figured out how to do Zoom calls or virtual appointments, we agreed to take a break from sessions for a bit, which was fine by me. Besides, when I returned from our cruise, I had better things to do—like play my own real-life version of *The Hunger Games* since while we were gone, everyone decided to start hoarding toilet paper, eggs, and every cleaning product known to man.

Eventually, Ms. Manager from the county shelter called back, saying she'd be happy to help in any way she could, but we agreed to hold off until things settled down pandemic-wise, not knowing that would take years.

I saved that voicemail. I have no idea if she even works there anymore, but I kept it, hoping one day I'd find the courage again to take her up on her offer.

155. VACATION

I'd gone from the dog attack to dealing with PTSD to a full-blown pandemic. My stress levels had been through the roof for over seven months, and I was mentally exhausted. I needed a vacation.

In the years prior, Dale and I traveled often. We aimed to squeeze in a little getaway each month, and even though it rarely worked out that way, we had fun trying. Being cooped up had been driving us both nuts, and we longed to look at something other than each other.

We got vaccinated as soon as we were able to. Not because we were afraid of getting sick or dying but because we'd hoped it would be the ticket back to normal. Plus, some of our friends were pretty freaked out over the whole thing, so we thought we could lure them out of their hidey-holes if we got jabbed.

A road trip hitting Utah's national parks—The Mighty Five—promised fresh air and expansive views, and let me tell you, it did not disappoint. Every day, we hiked from dawn to dusk, and the scenery was beyond spectacular.

I had my heart set on a notoriously treacherous hike called Angels Landing. Its ridge is so narrow and rocky that there are chains bolted into the ground for people to hang onto so they don't fall over the side. Yet, despite the chains, more than a dozen people have died trying. Unfortunately, or should I say fortunately, that part of the hike remained closed when we were there because the park couldn't properly sanitize the chain. Old Me, Daredevil Me, was disappointed, while New Me, PTSD Me, was secretly relieved.

The hikes were all strenuous but for different reasons. Some were long, and some had a wicked incline. Others had us up to our waists in water. Not to mention, it was June and a thousand degrees outside. Dry heat, my ass.

Overall, I was more entertained and amazed by the beauty of our surroundings than stressed about going over a cliff or winding up in some other situation requiring a search and rescue effort. However, I'd be lying if I said it never crossed my mind. But since I'd never hiked at those elevations and on such skinny little paths with nothing stopping me from tripping and falling to my death, I just assumed everyone thought about that kind of stuff. Let's just say, at the time, it didn't *feel* like anxiety.

156. CITY SLICKERS

In Canyonlands National Park, we had the bright idea to drive the Shafer Trail. Okay, technically, the idea was all mine, but Dale totally agreed to go along with it, and since he was the one driving, I'd say that puts him at sixty-forty in terms of blame. Not only was I utterly overwhelmed by thoughts of rolling down the cliff, the feeling was so thick I was convinced it was imminent.

The Shafer Trail winds up and down the side of a canyon and dates back to the Native Americans. When I say trail, I'm talking skinny and one hundred percent dirt. To be more precise, it's reddish sandstone, complete with big, long ruts. Some of those holes ran parallel to the road, so we had to be careful not to wedge our tires in them. Others ran perpendicular; when we hit one of those, it was like ramming a city curb head-on. On top of that, we also had to maneuver around the various rocks that had fallen from the cliffs above *and* avoid the missing sections where the road had apparently broken off and slid down the mountain in the last rainstorm. The scene was straight out of a Road Runner and Wile E. Coyote cartoon.

It was supposed to be a scenic way to drive to Moab, where we were scheduled to hit Arches National Park later in the day. The views over the expansive canyon were breathtaking, but the road itself was downright terrifying, especially when another vehicle came along. Since it was only wide enough for one car, someone would have to back up until they got to a somewhat wider section. If avoiding all those obstacles was hard to do driving forward, try backward—with a back window completely covered in dirt.

What was our reward when we got to the bottom? Wait for it—a few signs telling us we weren't even close to where we wanted to go and a park volunteer dude in a beat-up pickup truck who freakishly just so happened to be there doing his once-a-month rounds.

When we asked for directions, the volunteer dude laughed in our faces because, and I quote, "That so-called SUV is just a grocery getter and kid hauler made for city slickers." He then motioned toward our rental, a GMC Terrain with cruise control, power liftgate, and heated seats.

As I'm half expecting Curly Washburn or Billy Crystal to come bounding out from behind a rock, he goes on to explain that it doesn't have anywhere near the ground clearance we'd need to make it any farther. In fact, he was shocked we'd made it this far without a tire falling off. "Oh, and by the way, the only way out of here is to go back the way you came."

Fanfuckingtastic. And here I thought this was going to be a relaxing vacation.

157. DRIVING ME CRAZY

Heading back up the canyon wall, I was a basket case—oohing, ahhing, sucking in air, covering my face, and swearing. There was lots of swearing.

When I turned sixteen, my mom tried teaching me how to drive. Preferring that I drive like her, twenty miles under the speed limit, she'd constantly jam her foot into the floorboards as if trying to brake despite there being no pedals on her side. She couldn't see how stomping and bracing herself in her seat was distracting and made me way more likely to crash than my going twenty miles an hour in a thirty.

So every time she did it, instead of braking, I hit the gas just to prove my point. I was trying to convey, *See? I'm totally in control, so much so I can even go a little faster and still not crash, so chill out over there because I can't concentrate when you're being an overreacting drama queen!*

The next day, she hired a professional driving instructor. But that's not the lesson here.

My point is, I knew all my gasping and door-clutching had to be driving Dale crazy, so I checked in on him periodically. I'd remind him to go slow because we weren't in any hurry. I'd also casually mention that there wasn't a tow truck within thirty miles. And then, not so casually, I explained that even if we found a tow truck, Tripadvisor said they often charged thousands to rescue people on sketchy roads like this because, frankly, those people should have known better.

On top of that, although more so for my own reassurance, every few minutes, I'd also ask, "Are you okay driving?" Yeah, right, as if allowing *me* to drive would have *ever* crossed his mind since I was just as heavy on the gas pedal at fifty as I'd been at sixteen. I even had the tickets to prove it.

I never expected Dale to take me up on my offer. I merely asked like one does when both drivers are tired, a psychological diversion designed to keep everybody awake—because I didn't want to die. It didn't matter that Dale wasn't the least bit sleepy. Yapping at him made me feel better. I doubt Dale felt the same.

God bless this man for not pulling a Cheryl. He could've easily rammed that gas pedal, and Thelma and Louise'd us straight over the edge, even if only to put an end to my nonsense once and for all. Whoops, apparently, I'm full of spoiler alerts—sorry.

Needless to say, by the time we made it back to actual pavement, my nerves were shot. Even Dale agreed that the drive was "a little much" and "somewhat nerve-wracking," but he definitely wasn't having the same overwhelming reaction I was. I felt like I'd run my half marathon. I was exhausted, nauseous, and had a pounding headache.

Since Dale wasn't nearly as freaked out as I was, I didn't associate my feelings with the drive. Instead, I just assumed the last four days of intense hiking, skipping meals, and possible dehydration had caught up with me, so I grabbed a snack, a bottle of water, and a couple of ibuprofen. It *still* didn't register as anxiety.

158. PASSING

Of course, it happened again. This time, we were on a rural road in Texas. We'd driven Harry's car out there after storing it for him while he'd been away for a few months. It was rural, as in there wasn't a lot of traffic. However, it was probably considered a major road in this area, as it was one of the few that was paved, had one lane going in each direction, and painted lines running down the middle.

As we came up behind a car going way under the speed limit, Dale moved to the opposite side of the road to pass him. And yes, it was allowed on that section of the road, and yes, he'd signaled properly. That wasn't the problem.

The problem was that because it was Texas, meaning flat and open, I could see a car heading toward us in the other lane. Even though it was off in the distance and Dale had ample time to pass a line of twenty cars, I clutched the dashboard for dear life and yelled for him to hurry up as if at any moment we were going to die in a head-on collision.

I'd probably passed a hundred cars like this in my lifetime, so this wasn't something I typically would have considered scary. I had no idea what had come over me, and I could tell Dale didn't appreciate the backseat driving. Because who does?

When we were safely back on the right side of the road, I apologized for getting all worked up and acting irrationally. However, I asked Dale to refrain from passing any more cars for the rest of the drive because, for whatever reason, my brain could no longer correctly calculate distance-to-danger ratio. He knew that wasn't like me, so he agreed, even if reluctantly.

159. SNAKES

On our last day in Texas, the three of us decided to hike a trail that ran along the river. It was an official trail in a state park, so it was paved and had benches and signs scattered here and there. Signs that mostly talked about snakes. But that didn't surprise or scare me. After all, we have snakes in Florida, even the kinds that could kill me, but I'd never lost sleep over it.

On this day, however, not only could I not get snakes out of my mind, I'd somehow convinced myself I was guaranteed to be bitten by one. So naturally, I did what any irrational, crazy control freak would do. I set about formulating our post-snakebite plan.

As we hiked along, I quizzed my son on the locations of the nearest hospitals and which were most likely to stockpile antivenom. I also periodically asked each of them to check their phones to see how many bars of service they had, forgetting that we all shared a cell phone plan, so ipso facto, we all had the same zero bars. This wasn't ideal, considering calling 911 was step one of my ingenious plan.

Rather than remind me that we shared the same, apparently crappy coverage, when asked periodically how many bars he had, our son would reply sarcastically with completely random numbers like "twelve and a half," "forty-four," or "six point five."

I silently cursed my mother, a devout Catholic, who had told me over and over again throughout my life, *I pray you have a kid just like you.*

Dale had left his phone in the car—or so he said.

"Fine," I said. "I'm not the one who has to carry me until we find a phone signal."

Everyone knows antivenom needs to be administered as quickly as possible, so as we hiked, I'd remind them of any noteworthy landscape features we passed and each of the turns we'd taken, like mental breadcrumbs marking where we'd come from. Since one wrong turn on the way back to the car, and I'd be dead.

I also reminded them to stop often for water breaks. It was hotter than balls out, and if they were going to scoop me up and sprint back to the car, their muscles had to be well-hydrated for peak performance.

In addition, we also—okay, mainly me—discussed the most efficient ways to carry me. There was piggyback, over the shoulder, or out in front. I was partial to hanging myself around the back of their necks, with my feet dangling down the one side and my arms dangling down the other. That was the way those sexy firefighters and marines did it. I thought we needed to practice each to see which version of carrying me they were best at.

They thought not.

I knew my thoughts were irrational, but I couldn't help myself. I *had* to plan for the impending snakebite. I hadn't prepared for the worst when I went to feed the dogs and look where that had gotten me. This time, I was leaving nothing to chance.

I knew I was annoying them, yet still unable to abort my wacky comprehensive plan, I began to make jokes about it. I'd ask them to guess the number I was thinking of, and whoever got the closest would be the winner and thereby get to suck the venom out of my ankle or ass. You see, while I knew a snake would bite me, I *didn't* know whether it would be because I'd stepped on it or sat on it.

The paved trail ended at an overlook where the river split a hundred feet below us. From there, we could either walk along the cliffs and take in the sights from above or climb down the gently rolling embankment to the river below. Dale and Harry rushed to peer over the edge, but I couldn't move.

Beyond the trail and scattered about the red dirt were various-sized rocks and plants. I was afraid to walk because, having no idea where Texas snakes lived, I didn't know where it was safe to step.

Shit. Who was I kidding? I hadn't the foggiest idea where Florida snakes lived, either.

Being cold-blooded, I assumed snakes sunbathed on rocks. But what about when it's ninety-nine degrees? I could only picture those YouTube videos of eggs frying on blacktop driveways. Then again, weren't there jokes about tiny reptilian brains? Maybe they *were* dumb enough to get themselves cooked on a rock.

But what if they had evolved? Nature programs on TV always talk about how creatures have had to adapt to survive. If Texas snakes had learned to stay out of the sun, maybe they were hiding under a bush. Or perhaps the snake *had* been under a bush, but the guys had scared it out when they walked past, which meant if I walked by after, the cranky snake would bite *me* because it's dumb and didn't know I wasn't the jerk that just woke it up from its nap.

They tried to tell me snakes were nocturnal, but since they rolled their eyes when they said it, I didn't know if it was because they were lying or just sick of my shit.

Every rustle of the wind was the sound of a rattlesnake. And every time my ankle rolled because of the uneven ground, convinced I'd just stepped on one, I'd jump a foot in the air.

My insides were also hopping—with anxiety, like those Mexican jumping beans they sold in gas stations in the 1970s. And before I knew it, I was down the rabbit hole like Alice in Wonderland. There was no fighting it. I just had to roll with it.

My family appeased me, and while I could tell they weren't crazy about it, they didn't say anything demeaning. I followed super close behind them, stepping in precisely the same spots as *they* had seconds before. And if I lost track of where they had stepped because I'd looked up to take in the view or stopped to take a photo, they'd walk back to where I was. Again, so I could follow in their exact footsteps.

The walk back on the paved trail was much easier, but I still jumped at the sight of a lizard or cricket. If I wasn't mistaking them for snakes, I was petrified a snake would come bounding out after them in hot pursuit of a meal.

Back at the car, I felt euphoric to have eluded the snakes, like I had tempted fate and won. However, I also felt like I had been run over by a Mack truck. I was mentally drained, but that didn't stop me from stewing about our hike for the rest of the day. I knew my behavior was not only unreasonable but borderline insane. I just hoped my goofy personality had allowed me to play it off as more quirky than psycho.

160. DONE

I had to admit my panic attacks were happening more often and growing more intense.

Riding my bike around my neighborhood, if there were rain clouds, even in the distance, I was afraid I'd be struck by lightning and die.

Walking down the street—any street—I'd suddenly be overcome with fear that a car would jump the curb and kill me.

When we went skiing, I was petrified that I'd fall from the chairlift and die.

I worried that a bird would hit the window next to me on the plane, causing it to shatter, and I'd be sucked out into the troposphere to die.

It always came down to me dying. Ever since the attack, it seemed my mortality was always there waiting in the wings, taunting me.

That day in Texas, after the hike, I was done. This new Cheryl was a freaking lunatic, and I was done with her fraidy-cat ways. I was done thinking the worst, I was done overreacting, and I was *definitely* done thinking everything in the world was out to kill me. Clearly, something was wrong with me, and I wasn't going to stop until I found someone to fix it.

161. RATINGS AND REVIEWS

When I sought the help of a professional this time, I was advised to opt for a forensic psychologist, as they generally have more experience with trauma victims. Armed with a list of individuals covered under my insurance plan, I googled each of them—albeit halfheartedly—and read all the reviews I could find.

Reading reviews always confuses me more than it helps me. One person will say the establishment was dirty, but someone else will say it was spotless. One says the service was impeccable. Another says it was atrocious. How is that even possible? Then I begin to doubt if they even reviewed the same place, thinking one of them clicked the wrong button and inadvertently left a review for an entirely different business, leaving me stuck wondering which got it right.

Some reviews are so spiteful I automatically assume it's the competition or a disgruntled ex-employee out for revenge. Meanwhile, others are so ass-kissy that I'd swear they were written by the owner's mother or a paid overseas professional reviewer. At least the latter would explain the questionable grammar, and I'd be somewhat relieved our country's educational system wasn't really as bad as some say.

None of the doctors' reviews stood out as being particularly good or bad. So, being the instant gratification girl I am, after confirming by phone with the actual therapist, not just his receptionist, that he accepted my insurance, I settled on the one who could get me in the soonest. The fact that he had an opening for the following week should have been my first red flag.

162. RED FLAGS

The second red flag was when the therapist wasn't on time for my appointment—as in not even in the building. He rolled in via the back door about a half hour after we were scheduled to meet. The Universe had given me a legitimate excuse to leave, and I can kick myself for not jumping at the chance.

The guy was a complete asshole. He started off by questioning me on what I wanted to get out of the therapy. That was easy. I wanted to get better, back to the me I was before the attack. In return, I expected an enthusiastic *Well, you've come to the right place.* Instead, I was lectured on why getting better wasn't in my best interests. *Say what?*

The so-called therapist thought it would be better to rack up a hefty bill for the insurance claim. I assured him that was the furthest thing from my mind, reiterating that I wanted to focus on ridding myself of the imaginary death threats I'd been conjuring up. And preferably as soon as possible.

During our session, he spoke in riddles, making it difficult to follow the conversation. However, I listened closely, not wanting to miss it when (or more like *if*) he finally got around to making a point. He also slid in several lewd comments throughout, but I brushed them off so as not to appear too sensitive, disrupt what little momentum we had going, or waste any more time than we already had.

Nice job, Cheryl. Of all the therapists, you had to pick the pervy leprechaun.

His analogies were so bizarre I had no idea how they supposedly applied to me or my situation. The best one being, "If I stuck my tongue in your mouth when you're six years old, you might find it disgusting, but if you're seventeen, you'd probably find it titillating." I nearly choked. *Wait! What?* For starters, how in the hell did *that* have *anything* to do with me being attacked by dogs and my subsequent thinking that nature was trying to kill me?

Second, and more importantly, he was talking about *minors!* This dude was older than me and a doctor, for Christ's sake. Well, *supposedly* a doctor—by now, I was already having serious doubts about that, too. Because what he was spewing wasn't "titillating." It was child molestation, even aggravated sexual battery in some states.

Right then and there, I should've jumped up and run out the door, but instead, I did what was expected of me, just like always. I pretended to listen, even politely nodding on occasion, just waiting for my hour to be up.

163. DR. EVIL

I don't even know how many red flags we were up to by now. But at the end of the session, Dr. Asshole asked for my credit card, which he wrote down on a scrap piece of paper and stuffed into his pocket. I tried confirming that he'd taken the number to remain on file, only to be used sometime down the road to cover whatever my insurance didn't. That's when he literally laughed in my face.

He then lied, saying he never told me over the phone that he accepted my insurance. Obviously, he didn't know my toxic trait is that not only can I remember specific entire conversations with people but also where I was standing *and* what I was wearing when we'd had that conversation. Even Dale remembered overhearing us on the phone, so I knew I wasn't crazy—at least about that.

I looked at the situation like those old Mastercard commercials—Therapy: One hour of my life and $150 down the drain. Lesson learned: Priceless.

Days later, I called Dr. Sleazeball and asked him to email me a copy of the bill or receipt to present to my insurance company so at least I could apply it to my deductible, and he agreed. However, his demeanor changed moments later when he asked, and I had to tell him there wouldn't be any subsequent appointments. He became belligerent, telling me that I better get help from someone if it wasn't him because I definitely needed it.

I could understand if he'd said so out of genuine concern for my well-being from a therapeutic or professional standpoint, but no, this was spiteful. He practically hissed those words, and his tirade was accompanied by a rousing assortment of name-calling, including calling me "crazy."

164. BULLY

To say I was pissed at Dr. Piece-of-Shit would be an understatement. While in the past I might have joked about being crazy at times, it had taken me *months* to come to terms with the fact that what I had was an actual medical condition and a debilitating one at that. After working so hard to get to where I was, he had no right to wave that word around, joke about it, or rub my nose in it, especially in such a condescending way.

I had opened up and confided in him that day, and the first chance he got, he turned it around and used it against me simply because his ego was bruised. Fortunately for me, my childhood, if anything, had made me gritty. *Bring it, Dr. Dirtbag. I'm not afraid of you.*

I grew up in the seventies. Back then, you'd be hard-pressed to find a kid who wasn't picked on for one reason or another. We may have been mean, but that also made us resilient. We just weren't very original. Ask any Gen Xer, and they'll tell you our favorite sassy comeback was always that worn-out "Sticks and Stones" rhyme. It was basically the battle cry of our generation.

Thanks to that rhyme, a few psychology classes, and forty years of experience, I knew his words were just that. Words. As rude as he was, I knew he'd only put me down to feel better about himself. His tirade was more about him feeling inadequate than it was about me. However, that didn't make me any less furious.

The condemnation had rolled off his tongue with such ease that I knew in my gut he'd delivered that line before, and I felt bad for the others, knowing how he supposedly specialized in trauma cases. Again, with the *supposedly* because, by now, I didn't trust a single word that came out of that man's mouth.

I hoped he didn't talk to his other patients that way. If he did, I prayed they weren't so broken or vulnerable that they couldn't see through his bullshit for what it was— some sick manipulation tactic—and that they didn't take it to heart as he'd intended.

No bill or receipt ever came via email, though I can't say I was surprised. I called my insurance company to let them know what had happened and suggested they remove him from their preferred list, seeing how he really *didn't* take their insurance. But he later told them my session wouldn't have been covered anyway because it was a "special" forensic exam that required him to take "extremely detailed notes." Yet he failed to tell them he never picked up a pen the entire session; that is, unless we count him writing down my credit card number.

It kills me. Someone like me goes to someone like that, hoping to feel better about themselves. Yet I ended up feeling violated in so many more ways than I ever thought possible. Not wanting others to fall victim to this pathetic excuse for a human, let alone a doctor, I gave him a one-star review and submitted a brief synopsis of my experience on a well-known healthcare provider website. To this day, it remains the only time I've ever submitted an online review of anyone or anything in my entire life.

165. GLINDA

After my New Year's Eve fiasco, I'd been given a list of several therapists, but I whittled it down in no time as they either didn't take my insurance, weren't taking on new patients, or their next available appointment was months out.

Since I'd gone the fast and cheap route with this last one, and that hadn't worked out so well, this time, I was sure to ask around. "If you could only recommend one person, who would it be? Who's the best? If you were me, who would *you* choose?"

One name kept popping up, and lucky for me, amid the pandemic, she'd recently switched to a virtual appointment system, so she had an opening the following Friday. Unlucky for me, she wasn't covered under my insurance, so this would all be out of pocket. She'd *better* be good.

If this woman had a theme song, it would be the airy, bubbly music they play when Glinda, the Good Witch, shows up in *The Wizard of Oz*. She kind of looks like her, too. Same age, same build, just swap out the pink toile for a cardigan, lose the tiara, pop on a pair of glasses, and bingo.

Right off the bat, I liked her approach. There were *so* many forms to fill out, including a thirteen-page "Patient Background and Current Functioning Questionnaire." Don't get me wrong, I despise filling out forms. However, because I'm also meticulous and detail-oriented, I was delighted that she wanted to know everything about me, including a relationship summary for every person I had ever known.

I also liked that while she wanted to see notes from any past therapists, she didn't want to see them until *after* our first appointment because she didn't want them to influence her initial impressions. I had to hand it to her; this woman was thorough. *Me likey.*

166. BAGGAGE

Glinda, the Good Doctor, started our initial call by asking me to elaborate on some of my answers on the forms. I paused, reluctant to delve into any childhood stuff. There was a lot of baggage there, and I was afraid if we started to unpack it, we'd never get to the real reason for my appointment.

It reminded me of when I go for a deep tissue massage, and they start by playing with my hair. Supposedly it's meant to relax me, but all it does is piss me off. If I'm there, it's because something is really hurting. And since my hair is *never* hurting, I'd rather devote each of my sixty minutes to the areas that are.

I don't need massage foreplay, nor did I need psychological foreplay, for that matter. I just wanted to get to the issue at hand. But I also didn't want to start off with Glinda on the wrong foot, especially since I was far from qualified to tell her how to do her job. However, this time around, I had expectations of my own, and for this to work, we needed to be on the same page. So I tiptoed my way into asking how much of that childhood stuff we'd be getting into.

She rolled her eyes and gasped all surprised-like, noting that it would probably take *years* to sort through that shit, and that wasn't why we were there. "Besides," she added, "you seem to be functioning pretty well despite all that."

Not bad for right out the gate, Glinda. Not bad at all.

When people learn I have a complicated relationship with my parents, I think they automatically assume there's something wrong with me, and that's fine. I'd rather they think that than have to air dirty laundry just to defend myself or prove a point.

However, if I'm being completely candid, it stung when a cousin implied that it hadn't been that bad. For starters, I'm no overreactor. In addition, nobody really knows what goes on behind closed doors. Some people have a knack for only showing others what they want them to see, so I suppose I can understand how she may have missed it.

I'd parked all of that on the shelf ages ago. I knew where to find it if I needed to go back to it, like for reference or if I felt nostalgic, but for the most part, I was cool with allowing that part of my life to just sit there collecting dust. Healthy or not, that's how I rolled.

It took almost forty years for people to confide in me that they'd seen it, too, and it wasn't until then that I began to feel that sense of closure.

167. HOMEWORK

My homework was to read the book *The Happiness Trap* by Russ Harris. Glinda wanted to focus on one principle each week, so I was instructed to only read specific chapters. But by now, we all know I'm an all-or-nothing kind of girl who doesn't like being told what to do. So you better believe I jumped ahead.

According to Psychology Today, "Acceptance and Commitment Therapy (ACT) is an action-oriented approach to psychotherapy that stems from traditional behavior therapy and cognitive behavioral therapy. Clients learn to stop avoiding, denying, and struggling with their inner emotions and, instead, accept that these deeper feelings are appropriate responses to certain situations that should not prevent them from moving forward in their lives. With this understanding, clients begin to accept their hardships and commit to making necessary changes in their behavior, regardless of what's going on in their lives and how they feel about it."[1]

My personal CliffsNotes version goes a little something like this: life isn't always wonderful, so I need to quit telling myself it should be because having those expectations will only set me up for disappointment. The book also went in-depth on how to recognize helpful and unhelpful thoughts, as well as outlining the various mindfulness exercises I could use to help guide me through any emotions I might have been trying to avoid. *Ding ding ding!*

---

[1] "Types of Therapy." Psychology Today, March 21, 2022. https://www.psychologytoday.com/us/therapy-types/ acceptance-and-commitment-therapy.

Thanks to Glinda, I'd come to find out I was the queen of avoiding feelings, so apparently, I needed all the help I could get.

168. WEDNESDAY

For as long as I can remember, I've never been big on feelings. Apparently, my past is to blame, but according to Glinda, it's all completely normal, considering the circumstances. Wow, how I wished I had learned that little nugget sooner rather than trying to make my way through the world like Wednesday Addams all these years.

Glinda said my childhood didn't equip me with the tools I needed to process big feelings, especially the kind of big feelings that showed up after three dogs tried to eat me alive.

Our sessions weren't about validating feelings. I wasn't seeking permission from Glinda to feel a certain way. If anything, I wanted her to tell me I was wrong for feeling the way I did. Instead, the therapy helped me see I was wrong to beat myself up over those feelings and wrong to feel like I was wrong when I beat myself up because that's . . . umm, wrong. As I said before, I was in no way qualified to do her job.

Over time, our meetings went from weekly to bi-weekly to once a month, and as I made progress, I grew to look forward to them. Glinda had two dogs, so she shared her funny dog stories, and I shared my not-so-funny dog stories. We also shared plenty of inside jokes, most of which revolved around how much I detested talking about my feelings, followed by her reminding me how ironic it was that it always came down to that. I felt like she really got me, and I can't say that about many people in my life.

It's hard for some people to realize an awkward truth about themselves, admit to their insecurities, or laugh about a bad experience. I get it. Sometimes that hurts. However, when others help me see, playfully through sarcasm, the ironic or silly in those instances, that negative hold on me seems to lessen. Not to mention, I appreciate the fast thinking and quick wit it takes to get a valid point across *and* get them to laugh at themselves, all at the same time.

I knew I'd found the right therapist when we'd be talking about some sappy feeling thing or some horrific dog thing, and out of left field, she'd fling a sarcastic comment at me. Call me crazy, but that always made me smile from the inside out, like a big warm hug. Being able to laugh about my bullshit felt like I was finally on the path to normal.

When the one-year anniversary of the attack came and went, and I failed to notice, we both cried happy tears when it hit me at our session a few days later. That's when I knew it was time to fly the nest.

169. TINFOIL

I'm not the me I used to be before the attack, and I probably never will be. Glinda likes to say it's like tinfoil. Once it's crumpled, no matter how much you try to smooth it out, it will never be flat, shiny, and new again. But as I like to say, it doesn't need to be pretty to wrap your leftovers. My tinfoil may be a mess, but I can make do.

I still feel anxious—a lot. And while I'm not thrilled about it, it's manageable. It's like bumping into an ex at a party. I nod so they know I've seen them, but then I ignore them the best I can and try to have a good time. Once I recognize my anxiety for what it is, I'll acknowledge it, and then I'll try to brush it aside so I can get back to whatever else I'd been doing in the first place.

Full-blown panic attacks aren't as cooperative. Those can't be brushed aside. They have to run their course. I liken it to someone continuously ranting in my face to the point I can't get a word in edgewise. I'll remain stoic the entire time, and then when that person finally shuts up, I'll ask all snotty-like, *Do you feel better now that you got that out of your system? Are you done?*

170. BUCKLE UP

For me, anxiety is a roller coaster. Sometimes it's like a kiddy coaster, and I'm squashed into a giant green caterpillar with my knees up to my chin while it drags my grown-up ass up and down gently rolling hills. I'm not necessarily having fun, and it's uncomfortable, but overall, it's not that bad. I can see the happy faces waiting for me at the end, and I know it'll all be over soon.

Other times, the roller coaster is the kind named after a venomous serpent. The kind where they bolt me in with a five-point crotch buckle and some sort of mechanical shoulder contraption that resembles gym equipment made for a linebacker. Those times, I *know* I'm not going anywhere anytime soon.

As my anxiety roller coaster climbs, *tick, tick, tick, tick, tick,* by the time I realize how ramped up I am, it's too late. There's no getting off. There's only one way down.

Mind over matter, mind over matter. Breathe. It'll all be over soon. Hang in there.

When the worst is behind me, it's a tremendous relief. But, like exiting an actual roller coaster, I don't feel quite right, so I have to take things slow and ease back into the world.

The major ones are so intense they're almost tangible. That's when that immense crushing anxiety feeling takes charge of the entire mothership, and I'm at its mercy for however long it decides to be an asshole. If I try to shove it out the door, it gets rowdy and takes a firmer hold, so I have no choice but to let it wander around until it finds the exit on its own.

171. WORK IN PROGRESS

I'm shocked by the number of friends who tell me I need to smoke marijuana or take CBD. Like every troubled teen, I tried it a few times in high school, but I never felt like it did anything. I joke that I was too strong-willed to fall for it, in the same way I couldn't be brainwashed to drink six-dollar iced coffees from Starbucks or hypnotized at the fair.

Besides, pot's just not practical. Am I supposed to carry it everywhere I go? How about when I'm on a ski slope, convinced someone will run into me and send me sailing off the side of the mountain? I can't stash a joint and lighter in my ski outfit. I can barely keep track of my ChapStick. What about lighting up at work? How do I transport it on a plane? Is there a trick to remembering in which states it's allowed and in which I can be arrested? Surrender my concealed weapons license for a medical marijuana card? It all sounds way too complicated. I'll pass.

I've made peace with my crazy. Dogs and I don't mix like we used to, and that's okay. While I may try to interact with them every now and then, if I choose not to, in the grand scheme of things, it doesn't matter. Win some, lose some. Life goes on.

I've had to adjust my expectations to be kinder to myself.

When the flashbacks hit, that's my cue to find a distraction. I either get a glass of water, fire off an email, take out the trash, or jump on social media for a minute . . . or twenty . . . or ninety.

The physical stuff is a little trickier to ignore. I go about life not forgetting but allowing other experiences and daily to-dos to take up most of the space. It seems I'll never stop noticing my scars, grabbing a fork the wrong way, struggling to open jars, or shaking out my aching wrists, but I *can* decide not to dwell on it.

There will always be reminders, like catching sight of my scars or feeling a pain in my wrists, and they are bound to trigger a barrage of thoughts.

It often takes me by surprise. So first up is usually; *How come...? Why does...?* Followed by dejected recognition; *Oh yeah...*

What usually comes next is; *Damn dogs*, quickly followed by other disturbing and intrusive thoughts centered around that day.

And since I still struggle with blaming myself, I'll toss in a few of these for good measure. *Poor dogs. Why did you ever agree to feed them? Why on Earth do you keep buying flip-top toothpaste? You should know better by now than to do (insert whatever action had brought this on).*

Worry often shows up in the form of; *Is this getting worse? What will all this look like in twenty years?*

Next comes the beating myself up portion of the program; *Dummy. You know you're not supposed to think about that. Enough. When are you going to get over this?*

Followed by understanding and being kinder to myself; *Be nice. I get it, this sucks. Take some deep breaths. You're fine.*

Those thoughts are like The Haunted Mansion ride at Disney World. If you've been on it before, you know where the ghosts are going to pop up. They come and go throughout the ride, just lots of foggy-looking spirits that make brief appearances, then drift off again. It's all relatively benign. They're not scary; it's just part of the experience, so the best thing to do is sit back, relax, and keep your hands inside the ride until it comes to a complete stop. After all, it could be worse. It could be the spinning teacups.

Sadly, My Friend moved away, so we're not as close as we used to be. We still talk occasionally, but we seem to be on a different level these days. Our conversations are more superficial, and we definitely don't discuss anything having to do with that horrible day. Perhaps that's because there's nothing left *to* say. I miss her, but she'll forever hold a special place in my heart.

I'm still an absolute control freak, but if anything, this entire ordeal has taught me how to let go—even if only a little. As of the writing of this book, I'm in my mid-fifties and very aware that life's too short to waste time beating myself up over the past or things I can't change. Yet I can't help but miss the carefree, dog-loving Old Me. She'll forever hold a special place in my heart, too.

THE END

Thank you for allowing me to take you on this journey. If you enjoyed reading *The Pits*, please consider leaving a review wherever you purchased this book, as reviews are very helpful for authors. Not only do I read every review, they'll help other readers discover my book.

You can also visit my website: <u>www.thecheryledwards.com</u>. There, you'll find photos, videos, book club resources, dog training tips, the recipe for My Friend's chicken chili, as well as links to purchase sarcastic gym tanks and *The Happiness Trap* by Russ Harris. It's also the best place to find announcements regarding book signings, speaking engagements, and my other upcoming books. See you there...

ACKNOWLEDGMENTS

Thank you to:

My friends and family, who saw potential in my funny, newsy Christmas letters. It's too bad it took thirty years of your encouragement to make this happen. Though you may have inadvertently created a monster as I already have big plans for book two.

Chris (Toelsin) Barone, Abby Barone, Theresa Lundquist, and Chris Stucchio for believing in me. You guys were the first ones I trusted to share my writing with WAY back when, long before the attack. Thank you for being my biggest cheerleaders, laughing in all the right places, and instilling in me the confidence to keep writing.

My parents. While my upbringing was not necessarily what I would have chosen for myself, I would not be nearly as strong, resourceful, and independent if it wasn't for you. My experiences have served me well in the long run, and I am grateful.

Charles "Chuck" Palmeri, for going first and planting the seed. Having the courage to write about a difficult subject and publishing your first book at age ninety-three was beyond inspiring. You were the kindest man I have ever met, the best stepdad a girl could ask for, and I miss you dearly.

Suzanne Butler, Stefanie Edwards, and Sharon Player; the OG beta readers. Putting myself out there was scary, but you made it less so. Thank you for not only being so helpful but also kind.

Liz Coursen, who told me, "You have something here." If she hadn't been so excited about it, this book would not exist.

The Sarasota Creative Writers group for enduring some pretty crappy first, second, and third drafts, as well as your collective knowledge, valuable feedback, and never-ending patience. I'd especially like to thank Karen Thomas, Diane Mechem Kinser, Philip Sherman Mygatt, and Valerie Fitzgerald for being tougher than usual. I am a better writer because of you. This book would be crap if it weren't for you.

My editor, Danielle Lange, for not only understanding my voice but for allowing it to shine through. Of course, I appreciated each and every one of your suggestions, but most of all, I'm grateful for your ability to delete what didn't belong. Thank you for saving me from me. However, rest assured your job is secure—I learned nothing.

Ken Dawson for designing the book cover of my dreams. A million revisions later, it is just as I imagined. I appreciate your expertise, advice, patience, and friendship more than you will ever know.

The good samaritans and hospital staff who saw me at my worst and did their best that fateful day. You and your efforts are forever etched in my mind. I cannot thank you enough for all that you did and all that you do.

All the friends, family, and doctors, too numerous to mention, but you know who you are. Thank you for caring enough to listen when I needed to vent. You have no idea how much I needed that and how much it meant to me. I couldn't have gotten as far as I did without you all.

Samantha Humprey & Chief, Katie Kramer & Porter, Kellie Humphrey & Jax, and Jennifer Bernthal & Bauer for the free therapy sessions and for tolerating all my overanalyzing and overthinking as I worked through my nonsense. I love you all . . . and your puppers.

My husband, Dale Edwards, for taking such good care of me in the aftermath of the attack. I know it wasn't easy, so your patience while I continued the battle long after is also greatly appreciated. I also thank you for your support and understanding while I took the time to devote to this project because you knew it was important to me that I get it right. You were also a champ for not only enduring what must have seemed like endless rounds of *Which sounds better? This . . .? Or this . . .? How about this . . .? Or should I say it like this . . .?* but also for playing along even when you didn't have the time or didn't care.

My readers. The scariest part about writing is putting your whole self out there for all the world to see. I've shared my raw truths and my most intimate thoughts in the hopes you might see a little of yourself or others. Regardless of the journey we find ourselves on, understanding is the key to forgiving ourselves and others. Please be kind to one another. I appreciate you taking the time to read my story. Let's be friends.

Last but not least, thank you to My Friend. Your life was also turned upside down that fateful day. I recognize all that you have been through and the sacrifices you have made. I still love you with all my heart, and I wish you and your family nothing but the best.

Cheryl Edwards is a humorist, entrepreneur, travel addict, and trauma survivor. Her brief stint as a stand-up comic was mainly to embarrass her two sons. In her free time, she enjoys hiking, skiing, drinking tequila, and boxing—provided nobody's trying to hit her back. She currently lives in Florida with her husband and two cats.

Made in USA - Kendallville, IN
75338_9798990508118
04.07.2025 2256